THE KING IS COMING

THE KING IS COMING

IT'S TIME TO PREPARE FOR THE RETURN OF CHRIST

JOHN BEVERE

W Publishing Group
An Imprint of Thomas Nelson

The King Is Coming

Published in Nashville, Tennessee, by W Publishing, an imprint of Thomas Nelson. W Publishing and Thomas Nelson are registered trademarks of HarperCollins Christian Publishing, Inc.

Thomas Nelson titles may be purchased in bulk for educational, business, fund-raising, or sales promotional use. For information, please email SpecialMarkets@ThomasNelson.com.

Emphasis in Scripture quotations has been added by the author.

ISBN 978-1-4003-4967-8 (HC)
ISBN 978-1-4003-4969-2 (audiobook)
ISBN 978-1-4003-4968-5 (eBook)
ISBN 978-1-4003-4967-9 (ITPE)
ISBN 978-1-4003-4965-3 (TP)

Library of Congress Control Number: 2025946287

I dedicate this book to two groups of people:

First, to our Messenger International Team, thank you for laboring with Lisa and me to glorify our Lord Jesus. Each of you are very gifted and talented in what you do. Thank you for your faithfulness; I admire and love each of you. May your eternal reward reflect the love and devotion you carry for our dear Savior.

Second, to our legacy partners of Messenger International. God joined our hearts together as teammates to glorify His Son. The fact that you would give your resources and entrust us to be faithful with them overwhelms us. May your eternal reward be greater than you imagined. You are heroes in the faith.

CONTENTS

WEEK 3: THE UNITING OF THE BRIDE AND GROOM

WEEK 4: PREPARE FOR HIS RETURN

HOW TO JOURNEY THROUGH THIS BOOK

Dear Reader,

This is a message that has taken years to receive from the Holy Spirit, and several months to write. It's a critical and urgent message; one that, if believed and acted on, will prepare you for the soon arrival of our King. I know, because the truths contained within these pages changed my personal life, and I share vulnerably about this transformation in chapter 1.

Due to its importance, I took time and contemplative prayer to determine how to present it. I considered the ebb and flow of our present day—the demands of our schedules and the rapid pace at which we move, so I felt the need to adapt. I determined it would be beneficial to present the truths in bite-size chunks so you can deeply ponder them.

At first glance you may think this is a devotional. I assure you it's not. Let me explain. A devotional usually has different topics for each day that don't necessarily build into a concise and systematic message. Even though this book is structured like a devotional, each day builds on the previous day's chapter to form what we normally get in a nonfiction book. Now here is the great news: It certainly can be read in a day or two, if that is your preference, but I strongly recommend you read it in either a four-week or two-week time period. If four weeks, you'll read a chapter per day. If two weeks, you'll read a chapter for the morning and one for the evening each day. A hint for either choice to stay the course: Set a time (or times) and hold to it for each day.

HOW TO JOURNEY THROUGH THIS BOOK

At the conclusion of each chapter, you will find five tools to help deepen the benefit of its content. Let's call them the 5 Ps:

1. **Passage:** A passage from Scripture that is crucial to that day's message found in the body of the text, or one that was not brought up in the main body of that chapter but adds strength to what was presented. I recommend memorizing these passages.
2. **Point:** This is a main thought contained within the chapter to drive home its importance. Seeing it again will only strengthen its effectiveness and give you a quick reference for coming back and reviewing the chapter.
3. **Ponder:** This is crucial. The psalmist states, "I will meditate on Your precepts, and contemplate Your ways" (Psalm 119:15 NKJV). We meditate by rolling over in our mind how the Word of God applies to us in our present state. In doing so we are told our ways will be prosperous and we will have good success (Joshua 1:8; Psalm 1).
4. **Prayer:** A prayer that reflects the teaching of the chapter. It's so important that God hears our voice and that we give Him permission to change us according to His Word.
5. **Profession:** We are told that *death and life* are in the power of what we say (Proverbs 18:21). In speaking what He declares over us we come into alignment—spirit, soul, and body—with His will for us, which is the proven way to experience life to the fullest.

I recommend that you read the chapters and go through the 5 Ps with a journal alongside you. Put your thoughts and prayers into the journal day by day so that when you go back through the message later you will have all the Holy Spirit revealed to your mind on paper.

To enhance your experience, we have created twenty-eight four-to-five-minute videos that highlight the core truths from each chapter. These are meant to complement your daily reading and will not have the same impact if you don't read the chapter first before viewing. To access them, scan the QR code at the bottom of the next page.

A few more recommendations: Use your smartphone to time how long it takes to read the chapter, go through the 5 Ps, journal, and view the chapter's short video. Don't rush; it's not a race. The reason for the timer is that after three or four chapters you will develop an average time for wise planning for future chapters because they are all relatively the same length (with the exception of chapters 23 and 28; plan five minutes more for each of them).

Form a habit; don't allow anything to get in the way of your set time(s) each day. It's my prayer and hope that what God has done in me over the past several years He will do with you in four weeks, two weeks, or whatever time you allot to go through the book.

A few more thoughts. A message always brings the greatest benefit when I teach it or read it with a group of friends. Choose some close friends and go through it together. First go through the chapter alone, just you and the Holy Spirit, then set a time to talk with your friends about what He shows you. You can do this on a daily or weekly basis.

Scripture instructs us to "teach these truths to other trustworthy people who will be able to pass them on to others" (2 Timothy 2:2). To help you do that, we've also developed a weekly course that you alone or your small group of friends can go through together, available for purchase anywhere books are sold. This gives you even more tools to discuss the Word of God on this topic.

Finally, you will find other related messages on our easy-to-download app called MessengerX that will help mature your walk with our soon-coming King. You can download the app at no charge and benefit from dozens of books, courses, and other discipleship materials. Just scan the QR code on this page.

I pray you grow more intimate with God as you journey through *The King Is Coming.*

Sincerely,
John Bevere

WEEK 1

THE DIVINE MASTER PLAN

THEY WILL SAY, "WHAT HAPPENED TO THE PROMISE THAT JESUS IS COMING AGAIN? FROM BEFORE THE TIMES OF OUR ANCESTORS, EVERYTHING HAS REMAINED THE SAME SINCE THE WORLD WAS FIRST CREATED."

2 PETER 3:4

CHAPTER 1

WHY BOTHER DISCUSSING IT?

The return of Jesus. Dare we tackle such a controversial subject? But should it be referred to as merely a subject? Perhaps it's better identified as truth; more accurately an important truth, for it is one of the foundational teachings of our faith. It promises great hope and unimaginable blessings for His faithful followers. But before diving in, let's first discuss its relevance.

Wouldn't it be best to just leave this topic alone? Why address it? What's the benefit? After all, many generations of believers thought the King would return in their lifetime, so what makes ours any different? And even if the end of the age should occur in our lifetime, isn't it going to just play out in some mysterious way, one which only the Lord God knows? So how does discussing it affect anything or change the outcome? And furthermore, doesn't the ambiguity of it all just create uncertainty, tension, and even division among believers? These questions seem logical, but do they line up with the wisdom of Scripture?

Before answering, permit me to continue challenging its relevance by sharing my own journey. I've been teaching the Word of God on a regular basis for forty years. For most of that time—the first thirty-five years—I almost prided myself in avoiding *eschatology*. I know that's a big word and many don't know its meaning, because it's not a biblical word; rather, it's a theological term that simply speaks to the study of end times. I'm sure you've heard some of the applicable terms: last days, Antichrist, false prophet, tribulation, rapture, second coming, millennial reign of Christ, the new heavens and earth, and the list continues. In essence, eschatology centers on all aspects of the second coming of Jesus Christ back to the earth and what will follow.

In the past, I've steered clear of speaking on any facet of it, and quickly retorted to anyone's inquiry, "I don't teach on end times." In fact, I'm sad to say I don't think I've preached one message dedicated to this truth in my four decades of public ministry. Please don't get me wrong; I've always personally enjoyed reading the scriptures pertaining to Jesus' second coming, meditating on them, and even discussing them privately with family and friends. But to publicly speak on it, in my estimation, was too controversial and seemed to produce lazy people who were just waiting to be "raptured." Oh, how wrong I was! I didn't think or pray it through far enough. My assumptions were incorrect. But before uncovering my error, allow me to share what brought me to this mindset.

In the early days of our marriage, Lisa and I experienced and witnessed tragic tales from end time teachings, especially in the 1980s, when there were eighty-eight reasons for Jesus to return by 1988![1] Yes, that was a widely believed message in the American church. My wife wouldn't buy into it. I, on the other hand, as a young believer, took the bait—hook, line, and sinker. I was convinced He would be back in September of 1988, and a slew of my friends were right there with me.

Once that date came and went, rather than stepping back and learning from our blunder, further dates were set again and again. It didn't take long for me to realize how damaging attempting to pinpoint His return could be and therefore stop focusing on the teachings of eschatology altogether, especially from those who narrowed it down to a month or year. But others, and fortunately only a small part of the church, continued to listen to these "prophets."

As time passed, Lisa's and my view of the topic grew increasingly negative. We observed the fruit of the teachings to be more unfavorable than favorable. We heard the tales of people neglecting to pay their mortgages, quitting their jobs, or ceasing all plans and aspirations. There were many who ran up their credit cards thinking they wouldn't have to pay them off. We knew a young couple our age who chose not to have children and committed to the medical procedure to make it final because they thought He would return soon. We heard other wild stories of what people did or didn't do because they were certain His return was just around the corner.

Then there were those who got into heated debates and arguments over the rapture, whether it was pre-, mid-, or post-tribulation. There were discussions about the millennium (Jesus' thousand-year reign on earth)—is it real or allegorical? Then there were those who argued that all the events of Revelation had already occurred in the first century. Still others floated to the other extreme of interpretation. I distinctly remember one man saying, "John, we are in the tribulation." Another on our ministry team said, "John, we are already in the millennium." All these extremists seemed to have one thing in common: They were so consumed by talking about the second coming, they lost all motivation for being productive and fruitful in life.

Keep in mind, this was my personal observation and assessment. In my immaturity, I didn't fully process that people's behavior stemming from their inaccurate interpretation of Scripture shouldn't deem the truth invalid. We are explicitly told by the apostle Peter (and interestingly, these words are written immediately following his discussion of end time events):

> Therefore, beloved, looking forward to these things, be diligent to be found by Him in peace, without spot and blameless; and consider that the longsuffering of our Lord is salvation—as also our beloved brother Paul, according to the wisdom given to him, has written to you, as also in all his epistles, speaking in them of these things, in which are some things hard to understand, which *untaught and unstable people twist to their own destruction, as they do also the rest of the Scriptures.*
>
> 2 PETER 3:14–16 NKJV

Notice, these unstable people *twist* the truth of Scripture, and they reap serious consequences from not approaching the Word of God with humility, relying on the Holy Spirit to teach them. Often they are quick to listen to the YouTube prophets who interpret Scripture or current events inaccurately. These self-appointed ministers often exaggerate world events, twisting them to fit into their interpretation of the prophetic scriptures.

All of this helped solidify my stance on staying far from this subject. However, I was reacting instead of acting and seeking. I didn't like the effects I saw in many people, so I did an about-face and went the other way. Again, how wrong I was.

Approximately five years ago I felt a tug in my heart by the Holy Spirit to start paying closer attention to the numerous prophetic scriptures of Jesus' second coming. I began listening on a regular basis to balanced teachers of Bible prophecy. I'd listen in my car, while working out in the gym, and at various other times. I read books by sound prophetic authors, and my vision shifted and enlarged. The Holy Spirit started revealing important truths to me.

What was the result? I experienced significant changes. The more He revealed Jesus' imminent return in God's Word, the greater my passion became for ministry. I found my love for both Jesus and people growing stronger. It seemed the Holy Spirit was working in me both a greater awareness and compassion for a hurting humanity, with a stronger desire to see men and women birthed into the kingdom. My desire to teach on holiness grew, and my fear of the Lord was strengthened. I became kinder to my wife and family, and they affirmed they saw a change in me. I wasn't getting as easily upset during adverse situations as I had before. I became softer and more compassionate, but at the same time maintained a warrior's heart and posture. Best of all, the Lord became nearer and dearer to me than ever before.

There was something else I noticed. My desire for His return wasn't out of wanting to see the cataclysmic events mentioned in Revelation. Now it was out of a true, heartfelt desire to be with Jesus and His family, and to see Him glorified in this earth. Then I started discovering in Scripture why this was happening to me. What I thought would make me lethargic, lazy, and even obnoxious gave me greater zeal and purpose. Gradually the Holy Spirit opened Scripture to me as to why my life was changing for the better, and I want to share it with you in this message. However, I'm getting ahead of myself! I need to take this from the top and not jump to the final conclusions until we're properly set up.

I open this message by imploring you: Please don't make the error I made. Often when bringing up end time teaching with others, I hear the type of negative response similar to what I developed years ago. But let's look at some amazing realities in Scripture; hopefully they will help you come to the same conclusion.

First, the book of Revelation is the most prophetic book in the Bible. Many believers shy away from it. In fact, I was sitting with a lovely couple at dinner recently, and the man said, "John, it's the only book of the Bible I haven't read." I asked why, because I knew he loved God deeply. His response was that he was scared of it and confused by it. There are so many who feel the same way—is that you as well? Read what is stated at the very beginning of the final book of the Bible:

> God blesses the one who *reads* the words of this prophecy to the church, and he blesses all who *listen to* its message and *obey* what it says, for the time is near.
>
> REVELATION 1:3

There is a called-out, specific blessing connected with *reading, listening to*, and *obeying* the prophetic Word of God! This promise isn't articulated or written so specifically in any other book of the Bible. Why? Could one reason be the foreknowledge of God? That He foresaw end time teaching would be avoided, and even mocked, more so than any other doctrine in our time? Peter writes:

> Most importantly, I want to remind you that in the last days scoffers will come, mocking the truth and following their own desires. They will say, "What happened to the promise that Jesus is coming again? From before the times of our ancestors, everything has remained the same since the world was first created."
>
> 2 PETER 3:3–4

I didn't reach the level of a scoffer. A scoffer is someone who makes fun of this truth. I certainly never disdained eschatology, but I did avoid it. I didn't embrace wholeheartedly this major teaching of the church. It's so critical to understand that these mockers Peter discusses will make light of any aspect of the second coming of Jesus! He begins this warning with the words "Most importantly." Stop and ponder this for a moment.

This is an attention grabber! Why does Peter single out the return of Jesus over the numerous other truths spoken of in the Word of God? Why doesn't he write this regarding the baptism of the Holy Spirit, the gifts of the Holy Spirit, praying in tongues, women in ministry, laying on of hands, or other current controversial topics? We've seen people question these truths or contend that they've passed and no longer apply to today. Why does Peter single out the second coming by attaching "most importantly" to it? Could it be because it's a major foundational teaching of the Lord Jesus Christ, and our great adversary, the devil, knows the powerful potential of accurately studying and pondering it, and therefore seeks to discredit it?

Consider these facts. The return of Jesus is the second-most frequently mentioned topic in the entire Bible. It is mentioned 318 times in the New Testament alone! Only four books in the New Testament don't discuss the return of Jesus, which mean twenty-three do. And three of those four books are single-chapter letters to individuals: Philemon, 2 John, and 3 John. The only multichapter book that doesn't mention the second coming is Galatians. Bottom line: One out of every thirty verses in the New Testament mentions some aspect of the return of Jesus. Not only this, but other than the doctrine of salvation, it was the most frequent topic written on by the early church fathers.[2]

Luke and Matthew take practically two entire chapters to expound on Jesus' second coming, and Mark takes one full chapter. The entire last book in the Bible is dedicated exclusively to end time events. If all this isn't enough, here is the most outstanding fact: The season of Jesus' second coming is the most-written-about time period in Scripture.

In light of these facts, let's ask the big, overarching question: If God, who is perfect in wisdom, gives this much attention to the second coming of Jesus in the Holy Scriptures, what should be the fruit of our reading, teaching, and discussing end time events? Slothfulness and contention, or godly living and passion to advance the kingdom? I think we can agree that He would never emphasize that which makes us live contrary to His will. So it is safe to conclude that any of the former crazy behaviors spawned by eschatology were fostered by it being either taught or heard incorrectly. As Peter states, it was twisted by unstable people.

You are wise to take time to read, meditate, and pray about this truth. But set your heart now that the fruit of this message will see godlier behavior in you and a more focused kingdom mission, and I believe the Holy Spirit will concur and manifest this godly goal. This has been my heartfelt prayer for you while writing this book.

In this message I will not only address some of what the Bible states about the return of the King, but even more importantly, I will share what Scripture exhorts us to do to be *prepared—ready—*so that we are not ashamed when He appears. Let's begin our journey.

PASSAGE: Happy is the one who reads this book, and happy are those who listen to the words of this prophetic message and obey what is written in this book! For the time is near when all these things will happen. (Revelation 1:3 GNT)

POINT: If the return of Jesus is the second-most taught doctrine in the Bible, then we should not avoid it and especially not make fun of it.

PONDER: Have I ignored, or even mocked in my own thoughts, one of the most discussed topics of the New Testament? Have I thought, *This is not for me, there is too much ambiguity*? What practical changes can I make in my approach to prophetic scriptures?

PRAYER: Dear Father, I ask You to forgive me for any laziness I've developed in seeking You regarding the return of Jesus. I repent. I ask that Your Spirit show me what is to come so that I can obey Your prophetic words of instruction or warning. In Jesus' name, amen.

PROFESSION: I am determined to pay close attention to the words of Scripture pointing to the end times. I have the Holy Spirit as my Teacher; I trust His guidance in listening to and obeying the prophetic scriptures.

SUCH THINGS WERE WRITTEN IN THE SCRIPTURES LONG AGO TO TEACH US. AND THE SCRIPTURES GIVE US HOPE AND ENCOURAGEMENT AS WE WAIT PATIENTLY FOR GOD'S PROMISES TO BE FULFILLED.

ROMANS 15:4

CHAPTER 2

RECOGNIZING THE KING

In a speech to the British House of Commons in 1948, Winston Churchill made the famous declaration, "Those who fail to learn from history are doomed to repeat it."[1] Such a simple yet true and profound statement. Regarding our discussion, let's heed this great leader's remarkable words and glean from divine antiquity.

What history am I speaking of? None other than Jesus' first coming. It would be wise to mine some key truth indicators from this monumental event, which occurred a little over two thousand years ago—roughly 2 to 1 BC. It's mind-blowing to think the Creator of the entire universe, both the seen and unseen worlds, chose to take on a human body and be born in a stable near Bethlehem rather than in a palace or comfortable home.

No different from His soon-approaching second coming, His first arrival was a foretold event that also created controversy. Many, including faith leaders, foresaw the Messiah's coming quite differently than what actually transpired. They anticipated a conquering king who would free Israel from Roman tyranny and usher in the golden age of their kingdom. To make matters more complex, they had scriptures to back their beliefs. They were all too familiar with Isaiah's famous writings that a child would be born, a Son given, and the government would rest upon His shoulders, and of His kingdom there would be no end (see Isaiah 9:6–7). This was just one of many prophetic promises that shaped their view.

In those days, not too different from our twenty-first-century church, there were factions of religious groups in Israel—the Pharisees, Sadducees, Essenes, and Scribes, to name just a few. We didn't know much about the Essenes until the discovery of the Dead Sea Scrolls. We owe a debt of gratitude for their stewardship of the early writings. They were the group of devout followers who hid the sacred writings in the caves of Qumran.

Sadly, many leaders were adversarial to the Creator who came as a humble Servant. Though they professed loyalty to almighty God and the writings of the Law and Prophets, their hearts were proud, corrupt, and unteachable, thus blinding them to the arrival of the lowly King.

At the same time, there were others who did anticipate the time and whereabouts of His arrival. Simply put, they recognized Him. How did they know while most didn't? The simple answer lies in their sensitivity to the Spirit of God and attention given to the writings of the Old Testament, especially the prophets. Their hunger for God created in them an awareness of the times. What advantage was that? They knew what to do, whether it was waiting, speaking, or a specific action.

Consider just a few.

When King Herod asked the faith leaders the whereabouts of Messiah's birth, they were able to tell him exactly what city. How did they know? It was their knowledge of the prophet Micah's words that He'd be born in Bethlehem (see Micah 5:2). We can safely speculate that these leaders whom Herod consulted were not corrupt like those who would resist Jesus years later. More than likely, they were members of the Essenes, who were more like the man we are about to discuss.

When Jesus was a baby, He was brought to the temple for His dedication. To grasp the wonder of what transpired that day needs a proper setup. A young couple from out of town, who were not public figures, who didn't stand out in any unusual way, walked into the temple with their forty-day-old baby. Numerous other young parents had done so on a regular basis, so nothing was out of the ordinary.

The temple area was not a quiet place, as a cathedral would typically be in our time. There were several buildings in the complex, teeming with people and lots of activity at any given time. Yet there, among many others, Simeon suddenly and decisively approached this young unknown couple. He took their baby in his arms and proclaimed, "The Messiah!"

Jesus was an infant! He hadn't performed any miracles yet. He hadn't preached a sermon. He didn't have any followers, just two young parents! What prompted this man? How did he recognize God manifested in the flesh as a one-month-old baby? In our answer lies the key to understanding prophetic events, which is easy to miss. Simeon was

> . . . *righteous* and *devout* and was *eagerly waiting* for the Messiah to come.
>
> LUKE 2:25

There are three characteristics of this man listed that reveal our answer. First, he was *righteous*. It's the Greek word *díkaios*. It's defined as one who "conforms in his actions to his constitutionally just character."[2] Simply put, anyone who possesses this quality not only professes loyalty to the Lord God but lives accordingly. In essence, Simeon strived for holiness. He sanctified the Lord in his heart and lived in a way that honored Him as supreme.

Simeon's second identified feature is being *devout*. It's the Greek word *eulabḗs*, meaning "one who had taken seriously God's promises and God's Word."[3] Simeon didn't avoid or shrug off the prophetic words of God but read, listened to, meditated on, and most importantly, prayed about them. He didn't have the attitude, *When Messiah comes, He will just do it. Why should I give any attention to this matter?*

This Greek word *eulabḗs* pertains "to being reverent toward God."[4] It describes one who lives in the holy fear of God. Simeon held firmly to this virtue, and it enlightened him with insight that others didn't possess (see Proverbs 8:13–14).

The third aspect highlighted of Simeon stems from the first two. If someone takes God's Word seriously, pursues godliness, and possesses the insight of holy fear, he or she will be *eagerly waiting*—wholeheartedly anticipating—the arrival of Messiah, especially in the season of His coming.

Let's drill down further into Simeon's character. He embraced the healthy fear of God, which was a fountain of instruction, knowledge, and wisdom within him. We are told, "The fear of the LORD is the beginning of wisdom; all those who practice it have a good understanding" (Psalm 111:10 ESV). One who fears God is not afraid of Him; rather, he or she is terrified of being away from Him. We live in awe of God and esteem Him above everything and anyone else. We love what He loves, and we hate what He hates. What is important to Him becomes important to us. What is not important to Him loses importance to us. When a man or woman truly fears God, he or she will pursue walking in holiness and true humility; it's their passion. Now hear what the psalmist writes:

> The humble He teaches His way. . . . Who is the man that fears the LORD? Him shall He teach in the way He chooses. . . . The secret of the LORD is with those who fear Him, and He will show them His covenant.
>
> PSALM 25:9, 12, 14 NKJV

We see that the virtue of holy fear opens us to the awareness of what God is doing; it's the starting place, as well as the continuous flow, of the instruction of wisdom (see Proverbs 14:27; 15:33). Wisdom—which includes instruction, insight, knowledge, and understanding—is vital to understanding prophecy. Without it, we interpret statements incorrectly and make foolish decisions, not much different from the ones described in the last chapter. It's such a priority in life that holy fear is referred to as God's treasure (see Isaiah 33:6) and is Jesus' delight (see Isaiah 11:3). Volumes have been written on this vital virtue, and after writing *The Awe of God*, I discovered just how much people are craving it in their lives. I highly recommend that book as a companion to this message.

As we journey through this message, it will become more and more apparent that people who pursue the fear of the Lord, true humility, and holiness will have a passion for God's Word, including prophecy. These foundational characteristics of those who knew the details of His first coming are true for those sensitive to His second coming. This should be the *foundation* of any message, especially eschatology. If we don't pursue these virtues, we will become dogmatic in our knowledge and steadily veer off course. We will miss the hidden mysteries and nuances of the prophetic Word of God that only the Holy Spirit can reveal to us.

Continuing with Simeon, we read:

> The Holy Spirit was upon him and had revealed to him that he would not die until he had seen the Lord's Messiah. That day the Spirit led him to the Temple. So when Mary and Joseph came to present the baby Jesus to the Lord as the law required, Simeon was there. He took the child in his arms and praised God, saying, "Sovereign Lord, now let your servant die in peace, as you have promised. I have seen your salvation, which you have prepared for all people. He is a light to reveal God to the nations, and he is the glory of your people Israel!" Jesus' parents were amazed at what was being said about him.
>
> LUKE 2:25–33

After discussing this remarkable event in depth, it's easier to see what amazed Jesus' parents. How could this stranger know what Mary kept to herself and pondered in her heart? Only God could reveal to a man such wonderful insight and knowledge!

But that wouldn't be the only surprise of the day for this young couple, because before they left the temple, a woman named Anna approached them and gave thanks to the Lord. "She talked about the child to everyone who had been *waiting expectantly* for God to rescue Jerusalem" (Luke 2:38). Notice she didn't speak to all in the temple, but to those who, like Simeon and herself, were *eagerly looking* for the coming Messiah.

There are others we can speak of, and I encourage you to search the Scriptures for them. I'll also share more of another group of devout men and women who knew the timing and whereabouts of His arrival in an upcoming chapter—the Essenes.

Simeon, Anna, and Herod's informants were similar to another group of seekers of a different generation:

> The sons of Issachar who had understanding of the times, to know what Israel ought to do.
>
> 1 CHRONICLES 12:32 NKJV

Of course, the sons of Issachar lived centuries before the coming of Jesus. However, a similar principle applies: Those who understand the times are the ones who *know what to do*, whether it entails watching, waiting, speaking, or a required action. Not once but twice we run into a remarkable promise in John's apocalyptic book. I shared in the last chapter the first occurrence, at the beginning of Revelation; however, the same promise appears toward the end of his book:

> "Look, I am coming soon! Blessed are those who *obey* the words of prophecy written in this book."
>
> REVELATION 22:7

These words were not spoken by the apostle John or even an angel; rather, they came directly from the mouth of Jesus. Notice the words "*obey* the words of prophecy." There's action to be taken with numerous prophetic words in the Bible. The behavior of the sons of Issachar aligned with Jesus' command; they were not only *perceptive* but *obedient* to the wisdom of God according to the season they were living in. In essence, they knew *what to do*. Simeon, Anna, Herod's informants, and others who eagerly listened to prophetic words were all among those who aligned their beliefs and actions with the wisdom of God.

The men and women who feared God, took His Word seriously, and pursued godly living were those who anticipated Jesus' first coming. They got it right; they were not misled; they knew what to do! On the other hand, the Pharisees, Sadducees, and scribes, who were all experts in the Old Testament, were a different story. These men's training in Judaism required memorization of the first five books of the Bible. Think of it, Genesis through Deuteronomy! I don't know many today who've memorized the four Gospels, which are shorter. These spiritual leaders were diligent in their studies and ministries, yet they couldn't recognize the Messiah thirty years later when He healed the sick, raised the dead, and cast out demons right before their eyes. Not only did they not identify Him, but they accused Him of being demon possessed, a drunkard, and a friend of sinners. Though they knew the Scriptures, they were completely out of step with the prophetic insight of Scripture.

In light of this, let's recall from our last chapter Peter's warning of "Most importantly" (see 2 Peter 3:3). In hindsight, could the reason behind his strong emphasis be to keep us from not falling into the trap of taking lightly what should be taken seriously?

So, at the onset of examining the prophetic Scriptures, I encourage both you and me to position our hearts as hungry ones who are seeking truth in a humble way. Let's determine to listen to what His Word states rather than draw from our own points of view. Let's fully trust Jesus' words that the Holy Spirit "will announce and declare to you the things that are to come [that will happen in the future]" (John 16:13 AMPC). If we do this, we will be positioned to say and do what will keep us in alignment with the divine will of God in these final days.

In this book, we will address what's to come but even more importantly how to be prepared and ready for His imminent return. This is the most important aspect of knowing the prophetic scriptures. We certainly don't want to be knowledgeable yet unwise, like the foolish bridesmaids left behind when the bridegroom comes (see Matthew 25:1–13). It's a very eye-opening and sobering parable that warns us to be ready for Jesus' return.

The good news is, out of God's deep love for us, He has provided a clear path that will keep us prepared and ready for the coming of our King. I've prayed diligently that our dear Teacher, the Holy Spirit, will guide us in our quest to not only discover the truth but remain faithful to our soon-coming King.

PASSAGE: At that time there was a man in Jerusalem named Simeon. He was righteous and devout and was eagerly waiting for the Messiah to come. (Luke 2:25)

POINT: It is important to approach prophetic scriptures with a posture of humility, pursuing godly living and abiding in reverential fear of the Lord. This grants the wisdom to understand prophecy.

PONDER: Why did the Pharisees and many of the other spiritual leaders not recognize Jesus' first appearing? Was their knowledge of Scripture, fasting twice a week, paying tithes even of their garden herbs, and faithful synagogue attendance enough? If not, why? Am I more like Simeon or the Pharisees? What needs to change in my behavior to follow Simeon's example? How can I live with a greater awareness of His coming?

PRAYER: Dear Father, I ask You to forgive me for not developing an eagerness for the return of my Lord Jesus Christ. Please help me to pursue godly living and holiness, and to study the Scriptures on a regular basis. I choose the holy fear of God to be my treasure and the foundation of my walk with Jesus. In choosing holy fear, I will have a high regard for the prophetic words of God. In Jesus' name, amen.

PROFESSION: I am determined to pursue godly living and holy fear and to develop an eager anticipation of the coming of my Lord Jesus Christ.

FOR EVERYTHING THERE IS

A *SEASON*, AND A *TIME* FOR

EVERY MATTER UNDER HEAVEN.

ECCLESIASTES 3:1 ESV

CHAPTER 3

SEASONS AND TIMES

Suppose you're a filmmaker and you embark on producing the famous story of the Chronicles of Narnia, *The Lion, the Witch and the Wardrobe.* You've decided to film the age of winter scenes in New Zealand, and conversely, the springtime scenes in the lush land of Ireland. You've determined both locations carry a majestic and surreal vibe that well depicts C. S. Lewis's storybook description of Narnia.

Your assistant books the flights and accommodations for all the actors, directors, camera crew, and other necessary personnel to fly to New Zealand in January to capture winter over the next few months. Then everyone will travel to Ireland in early May to capture all the fresh foliage and flowers blooming in springtime.

What happens? You're shocked when your entire team lands in New Zealand only to find out it's summertime! You didn't account for the fact that the seasons below the equator are completely opposite of the Northern Hemisphere. You were ignorant of the season, so you did the wrong thing.

There are spiritual *seasons* and *times*, and God determines them. King David writes, "My times are in Your hand" (Psalm 31:15 NKJV). God holds our appointed times, and I imagine most of us face moments we wish were in our hands, but that's foolish thinking. Daniel gives additional insight by writing, "He changes the times and the seasons" (Daniel 2:21 NKJV). Our Creator both determines and holds the power to change either one.

God may choose to hide appointed times or seasons, and in other situations, He desires for us to know them. Just before ascending to heaven, Jesus said to His disciples, "It is not for you to know times or seasons which the Father has put in His own authority" (Acts 1:7 NKJV). Yet, on the contrary, God spoke through the prophet Jeremiah,

> "You will be in Babylon for seventy years. But then I will come and do for you all the good things I have promised, and I will bring you home again."
>
> JEREMIAH 29:10

These are not contradictions; rather, with some appointed times awareness is granted, and with others, they are kept secret. Our responsibility is to seek God. If He chooses to reveal the time or season, it can be in a general sense, or it can be specific. At any rate, one thing is for certain: Our filmmaker should have been aware of the natural seasons. In contrast, spiritual times and seasons are not obvious to human logic; to understand them, we must seek God.

Allow me to further illustrate the importance of knowing seasons. If it's January in Edmonton, Alberta, and you work in outdoor-park maintenance, how do you dress for the day's work? If you put on board shorts, a T-shirt, and flip-flops and then head to work, you are going to meet up with great adversity in the negative-ten-degree temperature you face outdoors. You'll suffer terribly and could experience consequences for a few days, or even long-term. This outfit may have worked well in July, but you acted out of sync with the current season. There is nothing you can do to change the season of winter; it's firmly set, and the wise person acts in a way that cooperates with the present season, rather than fights it.

How about appointed times? They exist in the spiritual realm and are like our natural appointed times. Imagine being invited to dinner with the president of your nation on Thursday, October 7, at 6 p.m., but you show up on Thursday the 14th. Or what if you waited until 5:30 p.m. on the correct day and merely threw on a pair of jeans and a polo shirt? Right time but wrong preparation. That would have been fine for the appointed time of a professional football game with your friends, but this appointment was set for a different event, and you foolishly neglected to prepare for it.

It is important to understand times and seasons. Perhaps this is why one-third of Scripture is prophetic. God has much to say so we can prepare, be ready, and act in alignment with either the time or season. Jesus rebuked the spiritual leaders: "You fools! You know how to interpret the weather signs of the earth and sky, but you don't know how to interpret the present times" (Luke 12:56).

We as believers get ourselves into trouble when we shout what God whispers and whisper what He shouts. Let me give you an example. Jesus, more than once, rebuked the Pharisees for getting the two backward. These leaders were sticklers for paying tithes and would even pay 10 percent of their garden herbs, yet they neglected the "weightier matters" of the Word of God, such as justice, mercy, and faith (see Matthew 23:23). So clearly there are more important matters in Scripture. Jesus acknowledged it was correct to pay tithes on their garden herbs. Obedience to any command is not to be neglected, but there are levels of importance, and justice, faith, and mercy are weightier matters.

When I did word searches for *justice*, *mercy*, and *faith* in Scripture, I found 856 verses addressing one of these three. A word search on *tithing* brought up forty-one verses. From this, we can see God shouted one and didn't shout the other. Why would the second-most discussed topic in the Bible be the second coming? Let me stress again: It's not intended to make us slothful or give us knowledge to argue with others; rather, it's intended to show us the importance of the time and season of His second coming and, thus, what to do about it!

To further elaborate, let's look again at Jesus' first coming to discover more key truths to assist us regarding His second coming. There were weighty consequences for not recognizing His first visitation. As Jesus approached Jerusalem the week of His crucifixion, He wept and lifted His voice:

> "If you had known, even you, especially in this your day, the things that make for your peace! But now they are hidden from your eyes. For days will come upon you when your enemies will build an embankment around you, surround you and close you in on every side, and level you, and your children within you, to the ground; and they will not leave in you one stone upon another, because *you did not know the time* of your visitation."
>
> LUKE 19:42–44 NKJV

Jerusalem was held accountable for not knowing *the time* of its visitation, and Jesus revealed the terrible consequences. Sure enough, four decades later, in AD 70, General Titus and the armies of Rome would lay siege to Jerusalem for four months. The event was horrid, first because of starvation as a result of the siege, and then because of the bloodbath from the killing. Once the wall was breached, several Jews hid their small valuables, especially gold coins, by swallowing them. When the Roman soldiers discovered this, the army went on a rampage disemboweling Jerusalem's inhabitants. Eventually, both the temple and the city were destroyed. The army pulled every stone apart looking for more gold that might have been hidden within the walls. Historians estimate the death toll anywhere from 600,000 to over 1,000,000.[1]

Later, in the year 132, the Romans officially desolated the country of Israel, and the Holy Land remained under the control of Gentile nations until 1948 for the nation of Israel, and 1967 for the city of Jerusalem. This also fulfilled Jesus' words:

> "For there will be disaster in the land and great anger against this people. They will be killed by the sword or sent away as captives to all the nations of the world. And Jerusalem will be trampled down by the Gentiles until the period of the Gentiles comes to an end."
>
> LUKE 21:23–24

Why did the Jewish people suffer such horrific consequences? Jesus says it was due to not knowing *the time* of their visitation. But we must ask, how were they supposed to know? If you go back several hundred years to 586 BC,[2] you'll notice another horrific event happened to the Jewish people and the city of Jerusalem. They were plundered by the armies of Nebuchadnezzar, king of Babylon; most of the inhabitants were killed, but a remnant was taken as captives to his homeland. One of the captives was a wise young man named Daniel.

Several years into captivity and a few rulers later, Darius the Mede (Babylon was overtaken by the Medes and Persians) was now leading the world-dominating empire. During Darius's rule, Daniel was reading the Word of God revealed to the prophet Jeremiah, given prior to the Jewish captivity.

Daniel, in reading Jeremiah (25:11 and 29:10), discovered that Israel's captivity would span seventy years. Daniel, knowing they were near the end of this appointed time, started seeking the Lord through fasting and prayer. He cried out for twenty-one days, and suddenly the angel Gabriel came and shared with him very valuable insight regarding times and events. The archangel announced:

> "Now listen and understand! Seven sets of seven plus sixty-two sets of seven will pass from the time the command is given to rebuild Jerusalem until a ruler—the Anointed One—comes. Jerusalem will be rebuilt with streets and strong defenses, despite the perilous times.
>
> After this period of sixty-two sets of seven, the Anointed One will be killed, appearing to have accomplished nothing, and a ruler will arise whose armies will destroy the city and the Temple."
>
> DANIEL 9:25–26

I'll attempt to make this as simple as possible. Three sets of seven-year spans are listed:

Seven 7-year periods = 49 years
Sixty-two 7-year periods = 434 years
One 7-year period = 7 years
Total = 490 years

The first span was the time it would take to rebuild Jerusalem after Babylonian/Persian captivity. The second would be how much longer from that point until the Anointed One—Messiah—would be killed (a total of 483 years).

According to Gabriel, Messiah's death would seem to accomplish nothing. This explains why so many of Jesus' followers, including the disciples, were distraught over His death (see Luke 24:13–21).

Gabriel continued, "A ruler will arise whose armies will destroy the city and the Temple." This of course references the exact terrible event Jesus foretold—Titus destroying the Holy City in AD 70. There is more in the revelation to Daniel, but we will discuss it in a later chapter. For now, our focus is the appointed time of 483 years.

The huge question is, When was the command given to rebuild Jerusalem? After Daniel's death, over one hundred years later, a new king ruled the world. He was the Persian King Artaxerxes Longimanus. Nehemiah, a Jewish man, was cupbearer to this king. We find in the book of Nehemiah that in the month of Nisan (March) of the twentieth year of Artaxerxes' reign, this great king gave the command and funded a group of Jews, led by Nehemiah, to go back and rebuild Jerusalem (see Nehemiah 2:1).

So what date was this? Artaxerxes began his rule in 464 BC. The twentieth year of his reign would have fallen in the year 444.[3] Some sources say the exact date of this decree was March 14, 444 BC. We now have the starting point of Gabriel's decree. Simple math dictates to add 483 years to March 14, 444 BC, and this will pinpoint the time of Jesus' crucifixion. I wish it was that easy.

Bear with me just a bit more. The calculation is difficult due to the differences between our Gregorian calendar and the ancient Jewish calendar (not to be confused with the modern-day Jewish calendar). Our Gregorian calendar consists of 365 days per year, while the ancient Jewish calendar consists of 360 days. For example, in the book of Revelation we see twice that a 3.5-year time span is specifically identified as 1,260 days. If it was according to our calendar, it would be 1,278 days. That's a big difference. Therefore, 483 years in our calendar (factoring leap years) is 176,416 days, but according to the ancient Jewish calendar, it's 173,880 days, a 2,536-day difference (almost a seven-year difference)!

A church father named Julius Africanus, who lived in the third century, wrote a book entitled *On the Weeks and This Prophecy.* Only fragments remain, but in one of the fragments, he tells how to calculate moving back and forth between the two calendars. To keep it simple, years must be converted to days from one calendar and then that number of days is converted back to years on the other calendar. That's dumbing it down, as it is a little more complex. Another man, Sir Robert Anderson, an English lawyer and head of Scotland Yard, did the same work centuries later in the 1800s. Interestingly, Julius's lost work was discovered in the twentieth century, so Robert didn't have access to it, but both men's findings matched.

These men, and others who are much smarter than me, have determined that if we begin at March 14, 444 BC (the time Artaxerxes gave the command to rebuild Jerusalem) and use the conversion formula from calendar to calendar, we arrive at April 6, AD 32![4] Remarkable!

It gets even more exciting. By examining the sun and moon sequences of AD 32 we discover it fell on Passover week, to be exact, the day Jesus came into Jerusalem riding on a donkey. This fulfilled Zechariah's prophecy:

> Rejoice, O people of Zion! Shout in triumph, O people of Jerusalem!
> Look, your king is coming to you. He is righteous and victorious, yet he is humble, riding on a donkey—riding on a donkey's colt.
>
> ZECHARIAH 9:9

Let's play this drama out. Jesus came into Jerusalem on a donkey, wept over the city, and pronounced its doom. However, two different responses occurred among the Jewish people. One group spread out their garments on the road ahead of Him and praised God (see Luke 19:28–40), and the other group—those who didn't know the time of their visitation—cried out "Crucify Him" days later.

Jesus' followers knew what Zechariah and Daniel had prophesied; all the rest of the city didn't care to know the time of His visitation. Those who knew the prophetic word of God knew exactly what to do because they knew the time and season they were in.

Once again, we discover from history the importance of knowing the prophetic scriptures. It gave the people insight on how to behave in line with the will of God. How is this important to us in the twenty-first century? By the leading of God's Spirit, we discern from the Bible the current times and seasons, thus empowering us to be ready and act in alignment with the will of God. Most certainly there will come a day we'll look back and see the great blessings resulting from our obedience that the various times and seasons required.

PASSAGE: Jesus went into Galilee, where he preached God's Good News. "The time promised by God has come at last!" (Mark 1:14–15)

POINT: There are appointed times and seasons in God's kingdom.

PONDER: How can I become more sensitive to the season we are in? What is God showing me about the present time? How should this affect my behavior?

PRAYER: Dear heavenly Father, I realize there are times and seasons You desire me to be aware of. Please make me sensitive to where we are now and where we are headed. I ask this in Jesus' name, amen.

PROFESSION: I will not be ignorant of the will of God for the season I'm in, both for myself and the church at large.

WHERE THERE IS NO PROPHETIC VISION THE PEOPLE CAST OFF RESTRAINT.

PROVERBS 29:18 ESV

CHAPTER 4

THE PROPHETIC VISION

I have a brother-in-law named Dale; he's one of those guys who can do practically anything with his hands. He loves vintage muscle cars and had a vision of owning a perfect 1966 Chevelle SS in the twenty-first century. After a diligent search, he found one that was in terrible shape and rusted out, but that was all he needed. He stripped it down to its bare frame and began the process of rebuilding his dream car.

In interviewing him, I was amazed by the time, effort, and money he put into this car. It took three years and well over one thousand hours of work. Numerous nights he labored nonstop until 10 p.m. My sister, Laura, would often bring his dinner to the barn/garage so his work could continue.

It was a difficult project. First he had to sandblast the rusted frame and repaint it; then he had to hunt for parts; and finally the most tedious task: rebuild the entire engine. Often he would drive miles and shop numerous stores just to find one part. There were seasons of delay from not having enough finances to purchase the more expensive parts.

I asked, "Were there times you fought discouragement?"

He replied, "Yes, many!"

I probed further. "Were there times you wanted to quit?"

Again, "Yes."

One of those times was after building the entire engine, when he discovered the rear engine seal leaked. He bemoaned, "I had to spend numerous days taking the entire engine apart to fix the problem." Yet he continued and didn't quit.

It was a constant hunt to find bolts, screws, and other small parts from other original Chevelles. Most were not in good shape, but rather than just insert them in their rusted and dirty condition, he chose to sand and polish them, even though they ended up in obscure places. He desired every aspect of the car to be restored to its original glory.

I distinctly remember the day I saw the finished product. I was in awe of its perfection. I thought to myself, *A meal could be eaten on this car, either on the body or on top of the engine*, both were so dazzlingly clean. It was as if I was transported back forty years and was looking at a brand-new Chevelle sitting in a new-car dealership showroom.

Were there days requiring hours of research, both online and over the phone, with no apparent progress? Yes. Were there appointments requiring long drives to get one part? Yes! Were there times he had to sacrifice other activities to work on the car? Yes.

What fueled his persistence and what kept him from giving up? His vision! It became a *positive restraining force* that kept him from becoming slothful, distracted, or discouraged.

There is a restraining force that's healthy. As a former athlete who played Junior Davis Cup tennis, the USTA Circuit, and started on the Purdue University varsity tennis team, I'm well familiar with healthy restraints accompanying a vision. In high school I would forgo many different pleasures and activities to diligently practice and train. I restrained myself from anything that would keep me from pursuing my dream of starting on a Division 1 tennis team. In like manner, Paul writes:

> I discipline my body like an athlete, training it to do what it should. Otherwise, I fear that after preaching to others I myself might be *disqualified*.
>
> 1 CORINTHIANS 9:27

Professional athletes, performers, artists, entrepreneurs, and others who excel in their field stay the course leading to their end goal. They're diligent and not easily distracted. In similar fashion, the heavenly prophetic vision creates a restraining force in our lives. It keeps us vigilant and gives us a sense of urgency, protecting us from slothfulness and distractions. Most importantly, it protects us from the disastrous end of being eternally *disqualified.*

Allow me to further elaborate. This world has a flow that's contrary to the way of God's kingdom. Scripture calls it the "course of this world" and it is powered by the prince of darkness and his legions of warriors (see Ephesians 2:2). Its effects manifest in the form of diversions, laziness, discouragement, enticements . . . and the list is too long to complete. Bottom line, it wants you out of God's purposes, out of sync with His appointed times and seasons. It's strong and deceptive, and without the restraints fostered by the prophetic vision, the flow can easily pull us out of sync with the kingdom of God before we know what's happened. Listen to the apostle Paul's words:

> We are instructed to turn from godless living and sinful pleasures. We should live in this evil world with wisdom, righteousness, and devotion to God, *while we look forward with hope* to that wonderful day when the glory of our great God and Savior, Jesus Christ, will be revealed.
>
> Titus 2:12–13

Notice the words "while we look forward with hope" regarding Jesus' second coming. Recall that Simeon was "eagerly waiting" for the Messiah. When we live with eager anticipation of His return to set up the kingdom, it creates a restraining force that protects us from godless living and sinful pleasures. These behaviors harden our hearts, which if not addressed can lead to disqualification. Does this give us additional insight into Simeon? Could the *hope* (or eager expectation) of Jesus' first coming be what fueled Simeon's holy fear, humility, and godly living? I believe it was!

The apostle John confirms this truth. He writes that our *eager expectation* (hope) of Jesus' return creates a healthy restraining force:

> We know that when He is revealed, we shall be like Him, for we shall see Him as He is. And everyone who has this *hope* in Him *purifies himself*, just as He is pure.
>
> 1 JOHN 3:2–3 NKJV

There is a *purifying force* connected to the *eager expectation* of Jesus' return. It's a restrainer that protects us from the onslaughts and pollutions of this world! In looking back, I've seen this truth exemplified repeatedly in many decades of ministry.

In 2016 I was asked to speak to a conference held in Brazil. It was a closed conference; only pastors or leaders of a church network were permitted to attend. It was held in the city of Goiânia. To my surprise, I entered an arena with over twelve thousand hungry leaders. They were vibrant and passionate; it seemed they might blow the roof off the arena with their energy.

The next day I had lunch with the eight top pastors of the network. I inquired, "Gentlemen, if those in attendance were just pastors and leaders last evening, how many people are in your churches?"

One responded, "Well over 300,000 people."

Amazed, I exclaimed, "Really? So when did this all begin and who was the founder?"

I anticipated hearing that it began well over one hundred years earlier, with the founder passing on to his heavenly reward decades or even a century ago. But to my amazement, their immediate reply was, "It started sixteen years ago with one man. You spent time with him last evening, but he couldn't attend our lunch today because of a previous appointment."

I wish someone could have taken a picture of my face at that moment. In shock, I dropped my fork, losing interest in my meal, and blurted out, "What? Wait a minute, you're telling me that just sixteen years ago one person started a church that today claims well over 300,000 people as members?"

They all responded, "Yes, exactly."

I quickly asked, "How do you do such a thing in a first-world nation?" (I thought I knew the answer to my question: It would be the effectiveness of their small discipleship groups.)

However, without hesitation, one of the pastors responded, "It's because we teach our people the second coming of Jesus, His assessment—judgment—of what we did with our lives, the ensuing eternal rewards, and how this will set our positions of leadership in the millennium and throughout eternity."

I was stunned and speechless.

The pastor could see my bewilderment, so he continued, "John, due to my ability to effectively communicate in English, I've been asked to minister at numerous Christian conferences in the USA. I've observed an interesting reality in most American believers. They see life through a seventy-to-eighty-year perspective, whereas our people see life through the eternal perspective."

His comment profoundly impacted me. I contemplated and prayed about it long and hard. Jesus says the light of our body is the eye, which is our perspective (see Matthew 6:22–23), and perspective directs our lives. Here's a crude example: If you were to walk into an exquisite Sunday brunch buffet and notice two tables filled with a vast variety of delicious desserts, what would you do? If you have a one-day perspective, you will eat one of each of the varieties. But what if you looked at all the same desserts with a one-year perspective? You will most likely eat one or none of them. Why? Your sight goes beyond that day; you don't want an upset stomach tomorrow, ten pounds of fat on your body next week, and compromised health. Your perspective fosters a restraint that will benefit your long-term health.

When we have the prophetic vision—an eternal perspective, rather than a seventy-to-eighty-year view of life—we have a restraining force that keeps us from making choices detrimental to our eternal state. Our present decisions are altered. Our template for making decisions is different, and the outcome is better and wiser choices. We endure things we wouldn't endure without the eternal perspective. We're willing to suffer the hardships, afflictions, and persecutions that are thrown at us by this world, rather than compromise obedience and godliness for short-term benefits, pleasures, or acceptance. In essence, we live differently!

In 2022 I learned of a major survey done by Barna that broke my heart.

This highly respected organization was investigating the health of the American church. Over ninety-five thousand people were strategically chosen to poll (most surveys involve three thousand to four thousand people; Barna sought greater accuracy in their findings).

The company gave percentages in their published report. I've converted the percentages to actual numbers to reveal their shocking discoveries. They put people into three categories:

1. **Practicing Christians**: Those who identified as Christian agreed strongly that faith is very important in their lives and have attended church in the past month.
2. **Non-practicing Christians**: Those who self-identified as Christians who do not qualify as practicing.
3. **Non-Christians**: US adults who did not identify as Christian.

They discovered that in the year 2000, approximately 126 million Americans identified as "practicing Christians." Over the next twenty years, 33 million moved to the "non-practicing Christian" category, and an additional 33 million moved from "practicing Christians" to "non-Christians," many of whom now are professing atheists and agnostics. Pause for a moment to think of the size of these two numbers.[1]

Most would say 33 million have fallen away, due to counting only the third category. That number alone is heartbreaking. However, consider more carefully the "non-practicing Christian" group. It can be contested that this group doesn't fall under the description of a New Testament follower of Jesus. With faith no longer a priority in their life, and neglecting God's Word to assemble with other believers (see Hebrews 10:25), it's a stretch to put the word "Christian" in this category. It seems they fell from the faith just as the third group did; they're just not admitting it.

This means 66 million people have departed from the faith. The population of the USA in the year 2021 was 332 million; 66 million represents one in five Americans. This is a disaster! The apostle Paul foretold this by writing:

> Let no one deceive or beguile you in any way, for that day will not come except the apostasy comes first [unless the predicted great falling away of those who have professed to be Christians has come].
>
> 2 THESSALONIANS 2:3 AMPC

This sign reveals two things. First, it shows we are near the return of Jesus (I'll expound on this later). Second, it tells us departing from the faith is a reality. In modern Christianity many believe it's impossible to fall away from faith. Yet Jesus warns that one of the main signs of the end days will be that "many . . . will stumble and fall away" (Matthew 24:10 AMPC).

Let's pause and ask, Is this another indicator of what happens if we neglect the prophetic scriptures? Did the early church fathers know something we don't, and is this why they strongly emphasized this aspect of our faith? We are told:

> Therefore let us go on and get past the *elementary* stage in the teachings and doctrine of Christ . . . not again . . . laying the *foundation* of . . . the resurrection from the dead, and eternal judgment and punishment. [These are all matters of which you should have been fully aware long, long ago.]
>
> HEBREWS 6:1–2 AMPC

As we will see later in this message, the resurrection from the dead is directly connected to the second coming of Jesus. I've highlighted two important words associated with His return.

First, *elementary.* What do we learn in elementary school? How to read, write, add, and subtract. Can you imagine building your college education without this knowledge? It would be very difficult, if not impossible. Let's bring this illustration over to our faith. How are we maturing in our walk if we don't have the basic building blocks? Does this explain why so many are being easily deceived?

The second word is *foundation.* What happens to a building that lacks a foundation? It's fine if the wind doesn't blow and storms don't come. In fact, it can be a bigger and more beautiful building than a smaller structure with a strong foundation. But once a powerful enough storm arrives, down it comes, while the smaller one stands. The bigger the building, the harder it will fall! How many who have walked away from the faith were at one time very outspoken and enthusiastic about Jesus? Did they lack the *foundation*, the *elementary* building blocks needed to become a true disciple?

We have different outcomes, and it would be prudent to compare them. In the first two decades of the twenty-first century, we have a Brazilian church growing at an exponential rate alongside an American church that's rapidly leaking oil, seeing masses of people walk away from the faith. The Brazilian church emphasizes eschatology. Do our American churches do that?

I admit that I stayed quiet on these important truths for years. In fact, for decades! Was this the scriptural choice for creating long-term disciples? I've had a change of heart; I've been compelled in my personal life and now in public ministry to speak out regarding God's prophetic Word.

PASSAGE: "When the Spirit of truth comes, he will guide you into all truth. . . . He will tell you about the future." (John 16:13)

POINT: The prophetic scriptures, when properly approached with the help of the Holy Spirit, create a healthy restraint in our heart and mind that keeps us in alignment with the eternal. It's imperative to be obedient to them.

PONDER: Has a lack of clarity kept me from seeking out the wisdom of prophetic scriptures? Have I been intimidated by their uncertainty? How can this change? Wouldn't it be wise to ask and trust the Holy Spirit to give me understanding regarding these truths?

PRAYER: Heavenly Father, Jesus promised the Holy Spirit will guide me into all truth and will tell me about the future. I ask that as I continue to seek, study, and meditate on the prophetic scriptures, Your Spirit will lead me into truth and show me what to do. I ask this in Jesus' name, amen.

PROFESSION: I am thankful that I can know the truth about the future because I have God's Spirit as my Teacher.

HE CHOSE THEM TO BECOME LIKE HIS SON, SO THAT HIS SON WOULD BE THE FIRSTBORN AMONG MANY BROTHERS AND SISTERS. AND HAVING CHOSEN THEM, HE CALLED THEM TO COME TO HIM. AND HAVING CALLED THEM, HE GAVE THEM RIGHT STANDING WITH HIMSELF. AND HAVING GIVEN THEM RIGHT STANDING, HE GAVE THEM HIS GLORY.

ROMANS 8:29-30

CHAPTER 5

THE DIVINE MASTER PLAN

With a basic understanding of times, seasons, and prophetic vision, we now possess the language to address the second coming of Jesus Christ. However, to fully understand what lies ahead, we first need to step back and look at the overall prophetic vision: the divine master plan for mankind.

To illustrate its importance, let's return to the story of my brother-in-law's 1966 Chevelle. Today's automobiles no longer use carburetors; they were replaced in the 1990s by fuel-injection systems. Let's assume you have no idea Dale is rebuilding a forty-year-old car. Your sole observation is limited to his tedious and time-consuming process of assembling a carburetor, including sanding and polishing every part, even the bolts and nuts that hold it together. You'd question, why all the hard work for something of no value; what's the use? Dale, on the other hand, sees a shiny and well-running '66 Chevelle. If you were assigned to rebuild the carburetor, you wouldn't be motivated to endure the arduous task, whereas he would eagerly continue to completion. The sole difference is that he sees the overall project—the master plan—while you see only one aspect of it.

The same is true for the second coming. If we look at Jesus' return through the perspective of a single event rather than through the eyes of God's glorious master plan, we'll lack the eager expectation that enables us to stay diligent in our obedience to the end. We are vulnerable—easy prey for distraction, discouragement, or deception.

God drew up this master plan for His kingdom before time began. There are numerous Scripture passages[1] confirming this truth, one being Isaiah 46:9–10:

> I am God, and there is none like me, declaring the end from the beginning and from ancient times things not yet done, saying, "My counsel shall stand, and *I will accomplish all my purpose*." (ESV)

The Lord God is the only One in the universe who wasn't created. He is from eternity past. As a sidenote, this truth is impossible to mentally comprehend, so don't go there; our brains are finite in their understanding. The good news is we can grasp this reality in our hearts, because God placed eternity there (see Ecclesiastes 3:11).

There are many characteristics that make God holy—set apart from all creation. One is that there is no other being that can foretell and control the future; only He can. He states through the prophet Isaiah, "I told you beforehand what I was going to do. Then you could never say, 'My idols did it'" (Isaiah 48:5). This statement separates His ability from all others. In fact, He makes the bold challenge: "Let them tell us what the future holds . . . tell us what will occur in the days ahead. Then we will know you are gods" (Isaiah 41:22–23). Have there been a few individuals who've accurately predicted future events by chance? Of course. Have there been familiar spirits who have heard things from God's throne, which He permitted, and subsequently revealed this knowledge to a few humans? Again, yes. However, He's the only One who truly foretells and controls the future.

God Almighty has a master plan that was formulated before time began, and in this regard He declares: "I will accomplish all My purpose." This explains why Jesus is referred to as "the Lamb slain from the foundation of the world" (Revelation 13:8 NKJV). This revealing statement tells us that God knew before He created our seen world that mankind would mess up and be in need of a Redeemer.

But hold on!

If God knew mankind would need a Redeemer before creating humans, and even more importantly, knew the pain and suffering that would be involved, both on His end and our end, why go through the trouble? Why not come up with a different plan altogether? This question causes us to dig deeper, to look further into the heart of His master plan.

It was all initiated from a strong desire in God's heart to have a family; to be more specific, a family that would inherit all He has, share in His glory, and govern throughout eternity with Him. This is His desire, will, and purpose, one He will not recant, nor can it ever be altered by anyone, whether it's an individual or a vast number of enemies.

The magnitude of wonder in this statement is both unfathomable and mind-blowing, so a pause to elaborate would be greatly beneficial. Allow me to illustrate. Let's imagine a global ruler—a king who is the wealthiest, wisest, and most noble in all the world, one who cannot be matched or defeated. He travels to one of his territories in the outer realm and during the visit decides to tour one of the most impoverished communities, a slum. In the process, he beholds an utterly poor and helpless young man (or woman) and is moved with empathy and compassion. Suddenly, to the surprise of his attendants and soldiers, he chooses to take this destitute, homeless young person into his family, not just to adopt but to make him (or her) heir to all he owns. A shocking move? It's almost unimaginable. This is merely a very weak example of what God has done for us. The apostle John writes:

> See what [an incredible] quality of love the Father has given (shown, bestowed on) us, that we should [be permitted to] be named and called and counted the children of God! And so we are!
>
> 1 JOHN 3:1 AMPC

The magnitude of love and generosity in His master plan is incomprehensible and generates greater astonishment the more we understand the glory of the One we're talking about. This is God Almighty, Creator of everything seen and unseen! The depth of His power, wisdom, and understanding revealed in just visible creation causes profound wonder and awe. Scientists have given their lives to understand both the intricacy and enormity of His handiwork and have merely scratched the surface.

As a high school student who had no relationship with God, I remember studying the universe as a hobby. As arrogant and prideful as I was, my investigation of His handiwork fostered awe and wonder within my dark soul. As a student of science, I knew it was utter foolishness to think it all happened by chance. I couldn't buy into the lie of evolution my teachers tried to instill in me. I knew even as an unsaved man that there was a Creator, and He was awesome, and the more I comprehended the science of the universe, the more I was convinced.

This glorious Creator has chosen to adopt us! Yes, we who are less than specks in a vast universe are the focus of His affection. And we must keep in mind, this is only the seen universe; there is an unseen realm that we can safely assume vastly trumps our seen world. Paul touches on this by writing, "By Him all things were created that are in heaven and that are on earth, visible and invisible, whether thrones or dominions or principalities or powers" (Colossians 1:16 NKJV).

Scripture records an exclamation of one who struggled to grasp the depth of love, compassion, and desire God has for such a seemingly insignificant part of His creation. His specific words:

> O LORD, our Lord, your majestic name fills the earth! Your glory is higher than the heavens. . . . When I look at the night sky and see the work of your fingers—the moon and the stars you set in place—what are mere mortals that you should think about them, human beings that you should care for them? Yet you made them only a little lower than God and crowned them with glory and honor.
>
> PSALM 8:1, 3–5

We wonder, what was the divine inspiration behind this cry—this passionate statement? I have a theory, and it can't be proven scripturally, but it bears mentioning. There are powerful angels called seraphim who are privileged to be next to God's throne. They are so mighty that when just one of them raises his voice, the entire heavenly arena, which most likely holds over a billion beings, shakes to its foundations from the magnitude of his voice (see Isaiah 6:4).

If God decides to travel, these four seraphim, also referred to as "living beings," travel with Him (see Ezekiel 1). That means when God came to the earth and formed Adam's body from the elements of the earth and breathed into his nostrils the breath of life, thus making Adam a living being, the seraphim were present. When they saw their almighty God's affection and love for this created human being, I imagine one of them crying out, "What are human beings, that You, God Almighty, should give such attention to and care so deeply for them!" I believe all four seraphim were shocked, amazed, and in awe; they struggled to comprehend the why behind such love directed toward such inferior beings. Yet God declared, "I have crowned them with glory and honor; they shall be My children, My heirs!"

The gap between our present state and who we actually are is monumental. But at Jesus' appearing, this will drastically change, for on that day who we really are will be unveiled. It's remotely, and I mean very remotely, like an ugly caterpillar transforming into a glorious butterfly on its given day, and I can't stress enough, that's a terribly weak example. We would be moving toward a better comparison if we were able to turn a gnat into a high-powered human athlete. Yet, as unfathomable as this is, it still doesn't come close! The apostle John continues:

> Beloved, now we are children of God; and it has not yet been revealed what we shall be, but we know that when He is revealed, we shall be *like Him.*
>
> 1 JOHN 3:2 NKJV

Like Him! Are you grasping the magnitude of what is being stated? When Jesus appears, His radiant countenance shall be so immensely profound that the sun and stars, even though they're still shining, will be darkened. The brilliant light of His glory will darken our blazing sun, no differently than when the same sun darkens the nighttime stars once it crests the horizon. They're still there—still shining, but the sun's magnitude of glory is so much greater than the stars that it darkens them. This is what Jesus' shining glory will do to the sun! Wow, what glory!

In that moment strong men and women "will crawl into holes in the ground. They will hide in caves in the rocks from . . . the glory of his majesty" (Isaiah 2:19). His brilliant countenance shall be so great that they will even cry out for the rocks to fall on them (see Revelation 6:16).

Now consider what we just read: We will be *like Him*! Are you grasping this? Are you in awe? Paul confirms by writing, "When Christ, who is your life, is revealed to the whole world, you will share in *all his glory*" (Colossians 3:4). *All His glory.* Not a small speck of it, nor even some of it; rather, we will share in "all His glory." We will be one with Him, He in us and we in Him. In the same context, Daniel also writes, "Those who are wise will shine as bright as the sky, and . . . shine like the stars forever" (Daniel 12:3). Our sun is a star; it's no different from the other stars. Jesus will forever have preeminence, we will forever worship Him; yet we have been welcomed as joint heirs with Him to share in His glory. It's too incomprehensible to fully grasp, but nevertheless, it's the truth.

I hope the Holy Spirit is giving you a greater glimpse into the magnitude of what He's bestowed upon His children. But let's not get ahead of ourselves. Let's back up to the inception.

God desired sons and daughters who would freely choose to love and obey Him. So, before this entrustment could be given to those He would adopt into His family, a test of loyalty would be required. He would not author the temptations of unfaithfulness, for He could never do such a thing. Rather, He would permit Satan and his hosts, those who had already revolted against Him, to be the proving instruments.

It began in the garden, called Eden, where there were two highlighted trees. One, the Tree of Life, which represented absolute trust in God's wisdom. To partake of this tree acknowledged nothing good could be found outside of His will. The other, the Tree of Knowledge of Good and Evil, represented the choice of determining "what's best for me" independent from the counsel of His will. To partake was forbidden; it would bring separation between God and mankind.

The Lord God knew in advance that the father and mother of all human beings would betray Him. They would disobey and choose independence from the counsel of His will. In doing so they would be separated from Life Himself and enslave themselves to the ruler of darkness. They would choose a corrupt nature of sin and death, no longer able to live in God's presence. This nature would pass on to all of Adam's descendants—all of mankind.

Yet God's love is so profound that even though humanity chose to rebel and commit high treason against their Creator, He still desired human beings to be adopted as family members. So God decided to take on a human body and pay the price with His own life to purchase us back to Himself—back to freedom. He couldn't do it as God Almighty, because He had given the earth to mankind. For Him to come and directly rescue us would be a violation of His Word, and God cannot lie.

This is why Jesus had to be born of a virgin, a woman who had never known a man sexually, impregnated by God's Spirit. This would make Him free from the nature of sin that was passed on from generation to generation through Adam's rebellion. It would make Him 100 percent man, being born of a woman, but also 100 percent God, being fathered by the Holy Spirit. Even though He was equal with God, the plan was for Him to walk this earth as a Man with a sin-free, divine nature filled with God's Spirit. His faithfulness would be tested in every aspect, yet not once would He fail in disobedience.

He would be the forerunner of a breed of people who would give their allegiance, trust, and obedience to Him. A phenomenal invitation would be extended to them, and we'll expound on this as we continue to unfold the master plan behind Jesus' second coming.

PASSAGE: Since we are his children, we are his heirs. In fact, together with Christ we are heirs of God's glory. (Romans 8:17)

POINT: God predetermined that the faithful would inherit all that is His.

PONDER: Stop and think of the glory Jesus gave up by taking on a human body and being birthed in this world. Yet He did it so that you could be a joint heir! What does it mean to be an heir? Can you imagine what being an heir of God entails? What does it mean that we inherit God's glory?

PRAYER: Dear heavenly Father, Your Word states that You want me to know what is the rich and glorious inheritance that You have given to us—to me (see Ephesians 1:18–19). I ask that You open my eyes to see this master plan and that the fruit of this knowledge would be evident in my life. In the name of Jesus, amen.

PROFESSION: Knowing God's master plan will help protect me from fainting, quitting, or being deceived into walking away.

THE WISDOM WE SPEAK OF IS THE MYSTERY OF GOD—HIS PLAN THAT WAS PREVIOUSLY HIDDEN, EVEN THOUGH HE MADE IT FOR OUR ULTIMATE GLORY BEFORE THE WORLD BEGAN. BUT THE RULERS OF THIS WORLD HAVE NOT UNDERSTOOD IT; IF THEY HAD, THEY WOULD NOT HAVE CRUCIFIED OUR GLORIOUS LORD.

1 CORINTHIANS 2:7-8

CHAPTER 6

UNFATHOMABLE LOVE

Imagine hiding a wonderful secret from those you love—a plan you've devised for their best interest, keeping it a mystery not just for a few months, years, or even decades, but longer. You'd give them clues along the way, but during this long stretch of time you'd refrain from sharing your magnificent strategy with the very ones for whom it's intended.

Not an easy thing to do, yet the Lord did exactly this!

God kept His grandest plan, the one He made "for our ultimate glory," a secret, not just for decades or centuries but for thousands of years. He knew if it leaked out, the dark rulers of this world wouldn't have played into it so perfectly.

Our opening scripture once again shows that when the prophetic vision is unknown, not only humans but even spirit beings end up doing the very opposite of what they would have done had they known. Sorrow will ultimately prevail from ignorant actions. But for Christ followers, here is the fabulous news. The apostle Paul continues:

> But as it is written, "Eye has not seen, nor ear heard, nor have entered into the heart of man the things which God has prepared for those who love Him." But God has *revealed them to us* through His Spirit. For the Spirit searches all things, yes, the deep things of God.
>
> 1 CORINTHIANS 2:9–10 NKJV

The master plan, which includes what lies ahead, is no longer a secret; it's been *revealed*! Most people quote only the first half, verse 9, implying it's still hidden. This is not true! If there's ignorance, it's from a lack of seeking and searching out what the Spirit of God opens our eyes, ears, and heart to in His Word.

In light of this, let's continue our journey. Again, it's important to emphasize the need to first look back to grasp the magnitude of what lies ahead—Jesus' second coming. So let's continue this journey together.

As already noted, in the garden of Eden, Satan successfully captured humanity through Adam's betrayal. It didn't just affect human beings but all visible creation (see Romans 8:20). The Lord God was ahead of the problem as He had previously devised a plan to recover what had been lost. He gave the first clue in the garden when He promised that the woman's Seed—the Messiah—would destroy Satan's works (see Genesis 3:15).

As generations passed, promises were made and covenants cut with select individuals. God's tactical moves with these faithful men and women were all part of His end goal of bringing forth the Seed—the Lamb slain from the foundation of the world. Some of the key figures were the following:

- Noah, whose obedience preserved the lineage of the Seed
- Abraham, who, in cutting covenant with the Almighty, secured the Seed
- Moses, who showed the necessity for the Seed
- King David, who received the promise of the Seed's eternal throne
- The prophets, who would give glimpses of the Seed's work, sacrifice, and the glories that would follow
- Mary, the woman blessed of all women, who was impregnated with the Seed
- And finally, John the Baptist, who prepared the people for Messiah's arrival

Bits and pieces of God's strategic plan were revealed right up to Messiah's first appearance. The wonder and depth of love in the divine plan is too marvelous to fully articulate, so please bear with me as I attempt to put it in words, in real time.

Our Creator makes the decision to leave the unimaginable, magnificent glories of heaven. He enters a cursed earth by being miraculously conceived in a woman's body—God becoming flesh and blood! His name is Yēshūʿa, known by us who speak English as Jesus.

The Lord, like any other human, develops and grows in His mother's womb, is birthed, and comes forth as an infant no different from any of us. He requires the parenting of His mother and stepfather! Are you getting an initial glimpse of the wonder? Our Creator put Himself into the care of His creation. He will require His mother's breast milk and nurture along with His stepfather's protection and provision.

Even though He is God, He doesn't hold on to His divine privileges but sets them aside and lives as a Man filled with God's Spirit. He doesn't bring obedience to earth; rather, He learns it by what He suffers. He is tested—enticed to disobey His Father, God Almighty, in every way. The Enemy throws his shrewdest, meanest, and most difficult temptations at Him, but not one succeeds (see Philippians 2:6–7; Hebrews 4:15; 5:8).

Jesus spends three years teaching and revealing two main truths: first, who God is; and second, how man should live before Him. In the process He becomes incessantly resisted—lied about, slandered, labeled a heretic, and even threatened. This persecution only escalates right up to the climactic purpose of His coming.

He is keenly aware of the unfathomable agony He will face to finish His assignment, giving small bits of insight to His close followers in advance. He reveals that a trusted friend will betray Him, another will deny Him, and the rest will abandon Him in the critical hour.

What Jesus faces brings such turmoil in both soul and body that His sweat becomes drops of blood (a phenomenon documented as medically occurring under horrific pressure[1]). He pleads with His Father that if there is any other way to accomplish mankind's salvation, He would alter the course, but there isn't another path. It is Jesus' greatest temptation: knowing He can call for legions of angels to deliver Him from the gruesome treatment that awaits but that doing so will forgo the very purpose of His coming and lose those He deeply loves. He chooses to stay the course and face unspeakable suffering.

Jesus is quite aware of what He'd revealed to Isaiah hundreds of years earlier:

> "I gave My back to those who struck Me, and My cheeks to those who plucked out the beard; I did not hide My face from shame and spitting."
>
> ISAIAH 50:6 NKJV

The extent of the horrific evening and morning following His arrest is easy to miss. The full picture is woven throughout the four Gospels, and only in putting them all together do we get a comprehensive account. As you read, don't skim or speed through it, but ponder deeply what He did for you. Keep in the forefront of your mind that this is our Creator and He willingly endured this cruelty.

Jesus gets no sleep that evening as He is moved five times to four different locations. He is unfairly examined and beaten in each of them. It starts at Annas's house (father-in-law of the high priest), where He is tied up and verbally and physically assaulted.

Once they finish, Jesus is transferred to the temple to stand before the high priest himself, Caiaphas, as well as other leading priests, supported by the temple guard. Everyone assembled vehemently hates Him, and no one stands by His side or comes to His defense.

Caiaphas's trained soldiers blindfold Jesus so He does not know when the blows will be administered. They proceed to spit in His face and slug Him with their fists. They ruthlessly and relentlessly beat and ridicule Him—hurling all sorts of insults as they whale on Him. This continues for hours until the light of morning, only for Him to be moved again to the next round of brutality.

Next, He stands trial before the Roman governor, Pontius Pilate. In due process, Pilate discovers Jesus is a Galilean, under Herod's jurisdiction. Therefore, he sends Jesus to Herod, the notorious corrupt king who murdered the Lord's cousin. If that isn't enough, to make matters worse, many of the chief priests follow along to continue their scathing insults and false accusations in hopes of inciting Herod to even greater brutality.

The king's squad of soldiers, who are called "men of war," begin a fresh round of verbal and physical assaults, similar to what Caiaphas's soldiers exhausted themselves doing all night long. This fresh batch of warriors unmercifully beats and ridicules Him, even dressing Him in a mock royal robe. Once Herod's warriors wear themselves out, Jesus is sent back to Pilate, where He faces the greatest brutality yet.

Pilate's soldiers are another level of fierce; these men are part of the most dominant military force on the planet, their skill and strength exceeding the brigades of both Caiaphas and Herod. To make matters worse, these Gentile warriors are most likely frustrated over the extra time on duty due to the Jewish festival—Passover.

Pilate turns Jesus over to his trained warriors. The captain calls for the entire regiment of soldiers to come and participate in the brutal torture. They strip Jesus naked, spit on him, rip out His beard, and vehemently thrash Him with their fists, the reed, and other instruments of torture until they are exhausted. Think of the intensity and time involved—an entire regiment of trained and highly skilled soldiers brutally torturing a Man until they're "worn out." It's unfathomable!

The flogging is without a doubt the worst phase of the beatings. The soldiers tie him naked to a short scourging post made of stone. His hands are tied over His head to a metal ring and His wrists securely shackled to restrain His body from movement.

Once He is harnessed and stretched out over it, they proceed to thrash Him at least forty times, and some believe more, because the Romans had no laws limiting the blows. One commentary reads: "Scourging was a brutal affair. It was inflicted by a whip of several thongs, each of which was loaded with pieces of bone or metal. It could make pulp of a man's back."[2]

Then they weave together a ring of thorns, each at least an inch long and so sharp and strong that they might as well have been nails. They press the crown into His scalp, causing severe lacerations. Blood pours down Jesus' face while they put a bogus scepter in His hand, a reed, and proceed to taunt and mercilessly beat Him.

Ponder this: The soldier (or soldiers, because often it was two men each with a whip administering blows consecutively) executing this torture is demonized and most likely hates Jewish people. He is skilled and knows how to inflict the greatest pain and damage. No mercy is extended. Rick Renner writes, "Historical records describe a victim's back as being so mutilated after a Roman scourging that his spine could actually be exposed."[3]

The total approximate time of brutal torture, in four different locations, lasts close to ten hours! Jesus is unimaginably beaten. The prophet Isaiah wrote hundreds of years earlier:

> Many were amazed when they saw him. His face was so disfigured he seemed hardly human, and from his appearance, one would scarcely know he was a man.
>
> Isaiah 52:14

Jesus is so physically abused, for so many hours, by different regiments of warriors, that by the time He heads for the crucifixion He no longer looks like a human being. A horrifying, dreadful sight to all bystanders.

Jesus knew beforehand that this inhumane torture awaited Him, which is why He sweat great drops of blood in the garden of Gethsemane, crying out for a possible alternate path for mankind's salvation. The level of stress and cruelty endured by our Creator is unimaginable.

Yet the worst is still to come.

He stands before the people in His final trial. Pilate hopes the scourging will pacify the angry crowd (see John 19:1–16). Yet His own people—fellow Jews—vehemently cry out, "Crucify Him!" The Gentile governor comes to Jesus' defense, wanting to release Him; however, the people cry out louder, making threats if their desires aren't satisfied. They choose a notorious criminal to free instead of their Messiah, thus intensifying the insults.

Once sentenced, Jesus carries the crossbar of the crucifix, which some estimate weighed over one hundred pounds. He is forced to carry it on His shoulders, and if He falls, this heavy log will inflict unimaginable pain from the multiple beatings and wounds He has already sustained.

Once out of the city He is laid on the cross, and huge nails are driven through His hands and feet into a wooden cross. He is pierced in the base of the hand where the median nerve is located, one of the most sensitive and potentially most painful places in the human body. The nails create pressure on this highly sensitive nerve so that when He pulls himself up to breathe, to avoid asphyxiation, the pain is beyond imagination. The crucifixion lasts for six long hours. He slowly bleeds out in agonizing pain, suffering the most gruesome death a human being could experience in that day.

There's quite a bit more I've omitted, but this overview makes an important point, one that cannot be properly comprehended without awareness of what our Creator willingly faced and endured to bring us back to Himself. And that point is this: He didn't do it all for Himself; He did it for you and me.

The overarching question lingers: Why would He undergo such agony and sacrifice to rescue us when we were totally at fault, when we betrayed Him? We read:

> Because of the joy awaiting him, he endured the cross.
>
> HEBREWS 12:2

He saw something that kept Him going. It was the prophetic vision of a faithful bride! He foresaw beautiful, intimate companionship, deep love, and trust between Himself and His bride in the ages to come. He saw the wedding and the celebration of our lives being united as one. He saw us reigning together for the rest of eternity.

His devotion to you and me is affirmed by His suffering for us, and our dedication to Him would be affirmed in our suffering for Him. So many miss this deep truth, and consequently numerous corresponding scriptures elude their understanding. One of these is Romans 8:17:

> We are . . . heirs of God and fellow heirs with Christ [sharing His inheritance with Him]; only we must share His suffering if we are to share His glory. (AMPC)

Why suffering? And why did He have to suffer so severely? Why couldn't He have planned it out differently? If He is God, why couldn't He have devised a pain-free salvation for both Himself and us? These important questions lead to answers that amplify the beauty of His second coming.

At this point, are you overwhelmed by what He endured for an intimate relationship with you and me—His bride-to-be? It only gets richer as we continue this love story of the ages.

PASSAGE: I bared my back to those who beat me. I did not stop them when they insulted me, when they pulled out the hairs of my beard and spat in my face. (Isaiah 50:6 GNT)

POINT: Jesus loves you so deeply that He was willing to be beaten to the point of no longer being recognized as a human being. Then He died for you.

PONDER: Why was suffering needed? And why did He have to suffer so severely? Why couldn't He have planned it differently? If He is God, why couldn't He have given us a pain-free salvation, for both Himself and us?

PRAYER: Dear Father, You gave Your Son to be sacrificed in my place. Jesus, You willingly endured brutal torture and death in my stead. Please help me to comprehend the depth of Your sacrificial love so that I can also walk in this same love toward You, as well as those You died for. In Jesus' name, amen.

PROFESSION: God has poured out His love in my heart so that I can love others as He loved me.

I PROMISED YOU AS A PURE BRIDE TO ONE HUSBAND—CHRIST.

2 CORINTHIANS 11:2

CHAPTER 7

DIVINE BONDING

The Lord God of all creation became a man to bring forth a family and to win Himself a faithful bride. The level of agony and suffering He endured to accomplish this mission is beyond comprehension, yet nevertheless true. Now let's turn our attention to His bride. To set this up, allow me to share Lisa's and my experience as a bride and groom.

As a sophomore at Purdue University, I gave my life to Jesus Christ in my fraternity in 1979. Immediately after being filled with God's Spirit, a burning fire was ignited in my soul to share the Word of God with lost students on campus. This eventually led to starting a Bible study that rapidly grew and lasted for years past my graduation. Many lives were transformed, and the weekly gatherings would be instrumental in meeting my bride.

It was in my final semester that I met Lisa, only to quickly discover she was a full-on party girl and possibly an alcoholic. After my conversion, I had committed to not date, as I didn't want to waste time, and, more importantly, I didn't want to get romantically entangled with a girl who wouldn't become my wife. I hadn't been on a date for over two years but felt strongly in my heart that I was to ask her out. I assumed it was only for the purpose of sharing the gospel, but God had more in mind. Many of the students were perplexed by my first date with a girl who was one of the wildest on campus (this was a comment made by one of my friends).

That evening after the gathering, Lisa and I walked around the campus.

I shared the gospel with her, and she was gloriously saved. To this day hers is one of the most radical conversions I've witnessed. If you saw a picture of her one month before and a day after she gave her life to Jesus, you would hardly recognize her as the same person.

We fell deeply in love, and a little over a year later, we were married. All through our engagement we dreamed of married life, a family, and what ministry would look like. At that time there weren't many couples laboring together in ministry, but we desired it, and even more so, we felt called to it. Our dream was two hearts becoming one, not only in marriage but in ministry too.

The first few decades of our marriage were filled with struggles to stay united and in love. There were numerous and intense attacks against our union, both within and without. As far as internally, there were seasons we were so at odds with each other that if it weren't for knowing God's will for marriage, we could have easily separated. But we both feared God, and we had made a vow not only to each other but to Him.

The external attacks came through people whose intent was to separate and sometimes even destroy us. What made it so difficult is that most were professing Christians. Not only that, but we also faced situations and circumstances of such great pressure that it would have been easy to give up on our dream. There were many seasons the pain was so intense it seemed unbearable.

I look back now and realize the multiple challenges we faced were targeted to either thwart our effectiveness or end the union of two with one heart. They could have easily done so, but we endured the struggles through strong faith and steadfast love, coupled with fervent prayer, genuine repentance, and forgiveness. The pain of these earlier trials has since passed. It has been replaced by a sweeter and stronger bond that emerged out of the suffering we endured. There is a depth of trust, intimacy, and companionship that didn't exist before the many hardships and suffering. We are much closer now than the day we married.

Walking this path for decades led me to a question: Is there a hidden benefit, one that cannot be fostered in any other way, from suffering pain and hardship? Recall, we asked at the conclusion of our previous chapter, Why didn't God devise a pain-free plan for our salvation? Why did He submit to such gruesome suffering? Of course, with Lisa and me, much of the pain in our marriage was due to our immaturity, stupidity, and selfishness; this behavior absolutely doesn't apply to our Groom, Jesus.

In addressing this question, we'll uncover a greater depth of beauty in God's master plan, which will amplify our eager anticipation of Jesus' second coming. What I'm about to write I would not have agreed with in my early years. My immaturity and lack of knowledge would have insisted that suffering is not necessary to create a sweeter, stronger, and more mature relationship. Yet Scripture teaches otherwise, and only in recent times has research confirmed this truth. Scientific findings explain:

> The research suggests that, despite its unpleasantness, pain may actually have positive social consequences, acting as a sort of "social glue" that fosters cohesion and solidarity within groups: "Our findings show that pain is a particularly powerful ingredient in producing bonding and cooperation between those who share painful experiences," says psychological scientist and lead researcher Brock Bastian of the University of New South Wales in Australia. "The findings shed light on why camaraderie may develop between soldiers or others who share difficult and painful experiences."[1]

Other research has shown similar conclusions, and psychologists coined the term "trauma bonding" to identify it. Studies show a mother's bond to her baby is greater than a father's. Think of it: A mother experiences a considerable amount of discomfort for a long period of time in carrying her child, and most often, the greatest agony a woman will face in her lifetime is giving birth to her baby. One would think this discomfort and pain would create resentment and bitterness in the mother. Yet it does just the opposite: It fosters a strong and deep bond.

Is this a reality regarding Jesus' suffering? We read:

> It was only right that he [God the Father] should make Jesus, through his suffering, a perfect leader, fit to bring them into their salvation.
>
> HEBREWS 2:10

The Greek word for *leader* is defined as "one who causes something to begin—'initiator, founder, originator.'"[2] Just as a mother through pain brings forth a child without any involvement of the child, so, too, Jesus paid the costly price needed for our salvation independent of our involvement. All true believers know and understand this fact.

However, there is another "initiating" aspect of His sacrificial act. He's the founder—or forerunner—of embracing pain that fosters a closer bond in a relationship. This is almost too wonderful to comprehend: Our Creator willingly embraced excruciating suffering not only to redeem us but because He desired the closest possible bond with His beloved—His bride, the church! Oh, the wonder, the depth of His love and His desire for us!

But is this truth isolated to Jesus only? In God's great wisdom, the same is true for us. We certainly could never suffer enough to purchase our salvation, and all true believers know this. However, how is a closer bond achieved on our part? Recall, studies have shown mutual suffering makes the connection of love deep.[3] Jesus (the pioneer) suffered first for us, but it's followed by His bride's willingness to suffer for Him, which fosters in us a deeper bond for Him! This seems ludicrous to the Western mindset, but let's go to Scripture for confirmation. The apostle Paul writes that he counts all his accomplishments and accolades as garbage so that he can *press on* to the highest calling:

> I want to know Christ. . . . I want to suffer with him, sharing in his death.
>
> PHILIPPIANS 3:10

Did we read this correctly? He wants to suffer with Christ, even share in His death. In fact, he's not passive in this pursuit, as he writes, "I press on to make it my own, because Christ Jesus has made me his own" (Philippians 3:12 ESV). For what purpose does Paul want to suffer with Jesus? The answer is to know Him more deeply—to have a stronger connection with Him. Here are his words out of the Amplified Bible:

> [For my determined purpose is] that I may know Him [that I may progressively become more deeply and intimately acquainted with Him] . . . and

> that I may so share His sufferings as to be continually transformed [in spirit into His likeness even] to His death.
>
> PHILIPPIANS 3:10 AMPC

Why do Peter and John, after being threatened and beaten (flogged) by the very same leaders and soldiers who unmercifully beat Jesus, come away so happy? We read:

> So they departed from the presence of the council, rejoicing that they were counted worthy to suffer shame for His name.
>
> ACTS 5:41 NKJV

Were they aware that the more they suffered in their obedience to God, the more they would bond with our Lord? Again, Paul writes:

> For to you *it has been granted* on behalf of Christ, not only to believe in Him, but also to suffer for His sake.
>
> PHILIPPIANS 1:29 NKJV

To the person who doesn't see God's wisdom in this, Paul's statement seems absurd. What does he mean, "granted"? If you are a parent, can you imagine looking at your child and saying, "For to you it is *granted* on your birthday to get a root canal at the dentist!" A child would resent that kind of twisted humor from his or her parent. Yet it wasn't masochism on the part of these early church leaders; rather, they sought the greatest prize: being closely bonded with our Lord Jesus.

Sin is rooted in selfishness, which is the greatest obstacle to intimacy. It hinders the formation of a strong bond. The very opposite of sin is unwavering obedience to our perfect, loving God. Please remember, Adam didn't jump in bed with a prostitute in the garden. He made a selfish choice by disobeying what kept him close to the Lord God. It separated him from his Creator, and it's no different today. The New Testament exhorts us, "You must warn each other every day, while it is still 'today,' so that none of you will be deceived by sin and hardened against God" (Hebrews 3:13). Sin (disobedience) hardens and, in turn, distances us from an intimate bond with our Lord or with people. In the same light, Peter writes:

> So, since Christ suffered in the flesh for us, for you, *arm yourselves* with the same thought and purpose [patiently to suffer rather than fail to please God]. For whoever has suffered in the flesh [having the mind of Christ] is done with [intentional] sin [has stopped pleasing himself and the world, and pleases God], so that he can no longer spend the rest of his natural life living by [his] human appetites and desires, but [he lives] for what God wills.
>
> 1 PETER 4:1–2 AMPC

Handling suffering correctly matures us in Christlike character. We are to be *armed*; this means we are mentally prepared to suffer adversity, hardship, or persecution in our obedience to God's Word. Those who are *unarmed* will react incorrectly to trials in self-preservation and veer toward compromise. Whereas those who are armed obey no matter what opposition they face. They gladly suffer the loss of all things—reputation, self-protection, self-promotion, or anything else to do with preserving one's life.

We must make a very important distinction between *true biblical suffering* and *perverted religious suffering.* When I write "religious," I am referring to someone who has the form of godliness but doesn't walk in close fellowship with Jesus.

A religious mindset will seek out suffering. For this person, pain, not obedience, becomes the focus—the way to please God. They will embrace conditions that Jesus paid a high price to set us free from rather than resist the Enemy and his works. They do not fight the good fight of faith; instead, they have become prisoners of war.

Blind Bartimaeus somehow knew Jesus had come to destroy the works of the devil, and a loss of sight fell under that category. He also knew the Lord of the kingdom of heaven was passing by. If he'd had a warped view of suffering, he would have been content to stay in his blind condition. Yet he fought the good fight and cried out for the will of God. People told him that he was out of line, to be quiet, to not disturb the Master. Yet he cried out even more, and consequently Jesus halted His mission and called for him. Once he was healed, Jesus commended him by saying, "Your faith has healed you" (Mark 10:52). The Master gave similar commendations to the Canaanite woman (see Matthew 15:21–28), the Roman centurion (Matthew 8:5–13), and many others in the Gospels.

Regarding Jesus, He didn't bring obedience to the earth—He had to learn it. Yes, we are told:

> While Jesus was here on earth, he offered prayers and pleadings, with a loud cry and tears. . . . Even though Jesus was God's Son, he learned obedience from the things he suffered.
>
> HEBREWS 5:7–8

What is the suffering He endured? He was tempted in every way to compromise the will of God, yet He never disobeyed (see Hebrews 4:15). Obviously, it wasn't easy, as He cried out with tears. We have never experienced the intensity of trials or temptations that He faced.

True biblical suffering is simply this: We live in a fallen world, one that opposes the truth of God—the ways of His kingdom. A true believer chooses to obey God's Word in the face of any resistant force. It can come from a temptation, a trial, or persecution for our faith. The fruit is we will live "no longer for human passions [*whether our own or others'*] but for the will of God" (1 Peter 4:2 ESV).

Stop and ponder the wonder of God's master plan. He chose to suffer from a world that hates Him. In doing so, He would pay the price needed to free His bride from sin and death, but also in the process would bond deeply with her. She in turn would deeply bond with Him through the sufferings she'd face in a very perverse and cruel world. This strong bond would intensify the desire He would have to be reunited with her and she with Him. The second coming isn't just an event; *it is the uniting of two lovers*, a Groom and bride-to-be who deeply long for each other. Oh, how marvelous is the wisdom of God!

Do you feel deeply loved by your Creator? Do you see how much He longs for true intimacy with you and me? As we proceed, we'll turn to a great promise, one that's a mystery to so many. Yet what we've discussed unlocks its truth. The depth of this statement is elusive without the understanding of true biblical suffering:

> If we endure hardship, we will reign with him.
>
> 2 TIMOTHY 2:12

Within this statement lies the climax of God's master plan and creates a greater anticipation of His soon return and the ages to come.

PASSAGE: Christ also suffered for us, leaving us an example, that you should follow His steps. (1 Peter 2:21 NKJV)

POINT: When we suffer in obeying God, if we don't become bitter, the result is a deeper bond of love.

PONDER: How do you view trials and temptations? Do you see them as joyful opportunities? (See James 1:2.) Are you quick to please those you see instead of One you don't see? How can this be changed? What is needed to get through trials and temptations?

PRAYER: Dear heavenly Father, Your Word states that when I meet up with trials, I should consider them an opportunity for great joy. I've not done this in the past. Please forgive me! I ask that You give me the strength of Jesus to see the joy beyond the trials, the joy of being closely bonded with You. In Jesus' name I pray, amen.

PROFESSION: The joy of the Lord is my strength!

WEEK 2

THE BRIDE AND GROOM

IF WE ENDURE HARDSHIP,

WE WILL REIGN WITH HIM.

2 TIMOTHY 2:12

CHAPTER 8

THE BOND OF TRUST

I've experienced the noticeable difference between living as a single man and living as a married man. The joys and benefits of life are so much richer alongside my wife and dearest friend. I love her companionship in our adventures, play, and work. We've taken many ministry trips to beautiful locations, met fabulous people, eaten wonderful food, and been treated to incredible experiences. If Lisa doesn't accompany me on a trip, I think dozens of times before returning home, *I wish we could experience this together.*

Then came our four sons, who when grown became a part of our ministry. All four have served on Messenger's team for at least eight years. To witness them flourishing in their responsibilities carries a joy and satisfaction that only a parent can understand. However, the pinnacle of gratification came when they proved themselves faithful and we started working together at higher levels. Whether it was planning, leading the team, or ministering together at a conference, it brought life to another level of enjoyment and fulfillment.

From these experiences, I've gained insight as to why the Lord desires a family and bride. He longs to experience eternal life together; to build, and even govern, together. It's quite amazing when you step back and ponder who it is we're discussing.

Most people haven't spent the time to investigate and contemplate the ages to come. There are believers who are concerned they're not going to like the eternal state as much as this present life. Many imagine us being transformed into some sort of ethereal beings, living in a world without substance and void of anything exciting to do. They imagine we will all be part of a nonstop church or worship service. Oh, how far that is from the truth!

Let's remember that all that's seen has been created by what cannot be seen. If we think it through, we will realize it's ludicrous to imagine our world coming forth from a boring or inferior one in recreation, adventure, creativity, development, expansion, innovation, the arts, or any other exciting aspect of this life. It's laughable when you say it out loud, yet some wrestle with these very deep-seated concerns. The eternal will consist of all the godly pleasures, joys, excitement, and beauty of this life but will be considerably better and perfect in every regard. On top of that, there will be many aspects of living—wonderful experiences this life could never support. Best of all, there will be no fear, pain, lack, turmoil, or any of the other corruptive or unpleasant aspects of this life.

Scripture gives glimpses of insight as to what's coming. We glean from the parable of the minas that there will be multiple cities, and even more remarkable, some of us will manage communities. Others will oversee groups of cities (see Luke 19:11–19). Where are these communities located? Who are their inhabitants? What will life be like in the neighborhoods, the towns, and the cities of the new earth? Will there be civilizations on other planets, other galaxies?

Jesus shared that there are *mansions* being prepared for us (see John 14:2).[1] If our eternal homes are this magnificent, what do the other structures look like? Will all buildings have the same architecture? What materials will they be made of?

Let's probe deeper. Will communities have identical cultures and environments? If we have such diverse civilizations in our present world, why not in the new earth and heavens? The apostle John saw "a great multitude which no one could number, of all nations, tribes, peoples, and tongues, standing before the throne" (Revelation 7:9 NKJV). If, as some suppose, there are no diverse societies in the next life, why are there different ethnicities called out before the throne of God? If we maintain our ethnic identity, then in what way will the communities vary in the eternal state?

What's more—and this is mind-blowing—we will judge the world! What will this look like, and what will be the results? Going even further, we will also judge angels! Can you fathom this reality? Yes, we will decide alongside our King how the seraphim, cherubim, archangels, and other ministering spirits will be rewarded. Our decisions will be based on how they served us. These mighty beings have been assigned to us; they are all sent forth from God's throne to minister to the heirs of salvation—us (see 1 Corinthians 6:2–3; Hebrews 1:14).

In essence, there will be much to do throughout eternity; we will never be bored! The most staggering reality is that our eternal "job positions" are being determined by how we live now in this life. Allow me to elaborate by returning to our family. Two of our sons, after years of faithfully serving and proving themselves, now have high-level leadership positions on our team. Addison started in an entry-level position over twenty years ago and eventually moved into senior leadership. Arden began as a travel assistant and now leads our Nashville team. Both proved time and time again their faithfulness, mature character, and obedience before they were promoted. In a similar way, as believers, this life is our proving ground; we are determining by our choices our roles for eternity, and Scripture shows there will never be any changes made to Christ's decisions, which will be further elaborated on in the final chapter. (As a sidenote, our other two sons initiated their own businesses. We are delighted and celebrate with them in their success.)

There's one important, lingering question in God's master plan that must be addressed. In the future, what prevents another colossal tragedy of a mutiny, such as the insurgence of Lucifer and his comrades ages ago? Can you imagine the heartbreak the Lord God experienced when His worship leader and many other angels rebelled against Him? The short answer is that these mutinous angelic hosts, who are so much mightier and smarter than human beings, never suffered adversity for His honor. They never had to fight to uphold God's desires. In essence, they were untested.

In God's wisdom, He determined that those who'd forever govern with Him would be those who proved their loyalty in hostile enemy territory. These coleaders refused to submit to pressures created by the rebellious forces, choosing to suffer and endure hardships in their obedience. Their trustworthiness would be forever sealed by enduring to the end. For this reason, Paul writes: "If we endure hardship, we will reign with Him" (2 Timothy 2:12).

Jesus chose to initiate the path; He, as Pioneer, faced the most severe testing. We read, "He humbled himself in obedience to God and died a criminal's death on a cross. Therefore, God elevated him to the place of highest honor" (Philippians 2:8–9). His loyalty was forever proven, so God declared to His faithful Son:

> Your throne, O God, endures forever and ever.
>
> HEBREWS 1:8

In the same way, God rejoices in the faithful ones who endure the testing of trials and temptations to the end. They will be His Son's bride and His children who will govern with Him for the rest of eternity, as Jesus states: "To all who are victorious, who obey me to the very end, to them I will give authority over all the nations . . . They will have the same authority I received from my Father" (Revelation 2:26, 28). Just as the Father gave Jesus an *eternal* throne, even so He will give us eternal authority, and "we will be with the Lord *forever*" (1 Thessalonians 4:17). It's almost too wonderful to comprehend!

The question arises: Why is testing necessary? The answer lies in one word: *trust*. In today's world, many lump the words *love* and *trust* together. It's sad when you hear someone question, "You know I love you, so why don't you trust me?" The two are not synonymous; we can love but not trust. Consider Jesus. He so deeply loved us that He agreed to take on a human body, suffer greatly, and finally die for us. What amazing love! In fact, it's the highest display of true love (see John 15:13). Yet regarding trust, let's look at what was stated at the outset of His ministry:

> Because of the miraculous signs Jesus did in Jerusalem at the Passover

> celebration, many began to *trust* in him. But Jesus didn't *trust* them, because he knew all about people.
>
> JOHN 2:23–24

Trust is an interesting word, defined in the Greek as "to believe to the extent of complete trust and reliance . . . 'to have confidence in, to have faith in.'"[2] Interestingly, trust is not reciprocated by Jesus. Even though people believed to the extent of complete trust and reliance on Him, He didn't *trust* them. He knew that human beings, unless tested, are not necessarily reliable. He loved them and served them but could not yet place His trust in them.

Three years later, at the Last Supper, He was with those who hadn't quit. In the previous three years of ministry, most who believed in Him were not reliable. Many followed secretly, others from a distance, or only when they benefited; many disciples left Him; and Judas betrayed Him (see John 3:1–2; 6:26, 66; 12:42; 19:38; Matthew 26:14–16). Does this give more insight as to why Jesus didn't reciprocate trust?

Jesus was now sitting with those who endured to His ministry's end. With gratitude and affection, He announced, "You are those who have stayed with me in my trials" (Luke 22:28 ESV). In essence, they had been reliable and suffered through all the hardships without quitting. Peter would have a major hiccup that evening, and so would the others, but they would all later repent and return with even more faithful and loyal hearts, and Jesus knew it. Jesus then said to these men:

> No longer do I call you *servants*, for a servant does not know what his master is doing; but I have called you *friends*, for all things that I heard from My Father I have made known to you.
>
> JOHN 15:15 NKJV

A servant is not someone you can confide in, work closely with, or entrust your heart to. You can give a servant many tasks but not lay bare your innermost desires and longings—your secrets. This you do with a friend—someone you trust.

Yet it would go further. After the resurrection He would now call us brothers and sisters (see John 20:17; Hebrews 2:11). Some siblings are not proven trustworthy. However, a sibling who is a dear friend is another level of closeness than a friend who's outside the family.

It gets even better, for the end goal for us is to become His beloved wife, one who is also His dearest friend. This is the strongest bond two can share. No one is more connected with me than Lisa. She's my dearest friend, levels beyond even my closest of friends both inside and outside my family. In essence, Jesus longs to be bonded as closely as possible with us—a bride who is His closest friend. How can we not respond with our entire heart and life!

Without a doubt, one of the greatest portions of Scripture regarding a noble wife is found in Proverbs 31. We rightly attribute it to a godly wife in this life, but is it possible there are aspects of these eternal words that apply to Jesus' bride?

> Who can *find* a virtuous and capable wife? She is *more precious* than rubies.
>
> PROVERBS 31:10

First, "Who can *find*" speaks of the fact that she must be sought out and identified. You don't stumble on her. However, if we look at the Hebrew word *māṣā*, we find something interesting, that "it is also used in a causative sense, to cause to find."[3] In other words, something caused this wife to be discovered, and for any wise man, it would be her *character*—her *heart*. This is not discovered by her words, but rather by her behavior. How she handles the tough issues of life. How she responds to difficulty.

Second, notice the great value Scripture places on her. Her worth is "*more precious* than rubies." This indeed was the joy set before Jesus that gave Him the strength to endure horrific suffering. He laid down His life for His loyal bride; He prophetically saw her and longed for her. This leads us to Solomon's next words:

> Her husband can *trust her*, and she will greatly enrich his life.
>
> PROVERBS 31:11

We see the two main points of this chapter in this one sentence. This is the wife He can *trust*, and she will *greatly enrich* His life. Jesus didn't entrust Himself to human beings until they endured with Him through His trials. The "trauma bond" of the previous chapter can be summed up in one word: *trust*. The greater the trust, the greater the bond. The NKJV states, "The *heart* of her husband *safely* trusts her." Jesus is looking for the bride He can fully give His heart to—He can safely trust.

Second, she will *greatly enrich* his life. My life has become progressively richer the longer Lisa and I have been married. In our days of courting, I repeatedly observed her loyalty and faithful heart manifest in given situations. Yet after years of walking with her, seeing the suffering she has been willing to go through in being my wife, a mother, and doing ministry together, my level of trust has greatly intensified. The result is that our time together is even richer. As stated in the beginning of the chapter, I've lived as a single man and a married man, and it's so much richer to share life with a trusted partner. For Jesus, He desires a queen to govern with, one who is a virtuous wife.

James writes:

> Blessed *is* the man who *endures* temptation; for when he has been approved, he will receive *the crown of life*.
>
> JAMES 1:12 NKJV

There is a crown awaiting those who have endured hardship. A crown speaks of authority, power, and governing. A queen wears a crown and she's given a throne. Just as our Groom was granted an eternal throne, the highest of all, even so His bride, through sharing in Christ's sufferings, will be granted an eternal throne.

> Then I saw thrones, and sitting on them were those to whom authority to act as judges and to pass sentence was *entrusted*.
>
> REVELATION 20:4 AMPC

To sit on one of those thrones means you've been entrusted with the

King's heart, and subsequently His authority, something very significant! He knows you'll rule as He would rule. It's the greatest honor given to a faithful Christ follower. You will forever be seen as His bride who showed unwavering devotion to the eternal King during the courting season of this earthly life.

Is it now even more obvious that the second coming is far more than an event? It's a royal marriage of the Son of God with His virtuous wife, and together they will enrich each other's lives throughout eternity to come as they build and govern together.

PASSAGE: "My servant Moses. Of all my house, he is the one I trust." (Numbers 12:7)

POINT: God loves us deeply and unconditionally; however, His trust in us must be earned.

PONDER: Think of someone you dearly love but don't necessarily trust. Why can't you fully trust him or her? Is it possible he or she can gain, or regain, your trust? How would he or she do this? Now consider this from God's perspective: Can He trust you? Why?

PRAYER: Father, it's my deepest desire to be a child whom You not only love unconditionally but whom You trust. Please give me the grace to obey You in the face of distractions, persecution, or hardship. Please give me the strength to never cave and disobey Your desires. In Jesus' name I pray, amen.

PROFESSION: My goal is to be well pleasing to God, and that is accomplished though my obedience to His will! (See 2 Corinthians 5:9.)

THE KINGDOM OF HEAVEN IS LIKE A CERTAIN KING WHO ARRANGED A MARRIAGE FOR HIS SON.

MATTHEW 22:2 NKJV

CHAPTER 9

THE ANCIENT JEWISH WEDDING

I remember, as if it were yesterday, the evening I proposed to Lisa. At the time, we lived in Dallas, Texas, and with both our families hundreds of miles away, I was on my own to prepare for the engagement. It began at one of the city's nicest restaurants, where I spent all my money that hadn't been spent on her engagement ring earlier that week.

After our dinner, we drove to a beautifully landscaped park. It was connected to a high-end shopping mall, smartly lit, with walking paths, flowers, and manicured trees. The mall was closed for the evening, so we had the area to ourselves. After walking a bit, I noticed a perfectly lit ornate bench, so we sat on it while continuing our conversation. Once the right moment arrived, I slid off the bench, got down on one knee, opened the ring box, shared my deep love for Lisa, and asked if she would marry me. To my delight, Lisa wholeheartedly said yes.

Her response not only evoked a great celebration but solidified the reality that our future would be spent together. Her acceptance would also initiate the engagement season—a set time to prepare for the monumental day of the wedding.

Over the next few months, we worked diligently, both together and separately. What I didn't anticipate is how this season would foster the sensation of time slowing down. The eagerness for our union caused days to seem like weeks, and weeks as if they were months. This feeling escalated as our final two months prior to the wedding were spent apart; Lisa had returned to Indiana to finalize preparations. Our engagement, even though it was only four months, seemed to last for years.

Once the long-awaited day arrived, I distinctly remember the blissful feelings flooding my soul. They continued to escalate, hour by hour, until the grand moment of watching, with tears streaming down my face, my bride coming down the aisle in her hometown church in Indiana. Nothing could have ever prepared me for the overwhelming emotions of that moment.

Although most couples share similar emotions and experiences, all weddings are not the same. Ours was a modern-day Western ceremony, much different from the weddings in Israel two thousand years ago. Therefore, to fully grasp the message of Jesus returning for His bride, we need to view what Jesus taught, and what the apostles wrote, through the lens of an ancient Jewish wedding.[1]

In those days, brides were often chosen by the father of the groom, and proposals were not initiated by the groom planning a special date and ending the evening by getting on one knee to ask the big question. The process was much different; it began with the *ketubah.* This word comes from the root word *katav*, which means "to write." The bridegroom, either with the approval of his father or accompanied by his father, would meet with the bride and her parents and present a written contract. The *ketubah* contained within it the terms of the proposed marriage, which always included the *bride-price*, referred to as the *mohar.*

In those days all the family members participated in running a household. A wedding would result in the daughter leaving her family and joining the groom's family. The *mohar* was given to compensate for the loss of her contribution in daily responsibilities; it could be paid in gold, silver, the currency of the day, valuable items, or even animals.

The tradition of the bride-price dates back thousands of years. We see glimpses in the Old Testament. Abraham's servant brought ten camels across the wilderness loaded with valuable gifts for the purchase price of

Isaac's bride. Jacob worked seven years for each of his brides. David's bride-price for Michael was one hundred Philistine foreskins (see 1 Samuel 18:25). And the list continues.

Once both parties agreed to the terms of the *ketubah*, the groom would then give gifts to his bride, and sometimes to her parents. Then he'd pour a glass of wine and offer it to his bride. Sharing the wine together officially declared her acceptance of the terms of the marriage covenant and sealed the agreement. From that time forward, they would not see each other again until the final stage of the wedding.

Once the *ketubah* was confirmed, it was considered binding; the couple was officially *betrothed*, which carries greater weight than our engagement. The difference being, *engagement* conveys the intent to marry, whereas *betrothal* officially joins the man and woman by covenant. They are now, in essence, married, with the exception of three privileges: seeing each other, physical consummation, and living together. At this point, the only way to separate is by a divorce. We see this with Joseph and Mary's betrothal. Once he learned of Mary's pregnancy during their time apart from each other, Joseph, being a kind and just man, planned to divorce her secretly and not to bring her to public shame (see Matthew 1:19).

After the completion of the *ketubah,* the groom would return to his home for an indefinite time period and begin to build the chamber the young couple would live in together. It was usually a room connected to his father's house.

This was his primary responsibility in the separation time, and once his father approved of the dwelling, he would commission his son to return to *snatch away* his bride. The separation normally spanned a year, give or take a few weeks. The exact moment wasn't known; however, there was a keen awareness of the time frame. The final decision was solely in the hands of the groom's father.

The bride had several responsibilities in preparing for the groom's imminent return. Most importantly, she would keep herself pure and remain faithful to him in their absence, as he would also do for her. Soon after his departure, the bride would experience a *mikvah*, a ceremonial immersion into clean water to publicly profess the separation from her old life to new life, from the life of a single woman to becoming a wife. Her other tasks were more involved; they included making her wedding garments, packing her belongings, securing an oil lamp with plenty of oil, and other preparations for leaving her home. It was critical that she live in a constant state of readiness to be taken away.

Like today, the groom and bride chose wedding parties—the groomsmen and bridesmaids. Their responsibilities were much more involved than our modern-day weddings. Once the appointed day arrived, the groom and his attendants would conduct a torchlight procession. Each would carry lamps, entering the bride's community with shouts in the streets along with the sounding of rams' horns—*shofars*.

They would come at night, sometimes as late as midnight. This was done for a couple of reasons. First, in those days people didn't go out in the dark of night as we do so easily today. They had no sources of light other than candles or oil-burning lamps. Coming in the evening ensured families would be gathered in their respective homes. Second, the dark would also keep their arrival secretive. If the procession were to take place in daylight, the approaching group of men might be spotted prematurely by someone in the community; it was intended to be a complete surprise.

Once the shouts of the groomsmen were heard, the bridesmaids would respond by lighting their torch lamps and joining the procession. Together with some alert family and friends, they would witness the groom catching away his veiled bride.

Once she was apprehended, the procession would lead back to the father of the groom's house. By this time, the parade would have significantly enlarged to include not only the bridal party but musicians, singers, and dancers, along with family and friends. The wedding party would escort the bride to the *huppah*. This is the name given to the canopy that covered the bridal chamber. (It's mentioned in Scripture in Psalm 19:5 and Joel 2:16.) She would enter the chamber where her groom, who'd hurried ahead, was now awaiting her arrival to reveal the place he'd prepared for her. In the privacy of the *huppah*, the groom would unveil his bride, and the couple would enter physical union.

The "friend of the bridegroom"—the best man—would remain outside the chamber awaiting the announcement of the consummation. The groom would come out and present the evidence of the blood-stained sheet. This was the final confirmation of her faithfulness. The best man would then join the other guests, make the announcement, and a seven-day wedding banquet celebration would commence.

During the entire seven days, the bride and groom would remain in the bridal chamber. Upon the week's completion, the groom would bring out his bride, now unveiled, and present her to all the wedding guests.

I think you'd agree, this is significantly different from our ceremonies today. In fleshing out this ancient traditional wedding, we see numerous scriptural correlations with Jesus and His bride. The first being His words:

> "Don't let your hearts be troubled. Trust in God, and trust also in me. There is more than enough room in my Father's home. If this were not so, would I have told you that *I am going to prepare a place for you*? When everything is ready, I will *come and get you*, so that you will always be with me where I am."
>
> JOHN 14:1–3

All the disciples were well acquainted with Jesus' idioms. They'd heard these exact wedding terms and phrases numerous times growing up. Families, friends, rabbis, and teachers would have often discussed or mentioned them. As young men, they'd most likely been to plenty of wedding celebrations. In essence, Jesus' words weren't a riddle or mystery; they were familiar and easily recognizable.

Let's touch on a few key points. First, His words "come and get you" are from the Greek word *paralambánō*, defined as "to take, receive. To take near, with, or to oneself, to receive to oneself."[2] He specifies that He personally will come and get us and we will be with Him in His Father's house. This tipped off the disciples about where He was headed in what was being shared.

Second, Jesus had to disarm the thought that there might not be enough room. A wedding celebration could only hold so many people at a typical family home. Jesus expands their thinking to the fact that this will be a very large wedding. In fact, Dr. Henry Morris, who has a PhD in science, reported that according to his mathematical calculations, the New Jerusalem, being 1,400 square miles, would be able to house twenty billion people, with each resident having a homestead of a third of a mile cubed.[3]

Third, "I'm going to prepare a *place* for you." The Greek word for *place* is *tópos*, and one of its definitions, in more than one Greek dictionary, is "a room."[4] At this point they are assured He is discussing a wedding, for it is the exact phrase a groom would comfort his bride with when they parted ways.

Finally, and most exciting, He declares, "When everything is ready, I will come and get you, so that you will always be with me." I can only imagine their minds went right to the exhilarating emotions hitting a bride once her long-awaited groom finally appears; she is now assured they will be together for the rest of their lives.

What about the *mohar*—the bride-price? Scripture states, "God bought you with a high price" (1 Corinthians 6:20). We are also told: He "purchased with His own blood" His Son's bride (Acts 20:28 NKJV). A very costly purchase!

What about the wine? Jesus announced to His disciples just before the crucifixion His eagerness to have the Passover meal with them. During the meal He offered a cup of wine to His disciples and stated, "I will not drink wine again until the Kingdom of God has come" (Luke 22:18). So similar to how the young couple confirms the *ketubah*.

Regarding the betrothal, Paul writes to the Corinthians, "For I am jealous for you with godly jealousy. For I have *betrothed* you to one husband, that I may present you as a chaste virgin to Christ" (2 Corinthians 11:2 NKJV). Now in understanding their traditional wedding, we can better understand the apostle James's strong words:

> You *adulterers*! Don't you realize that friendship with the world makes you an enemy of God?
>
> JAMES 4:4

Recall the difference between our modern "engagement" and a "betrothal." In light of this, James's words take on a whole different tone. To engage in friendship with the world, we are breaking the covenant of our marriage betrothal to Jesus—that's *adultery*!

Why doesn't James say befriending the world makes us enemies of Jesus? Why God specifically? When you understand the high price that the Father paid to purchase a bride for His Son (think back to the previous chapter about the excruciating suffering He watched His Son endure) and then He watches His Son's betrothed bride living faithlessly by befriending the world, you can better understand His anger.

We are not talking about a bride who is tempted, falls into sin, and then heartbrokenly repents. No, the blood of Jesus cleanses completely. Rather, James is talking about a bride who lives for herself and not her Groom—her pursuit in life is for whatever looks good, feels good, or feeds her pride of accomplishment (see 1 John 2:15).

In Paul's letter to the Ephesians, it sounds as if he's only discussing marriage between a couple in this life; he's not. He is using this as a metaphor to discuss our relationship with Jesus:

> For husbands, this means love your wives, just as Christ loved the church. He gave up his life for her to make her holy and clean, washed by the cleansing of God's word. He did this to present her to himself as a glorious church without a spot or wrinkle or any other blemish. Instead, she will be holy and without fault.
>
> 5:25–27

The bride He is returning for is one who is unspotted from committing adultery with the world. She is not pursuing self-pleasure, self-gain, self-promotion, or self-preservation. She has given her life to Him as He gave His life to her, no different from the groom and bride who will enjoy a wholesome marriage.

Notice she is washed by the cleansing of God's Word. The Complete Jewish Bible version translates this as "making it clean through immersion in the *mikveh*, so to speak." Recall, the *mikveh* is the clean water the bride is washed in. The New King James Version states, "that He might sanctify and cleanse her with the washing of water by the word." It is the Word of God that washes us from the contamination and filth this world attempts to stain us with. It keeps our minds renewed and uncorrupted.

There is so much more to unfold in this love story of the ages. We'll continue to refer to the ancient Jewish wedding as we further discuss His second coming; the understanding gleaned in this chapter will unlock previously hidden truths.

Is it becoming clearer that Jesus' soon coming isn't just something spooky to be afraid of or religious? We see how our eternal Groom longs to be permanently united with His beloved. Do you sense His profound love and desire for you?

PASSAGE: You have captured my heart, my treasure, my bride. . . . Your love delights me, my treasure, my bride. (Song of Solomon 4:9–10)

POINT: Jesus' heart is captured for the bride who loves Him the way He loves her.

PONDER: What should you be doing to prepare for your Groom's unexpected arrival? In the ancient Jewish wedding, the bride and groom hide away for seven days. What might this mean for Jesus' bride? We are not engaged to Jesus; rather, we are betrothed. Think of and list out the differences between the two.

PRAYER: Dear heavenly Father, I ask that You help me to prepare for the coming of our Groom. I forsake dating the world—following the paths of those who don't know Jesus. I ask that as I continue in Your Word, it would wash me from the filth of this present age. In Jesus' name, amen.

PROFESSION: I am my Beloved's, and my Beloved is mine!

YOU AREN'T IN THE DARK ABOUT THESE THINGS, DEAR BROTHERS AND SISTERS, AND YOU WON'T BE SURPRISED WHEN THE DAY OF THE LORD COMES LIKE A THIEF.

1 THESSALONIANS 5:4

CHAPTER 10

THE SEASON OF HIS RETURN

In the days of Jesus' first coming, those who walked with God knew the approximate time and place of His birth and death. In fact, the Essenes predicted it, not only to the year but to the week. How did they know? They gave prayerful attention to the words of the prophets, especially the angel Gabriel's message to Daniel. The prophecy's timeline was specific and turned out to be right on the mark.

Now we turn our discussion to the second coming of Jesus. Are we able to nail down the day, the month, or the year of Jesus' return? The answer is emphatically "No!" Jesus states:

> "But of that day and hour no one knows, not even the angels in heaven, nor the Son, but only the Father."
>
> MARK 13:32 NKJV

No different from the groom in the ancient Jewish wedding, even so with our Groom, Jesus. It's quite remarkable that He doesn't know, even though He is God. Perhaps the Trinity decided before the foundation of the world that only the Father would know. Pause and ponder the amazing reality of this: God put it in the hearts of the Jewish people thousands of years ago to conduct their weddings in a way that would reflect how Jesus would return for His bride. Remarkable!

Only God the Father knows the moment Jesus will return. What about the season? The generation? What do Jesus, His apostles, the prophets, and the Scriptures say regarding this? Up front, I will boldly state, "This we are expected to know."

Let's begin with Jesus. I'll pull statements from His same discourse from three different Gospels. Let's set it up. The disciples are admiring the temple complex, commenting on the stunning beauty of the buildings. Jesus seizes the moment to inform them of the approaching devastating destruction and goes so far as to say that not one stone will be left upon another. As discussed earlier, He's foretelling Titus and Rome coming forty years later and utterly destroying the temple and Jerusalem.

His disciples then ask three questions (see Matthew 24:3):

1. When will the temple be destroyed?
2. What will be the sign of Your coming?
3. What will be the sign of the end of the age?

Due to the nature of their questions, we consequently have two different time periods being addressed, AD 32–135 and AD 1967–unknown. Our discussion will focus on the second time frame. But first, let's look at Jesus' concluding words concerning the devastation of AD 70:

> "They will be killed by the sword or sent away as captives to all the nations of the world. And Jerusalem will be trampled down by the Gentiles until the period of the Gentiles comes to an end."
>
> LUKE 21:24

The initial and major blow of dismantling Israel's population occurred when Titus's army destroyed Jerusalem in AD 70. However, strongholds still lingered in Israel that Rome dismantled over the next sixty-five years. The final blow occurred with the defeat of the Jews' last leader of that era,

Bar Kokhba, in AD 135. This was the siege and fall of Betar, the final Jewish stronghold. The numerous Roman campaigns led to nearly the full depopulation of the Jews from Israel, with many killed, masses deported into slavery, and the remaining forced to flee. Eventually the Jewish people could be found in practically every nation of the world.

Jesus foretells that after this, Jerusalem would be "trampled down by the Gentiles." He simply means the city would be under Gentile rule until the time for Israel to return. The Romans, Byzantines, Arab Caliphates, Crusaders, Mamluks, Ottoman Empire, and finally Great Britain shared the Gentile rulership of the Holy City and Land for the next eighteen centuries.

However, on May 14, 1948, a remarkable event occurred: Israel was born in one day. This was foretold by the prophet Isaiah. We read:

> "Who has heard such a thing?
> Who has seen such things?
> Shall the earth be made to give birth in one day?
> *Or* shall a nation be born at once?
> For as soon as Zion was in labor,
> She gave birth to her children."
>
> Isaiah 66:8 NKJV

It was miraculous. A nation of people exiled all over the world, to practically every nation, for over eighteen hundred years, stayed intact. They kept their lineage pure, their customs alive, and today they're speaking Hebrew! No nation has ever done this in the history of mankind. The odds are astronomical; only with God's involvement could this have been accomplished. Isaiah again prophesied:

> In that day the Lord will reach out his hand *a second time* to bring back the remnant of his people. . . . He will raise a flag among the nations and assemble the exiles of Israel. He will gather the scattered people of Judah *from the ends of the earth.*
>
> 11:11–12

Take notice of Isaiah's words: *a second time*! This raises the question, When was the *first time*? Some think it's when God brought Israel out of Egypt to the promised land. But it couldn't be, for Isaiah specifically says a "remnant," which is a small surviving group. In the Egyptian exodus, the entire nation was brought out, not a remnant. The *first time* could only refer to the return from Babylon, because most of the people were killed by King Nebuchadnezzar's army. Before Babylonian captivity, the prophets repeatedly warned that only a small segment would survive their onslaught, thus confirming the *first time*.

When is the *second* time? It could only be the return of the Jewish people in the twentieth century. Isaiah is clear: In the *second time*, the remnant is not coming back from one place, Babylon, but rather *from the ends of the earth*. This began in the twentieth century, from nations all over the globe, and it is still happening to this day. It's mind-blowing!

Even though Jews were returning in the 1940s and '50s, and the UN recognized Israel as a nation, the Holy City of Jerusalem was still under Gentile control. It wasn't until the brief Six-Day War that took place June 5–10, 1967, that this would change. Israel's decisive victory over five allied Arab nations led to the recovery of the Old City of Jerusalem, which up to that time was under Jordanian control. Jesus' words were fulfilled; the period of the Gentiles had come to an end.

Jesus then stated:

> "And there will be strange signs in the sun, moon, and stars. And here on earth the nations will be in turmoil, perplexed by the roaring seas and strange tides. People will be terrified at what they see coming upon the earth, for the powers in the heavens will be shaken. Then everyone will see the Son of Man coming on a cloud with power and great glory."
>
> LUKE 21:25–27

Jerusalem, as well as the land of Israel, is now governed by the Jewish people, the first time in over eighteen hundred years. It's crystal clear: Jesus is now discussing the time period of 1967 and forward. There are some who think everything He says in this discourse dealt only with first-century events, but these three verses show clearly this is not the case.

Jesus speaks of the signs—birth pangs (see Matthew 24:8). This analogy is important to mention. Just as a woman's birth contractions become increasingly frequent and intense, even so the signs in the sun, moon, stars, earthquakes, tsunamis, plagues, pestilence, famines, and others Jesus speaks of have done the same. They will become even more frequent and intense as we approach His return. Then we come to the climax: *His coming in great glory*, and *every eye* will see Him. I love the words of the apostle John:

> Behold, He is coming with clouds, and *every eye will see Him*, even they who pierced Him. And all the tribes of the earth will mourn because of Him. Even so, Amen.
>
> REVELATION 1:7 NKJV

It will be both a glorious and terrifying day. Terrifying for those who refused to submit to His lordship—those who stubbornly would not obey His desires. On that day multitudes will cry out for the rocks or mountains to fall on them and hide them from the face of our glorious King (see Revelation 6:16). The wrath will be so terrible and decisive that before it's over, "People will become like walking corpses, their flesh rotting away. Their eyes will rot in their sockets, and their tongues will rot in their mouths" (Zechariah 14:12). Isaiah wrote,

> Scream in terror, for the day of the LORD has arrived—the time for the Almighty to destroy. Every arm is paralyzed with fear. Every heart melts, and people are terrified. Pangs of anguish grip them, like those of a woman in labor. They look helplessly at one another, their faces aflame with fear.
>
> For see, the day of the LORD is coming—the terrible day of his fury and fierce anger. The land will be made desolate, and all the sinners destroyed with it. The heavens will be black above them; the stars will give no light.
>
> The sun will be dark when it rises, and the moon will provide no

> light. "I, the LORD, will punish the world for its evil and the wicked for their sin."
>
> 13:6–11

God's wrath will be poured out, and the King whose face outshines the sun will be on a white horse, accompanied by His holy ones—the armies of heaven. No one on or under the earth will be unaware of this event.

John the apostle wrote of this moment, "I saw an angel standing in the sun, shouting to the vultures flying high in the sky: 'Come! Gather together for the great banquet God has prepared. Come and eat the flesh of kings, generals, and strong warriors; of horses and their riders; and of all humanity, both free and slave, small and great'" (Revelation 19:17–18). Scripture declares that on that day, humanity will be scarcer than gold (Isaiah 13:12).

It will be a horrific time; we have nothing in the past to compare it to. It's been forewarned by the prophets, apostles, angels, and Jesus Himself. There will never have been such dreadful days in all the history of mankind. Think of all the terrible natural disasters, hellish wars, horrendous genocides, devastating plagues, and other past horrific sufferings of the human race. None of them will compare to what is coming. Godly voices have been crying out for centuries, warning mankind to *flee the wrath to come*, but we go on as if that day will never come.

This should terrify anyone who is not abiding in Christ, and yet, so many play it down or put it off. On one extreme, they scoff at this warning, saying, "It won't happen, nothing has changed for centuries." On the other extreme, they say, "No loving God would ever do this!" This group doesn't know how truly contagious evil and wickedness are. If they were to go unchecked, they would pollute all of God's creation. They must be utterly destroyed to make way for an eternally pure kingdom.

God has been so patient, kind, and long-suffering, giving mankind every chance to embrace the needed sacrifice His Son paid to free us from the wrath to come. He can only wait so long. The end is at hand, and yet many think it is business as usual. It's this simple: When mankind chooses sin and rebellion over full submission to the lordship of Jesus, he or she sides with the full cup of judgment decreed for all the rebellion of generations past right up to the present.

It's serious, dear ones. Ponder this: If such a terrible price was paid by our Creator to free us from the tyranny of this world's system and its looming judgment, why would we think it's not a serious matter? It is, and too many ministers shy away from warning of it, thinking it will repulse and turn people away from God, that it's not palatable.

When Scripture warns, "Flee from the wrath to come" (Matthew 3:7 and Luke 3:7 NKJV), does it fall on deaf ears? Have we forgotten that we are forewarned?

> See, the LORD is coming with fire, and his swift chariots roar like a whirlwind. He will bring punishment with the fury of his anger and the flaming fire of his hot rebuke. The LORD will punish the world by fire and by his sword. He will judge the earth, and *many will be killed by him.*
>
> ISAIAH 66:15–16

Many will be killed by Him! How can a God of love do this? That is exactly why He must do this: *because* He is love. View "the nature of sin and death" as an extremely contagious disease. It will eventually pervert, corrupt, and destroy what is clean and holy. How can God put all that is pure and lovely in harm's way? How could He allow this? If He did, He would be cruel, not loving. Because He truly is love, therefore He protects.

When Adam chose the nature of sin and death, God quickly drove the first couple out of the garden to protect them. If they had partaken of the Tree of Life, they would have been doomed to keep their evil nature forever, thus making mankind forever an adversary to God's nature of righteousness and goodness. Mankind would have been eternally evil, as Satan and his hordes are. Love rescued those who would choose to worship Him.

God has been patient; He has been long-suffering; He wants everyone to repent and come to eternal life through the lordship of Jesus Christ. But as time passes, mankind's heart grows harder and harder, and there is coming a time—and it's so soon—when, if those who remain were given a thousand more years, they wouldn't change. In fact, even after the horrific seal judgments and six of the trumpet judgments of the tribulation, in which billions of people will be killed, we still hear these sobering words: "But the people who did not die in these plagues still refused to repent of their evil deeds and turn to God" (Revelation 9:20). In the day of His coming there will be no in-between. We read:

> Everyone will see the LORD's hand of blessing on his servants—
> and his anger against his enemies.
>
> ISAIAH 66:14

This speaks specifically to the great and terrible day the King returns to this earth, and we'll continue to discuss that in more depth later in this message. However, we need to get back on track. You most likely are wondering what happened to our discussion of our Groom coming back for His bride. Why are we hearing about terrible judgment? There is a reason. Many lump together the Groom coming for His bride with the judgment briefly described. The looming question with so many is, Do these events coincide as one, or are there two significant events coming in the near future?

We opened this chapter seeking to know the season, the generation, when all these things are going to happen. We'll continue this quest in the next chapter, and we'll eventually discuss whether Jesus is coming for His bride at the exact same time the earth is being judged.

Before closing, let's ask ourselves: *How will we, our children, or our children's children fare in what is rapidly approaching?* We can be prepared because the important matters regarding this time are clearly outlined in God's Word. I'm so delighted you're investing the time for this preparation. It's my heartfelt desire, and God's, for it to be to you and your descendants a great, and not terrible, day of the Lord.

PASSAGE: "Do not seal up the words of the prophecy of this book and make no secret of them, for the time when things are brought to a crisis and the period of their fulfillment is near. Let the evildoer still do evil, and the filthy still be filthy, and the righteous still do right, and the holy still be holy." (Revelation 22:10 AMPC and 11 ESV)

POINT: We have a choice: Will we be eternally evil and filthy or eternally righteous and holy?

PONDER: What does the above Scripture (Revelation 22:10–11) say in light of what I've read in this chapter? Why does God speak so much of the coming judgment and we speak so little of it? How can this be changed?

PRAYER: Dear heavenly Father, You are able to keep me strong until the Day of the Lord Jesus Christ. Please do this; strengthen me so that I may be found blameless on that great Day of my Lord's coming. In Jesus' name, amen.

PROFESSION: I will cling to the righteousness found in Christ and pursue holiness to be ready for the Day of His coming.

"I TELL YOU THE TRUTH, THIS GENERATION WILL NOT PASS FROM THE SCENE BEFORE ALL THESE THINGS TAKE PLACE."

MARK 13:30

CHAPTER 11

THIS GENERATION WILL NOT PASS

Picture a betrothed bride in ancient Jewish times. Her groom has been away for almost a year, and she's expectant and prepared for that special evening when the shouts and blowing shofars will ring throughout her community's streets. Her lamp is bedside, her trunk is packed, and her wedding garment and veil hang in a prominent spot in her bedroom. Though his return was imminent from their first day away from each other, she's keenly aware it's now the most probable time frame for him to catch her away.

Every true believer is in a similar place. There's a deep knowing in our hearts that His arrival is near; it's the season. Most importantly, can this be confirmed in Scripture? Yes, indeed! We embarked on this search in the last chapter. Let's continue.

We'll return to the words of Jesus and pick up from where we left off. After identifying the signs, He makes a statement that's eye-opening yet easy to miss:

> "Then everyone will see the Son of Man coming on a cloud with power and great glory. So when all these things *begin* to happen, *stand* and *look up*, for your salvation is near!"
>
> LUKE 21:27–28

When all these things—the birth pains—*begin* to happen. He does not say "once they are *finished*." No, He says "*begin*." The Greek word is *árchomai*, and it specifically means "to initiate an action, process, or state of being . . . 'to commence.'"[1] So at the commencement of these birth pains, we are told to do something.

When Lisa was pregnant with our second child (our first had to be induced), I learned about "doing something" that corresponded with the commencement of labor. I was in an administrative meeting at our church when one of the assistants suddenly interrupted our conversation and urgently declared, "Pastor John, you need to leave immediately. Your wife is in labor."

I jumped up, blurted "goodbye," drove home to pick up Lisa and her packed bag, and rushed to the hospital. Within two hours Austin was born. The beginning of her labor moved both of us into action. Jesus is instructing us, "When the labor of these specific signs begins, this is what you need to do."

We are told by the Master to do two things: first, to *stand*. In Greek the word is *anakúptō*, which means "to lift or raise up oneself from a bending posture."[2] I picture this "bending posture" representing not being engaged in the task at hand. In Jesus' parable of the virgins, while the bridegroom was delayed, they all slept (see Matthew 25:5). They were disengaged. I have to admit, in looking back, ten years ago I was asleep compared to what has awakened in my heart in the past five years. The Holy Spirit drew me to study the prophetic Word of God, and that created a greater urgency for this season, an intensified passion to love people, make disciples, and see the lost saved. I feel as if I've stood up and am more alert.

The second phrase is *look up*. It does indeed mean to lift your eyes and look up. However, another definition from the Greek word *epaírō* is: "to be taken up, be borne upward."[3] It's safe to say that, in essence, He's encouraging us, "Stop slouching. Stop growing dull by being too attached to the affairs of this life. I've called you to overcome the world, so get up! Look up! For you are about to be taken up!"

Regarding this, Paul writes:

> Since you have been raised to new life with Christ, *set your sights* on the realities of heaven, where Christ sits in the place of honor at God's right hand. *Think about the things of heaven*, not the things of earth. For you died to this life, and your real life is hidden with Christ in God.
>
> COLOSSIANS 3:1–3

Notice the words *set your sights*. The key word is *set*. When I'm driving a car, my *sight is set* on the road. I may look down *momentarily* at the instrument panel, glance over to a passenger riding with me or beautiful scenery, and even do a rapid glance at my phone's GPS, but I quickly return to where my sight should be *set*.

Similarly, we have things to accomplish in this life: work, various daily tasks, and needed rest, which could include periodic recreation or hobbies. It's necessary to attend to these things, but often they can be executed no differently than engaging in a conversation with a passenger in our vehicle; our sight is still *set* on the road. However, if our sights get *set* on the things of this life and we periodically glance at the realities of heaven, we are not *looking up*.

Paul instructs us to think about the things of heaven, not the things of earth. Wherever your sight is *set*, that is where your thoughts will go by default. If your sight is predominantly *set* on the NFL, entertainment, success, fame, popularity, politics, social media (the list is almost endless), you can be easily lulled to sleep.

Consider the bride-in-waiting, who has her daily tasks at her parents' home: prepare food, do laundry, get water from the well, or various other chores; however, in this season her sights are *set* on her soon-coming groom. Her thoughts go to his coming whenever they are not required for the daily tasks.

Where do you find your thoughts going when your mind is in neutral? This is where they are *set*. If you incessantly think about and are consumed by the stats of your favorite NCAA team, increasing your followers on YouTube or Instagram, making money, and . . . the list is almost endless . . . you're slouched over. Your mind is *set* on a world that is quickly passing away. If you belong to Jesus, you died to this world and your life is hidden with Christ in God.

Look at Paul's very next statement. If we heed the instruction to stand and look up:

> When Christ who is our life appears, then you also will *appear with Him in glory*.
>
> COLOSSIANS 3:4 NKJV

Okay, wow, *appear with Him in glory*! Take a moment to reflect on what we just discussed in the last chapter—the glory that will be revealed when Jesus comes in the clouds! Mighty men will cry out for the rocks and mountains to hide them from the One who is riding on the white horse. In light of this, John the apostle writes:

> Dear friends, we are already God's children, but he has not yet shown us what we will be like when Christ appears. But we do know that we will be like him.
>
> 1 JOHN 3:2

Hold on, Paul just wrote that *we will appear with Him in glory*, not at a distance from Him—we will be *with* Him. We will be *like* Him! We will shine bright like our King, our beloved Husband, our Lord and Master. With these words in mind, let's return to the statement of Daniel about the end-times judgment of the world:

> "Then there will be a *time of anguish* greater than any since nations first came into existence. But at that time every one of your people whose name is written in the book will be *rescued*. Many of those whose bodies lie dead and buried will rise up, some to everlasting life and some to shame and everlasting disgrace. Those who are wise will shine *as bright as the sky*, and those who lead many to righteousness will shine like the stars forever."
>
> DANIEL 12:1–3

Is your heart filled with hope and excitement? We will shine *as bright as the sky.* Those who heed His commission to make disciples within their world of influence will shine like stars forever! Jude and Zechariah both write:

> Behold, the Lord comes with His myriads of holy ones (ten thousands of His saints) to execute judgment upon all.
>
> JUDE VV. 14–15 AMPC

> The LORD my God will come, and all the saints with You [Him].
>
> ZECHARIAH 14:5 NKJV

Let's put all this together. Jesus says when you see all these signs *begin* to come to pass, stand up from a slouching position and look up by setting your sights on the things above, longing for and thinking of life in His kingdom. In doing so, He will *rescue* you; then our Groom, accompanied by us, will shine with His glory as bright as the sky. When we appear with Him, being revealed to all the world, every eye will see not only Him but His beloved bride!

Recall, after the seven days in their *huppah*, the bride and groom come out, revealing themselves. His bride is no longer veiled, and her beautiful face is seen by all the wedding guests. John's words come to mind: "It has not yet been revealed what we shall be, but we know that when He is revealed, we shall be like Him" (1 John 3:2 NKJV). With this understanding, Paul's words to the Roman believers become clearer:

> Everything God made is waiting with excitement for God to show his children's glory completely.
>
> ROMANS 8:19 NCV

I'm sure your excitement is mounting! Unless, of course, you are still slouching, tethered to this world's system, still controlled by your flesh. If so, just "awake, O sleeper, and arise from the dead, and Christ will shine on you" (Ephesians 5:14 ESV). Your Groom is waiting. He's longing for your love and devotion. He wants to trust you; it's every groom's desire.

Let's return to Jesus' words and continue our quest to know the season of His return.

> "So when all these things begin to happen, stand and look up, for your salvation is near!" Then he gave them this illustration: "Notice the *fig tree*, or *any other tree*. When the leaves come out, you know without being told that summer is near. In the same way, when you see all these things taking place, you can know that the Kingdom of God is near. I tell you the truth, this generation will not pass from the scene until all these things have taken place. Heaven and earth will disappear, but my words will never disappear."
>
> LUKE 21:28–33

Carefully examine His illustration: "Notice the fig tree, or any other tree." The NKJV states "and all the trees." Why does He choose a fig tree, and, even more interestingly, why does He mention the other trees? It's not common knowledge in the West, but at the end of World War I, several nations were formed after the collapse of the Ottoman Empire. Below are a few, along with the dates they were founded and the trees that represent these nations:

1. Saudi Arabia (1932), date palm tree
2. Lebanon (1943), cedar tree
3. Syria (1945), olive tree
4. Jordan (1946), Mount Tabor oak tree
5. Kuwait (1961), date palm tree
6. Israel (1948), fig tree

Up front I need to clarify an important point. Israel voted to name the olive tree as their national tree; however, often the Lord speaks of Israel as a fig tree (see Hosea 9:10; Jeremiah 8:13; Jeremiah 24).

In looking at the fig tree, along with the other trees—Israel and the other five nations listed in the Middle East region—we will get an indication of the season. It's remarkable their budding occurred in the same time frame, especially when we look through the lens of a two-thousand-year period. Jesus says once this happens, we will know the time of summer is near, and in this case, summer represents His return. For He continues:

> "I tell you the truth, this generation will not pass from the scene until all these things have taken place. Heaven and earth will disappear, but my words will never disappear."
>
> LUKE 21:32–33

There is so much in these statements! But before elaborating on them, let's first consider an eye-opening fact: In examining Jesus' full discourse, along with the books of Daniel and Revelation, we discover a significant detail that separates our generation from all others. The man of lawlessness, the global leader who will embody Satan, will at one point make a covenant with Israel and violate it three and a half years later by entering their temple and proclaiming that "he is god" (see Mark 13:14; Daniel 9:27). A Jewish nation must exist for this to happen. No other generation in eighteen hundred years has been able to say this. It's only been since 1967 that we can say Jerusalem is under Jewish leadership. It's remarkable when you think of it.

Now to Jesus' statements above. First, "I tell you the truth." Everything He has said to His disciples for three years has come to pass. He's never told a single lie or made a deceptive statement; they know this, but He still chooses to preface His statement with these words. But if that's not enough, He doubles down by declaring His words to be surer than the existence of heaven and earth! Therefore, we can safely say, our generation will not pass until He's returned.

Now the question arises, What is a generation? We see various time spans representing a generation in Scripture. It can be forty or seventy years, and in the Patriarchs' era, it could be argued it's one hundred years. *Nelson's*

Bible Dictionary defines it as "a body of people who live at the same time in a given period of history."[4]

If the starting point of the budding is 1967 (when Gentile rule over Jerusalem ceased), we can add one hundred years and safely come to a conclusion as to the timeframe when Jesus might return. Let me be clear, I am open to further investigation, discussion, or challenge about this; it's my intent to remain teachable! I also realize my statement is speculative, as I could be interpreting what He said incorrectly. But I've weighed out what I've said in the light of what other scriptures reveal—which we are about to see—as well as what respectable leaders have taught.

With this said, it's important to state: We should *plan and work* as if He is not returning for over two hundred years (because we are commanded to "do business till" He returns [Luke 19:13 NKJV]). However, we should *live* as if He's returning today. Hopefully this knowledge will create a greater sense of urgency to be engaged in what He's called you to do in His kingdom advancement.

When establishing doctrine, it's important to have more than one reference. The good news is we do, and we'll discuss other confirming indicators from the apostles and prophets in our next chapter.

PASSAGE: "So when all these things begin to happen, stand and look up, for your salvation is near!" (Luke 21:28)

POINT: You are called to overcome the world. So get up! Look up! For you are about to be taken up!

PONDER: In what ways have you been tethered to this world? How can you better set your sights on the things of the kingdom? What practical steps can you take to attain this?

PRAYER: Dear Father in heaven, forgive me for being slouched over in a sleeping position. I repent and choose to awaken to the call You've placed on my life to advance the kingdom. I will begin by setting my sights according to what You say is important in Your Word. In Jesus' name, amen.

PROFESSION: I will lift my eyes to where my help comes from.

FOR A THOUSAND YEARS

IN YOUR SIGHT ARE BUT AS

YESTERDAY WHEN IT IS PAST.

PSALM 90:4 ESV

CHAPTER 12

THE LENGTH OF A DAY

Have you ever moved forward on something important with only one source of information? Was it wise to do so? Did you consider the chance of misinterpretation of or possible error from your single source? Think of a time when, instead of seeking a second confirmation, you proceeded with the lone report. Afterward you found out that information was indeed unreliable. How did you feel?

I recently watched a team competition of professional golfers. They were playing on a big-screen simulator against another group of professionals. The team member whose turn it was thought he heard the yardage to the pin to be ninety-nine. He took out his sand wedge, a typical ninety-nine-yard club, and hit it with confidence, but the shot ended up half the distance to the simulated green. His teammates began to scold him because it was actually 199 yards. He believed wholeheartedly he had the right number, but he missed the mark considerably.

How about this scenario: Have you ever believed a report on social media or from a Google search and started to share it with others, only later to find out from a second source that it was fake news?

We know Jesus' words are perfectly accurate, but suppose we're misinterpreting His discourse on the sign of the fig tree and other trees. Even though our interpretation seems sound, wouldn't it be nice to have a second confirmation? Even Scripture teaches us, "The facts of every case must be established by the testimony of two or three witnesses" (2 Corinthians 13:1).

We *do* have other confirmations. First, many of the early Jewish and church fathers taught mankind's dominion on the earth would last seven thousand years. It correlates with the seven days of creation found in Genesis. They saw this time span broken up into four ages: the first three being two thousand years each and the final spanning one thousand years.

1. The Age of Creation: 2,000 years
2. The Age of the Law: 2,000 years
3. The Age of Grace: 2,000 years
4. The Kingdom Age: 1,000 years

It makes sense. On the fourth day God created the sun, and roughly four thousand years after Adam, Jesus was born. Interestingly, He is referred to as the "the Sun of righteousness" (Malachi 4:2). Another indicator would be that God rested on the seventh day of creation, and the Kingdom Age, the seventh millennium, is also known as the Age of Rest.

The span of the ages is delineated by key indicators. From Adam to Abraham is roughly two thousand years; from Abraham to Jesus approximately two thousand years; and from Jesus until now is right at two thousand years. The final one thousand years would apply to Jesus' reign of great peace on this earth (see Revelation 20:2–7). We are informed, "He shall deliver you in six troubles, yes, in seven no evil shall touch you" (Job 5:19 NKJV). This is an amazing correlation.

Along these lines Peter writes:

> I want you to remember what the holy prophets said long ago and what our Lord and Savior commanded through your apostles. *Most importantly*, I want to remind you that in the last days scoffers will come, mocking the truth and following their own desires. They will say, "What happened to the promise that Jesus is coming again? From before the times of our

> ancestors, everything has remained the same since the world was first created."
>
> 2 PETER 3:2–4

There's so much here to unpack. First, notice "Most importantly." We shouldn't ignore the stress placed on what he's writing. He has just emphasized remembering the prophets and the Lord's teachings and commands. Yet what he labels *most important* is the warning of professing believers making light of Jesus' second coming in our day.

How do we know that these "scoffers" profess faith? First, they refer to the world as being created rather than evolving. Second, if you read Peter's entire letter in context, along with Jude's companion letter, both write that these people will profess to be saved but, alarmingly, will teach "God's marvelous grace allows us to live immoral lives" (Jude v. 4; see also 2 Peter 2). They will not just pervert the teachings of Scripture but will live in a way that denies the power of the gospel. To put it simply, they will have the language of the New Testament yet live no differently than an unsaved person. They'll follow their fleshly instincts, rather than exhibiting the fruit of being filled with God's Spirit.

Their sensual lifestyles will lead them to the mental delusion of sneering at the thought of a holy God returning for His church in their lifetime. Peter continues:

> *They deliberately forget* that God made the heavens long ago by the word of his command, and he brought the earth out from the water and surrounded it with water. Then he used the water to destroy the ancient world with a mighty flood. And by the same word, the present heavens and earth have been stored up for fire. They are being kept for the day of judgment, when ungodly people will be destroyed.
>
> 2 PETER 3:5–7

In essence, they *forget* this is the same God who by just a word out of His mouth created the entire universe and destroyed the world with a flood. He also caused a nation to walk through an ocean on dry ground, kept them alive in the desert by raining food on the ground, and brought water from a rock to give millions of people and their animals a drink. He also brought two men to heaven alive, caused the sun to stand still, impregnated a virgin, raised Jesus from the dead, and a host of other mind-blowing acts. These deluded people think that just because no similar acts have occurred in their minuscule time on earth (compared to the history of mankind), God isn't doing mighty wonders any longer. Foolish indeed!

Then Peter seeks to protect those who pursue an authentic walk with Jesus. It's quite interesting how he protects us:

> But *you must not forget this one thing*, dear friends: A day is like a thousand years to the Lord, and a thousand years is like a day.
>
> 2 PETER 3:8

See the connection? I'll shorten his statements to make it more easily recognizable: "They deliberately *forget* . . . but you must not *forget* this *one thing*." What *one thing* is it that we must not forget? One day with the Lord is a thousand of our years!

We see a critical indicator here. What they "forget" and what we "must not forget" is the exact same thing: that God is sure to do what He says, but in His timeline, not ours. It's surer than the sunrise in the morning, but again, it shows the importance of knowing the revealed seasons and timings of God.

With this knowledge, we now go to the prophet Hosea. It's important to know the context before we read. He is speaking to the Jewish nation, but in doing so, we get a glimpse of the church's time period:

> "I will be like a lion to Israel, like a strong young lion to Judah. I will tear them to pieces! I will carry them off, and no one will be left to rescue them. Then I will *return to my place* until they admit their guilt and turn to me. For as soon as trouble comes, they will earnestly search for me."
>
> HOSEA 5:14–15

There are two major times that God permitted Israel and Judah to be torn into pieces. The first was the Babylonian invasion. If you search the Scriptures, you'll find out the Chaldeans were ruthless with the Jewish people, including women, children, and babies. A small remnant survived and were taken to Babylon, but most were brutally slaughtered. The other occasion was Titus's conquest of the city of Jerusalem in AD 70, culminating in Rome's utter depopulation of Israel over the next few decades.

The question is, Which incident is God addressing through the prophet Hosea? The simple answer: It's definitely the Roman devastation spanning from AD 70 to 132. There is a key statement in the above verses: "I will return to my place."

To "return" means you have to leave a specific location, go somewhere, and then come back to the specific location you started from. Jesus left "His place" with the Father approximately two thousand years ago and *returned* to His place thirty-three years later. Shortly afterward Israel was "torn into pieces" by Rome.[1] Continuing on:

> Come, and let us return to the LORD; for He has torn, but He
> will heal us; He has stricken, but He will bind us up.
> *After two days* He will revive us; on the third day He will raise
> us up,
> that we may live in His sight.
>
> HOSEA 6:1–2 NKJV

Israel as a nation eventually cries out, "Come, let us return to the Lord." When will this happen? After two days! Remember what Peter said we must not forget: A day with the Lord is as one thousand years. Hosea is saying "after two thousand years." We have the timing!

What happens during these two thousand years? In a general sense, the Jewish people are blinded to the redemption available to mankind. God focuses on the Gentiles during this period. This is the Age of Grace—the church age, in which the Gentiles (and most definitely some Jewish people) come to salvation.

Both Paul and James give us more insight. Starting with Paul:

> For I do not desire, brethren, that you should be ignorant of this mystery, lest you should be wise in your own opinion, that blindness in part has happened to Israel until *the fullness of the Gentiles* has come in. And so *all Israel will be saved.*
>
> ROMANS 11:25–26 NKJV

This was a mystery to the early Jewish church. It took a vivid heavenly vision to get Peter to go to the house of Cornelius, the Roman centurion. Once there, Peter didn't give the people the opportunity to receive Jesus, probably because he was leery of being in a Gentile home. So God caused His Spirit to fall on them without Peter's initiation (see Acts 10:44).

Peter was now fully persuaded the Gentiles could be saved and filled with God's Spirit. But most of the other Jewish leaders of the early church were not pleased with his actions. They called an emergency meeting, had a heated debate, and the lead apostle, James, concluded by speaking prophetically. More than likely, he didn't realize the extent of what came out of his mouth:

> "Brothers, listen to me. Peter has told you about the time God first visited the Gentiles *to take from them* a people for himself. And this conversion of Gentiles is exactly what the prophets predicted."
>
> ACTS 15:13–15

Take note of his words "to take from them," which speak of the harvest of the Gentiles occurring over a period of time. He most likely didn't realize the time would last two thousand years. In examining Paul's and James's words together, we understand once the "full number" of Gentiles comes to salvation, then God will turn His focus back on Israel, which will be Daniel's final week—the seventieth week of years. Their eyes will be opened to the reality that they truly did crucify their Messiah, and according to Paul, Hosea, and Zechariah (see Zechariah 12:10–11), all Israel will repent and turn to the Lord. It's beneficial to read Hosea's words again with this knowledge:

> Come, and let us return to the LORD; for He has torn, but He will heal us; He has stricken, but He will bind us up. After two days He will revive us; on the third day He will raise us up, that we may live in His sight.
>
> HOSEA 6:1–2 NKJV

Let's interpret his words in the light of what we've learned, the very thing *we are not to forget*! After two thousand years the Lord will revive Israel. It will occur within Daniel's final week (the seven-year tribulation). After that, He will raise up His people to live in His sight! The third thousandth year is the Kingdom Age, when Jesus Christ will rule and reign over the nations of the world. During this time Satan and his demonic hordes will be locked up and unable to wreak havoc among the nations (see Revelation 20:1–4).

The main point is that we have a timeline. God allowed Israel to be torn by Rome in AD 70, almost two thousand years ago. Then we are told that after two days—two thousand years—He would once again revive Israel. In adding the numbers, we come to the year AD 2070.

Remember what we discussed around Jesus' fig tree parable—that this generation would not pass until all was fulfilled? If a generation is one hundred years, we arrived at 2067 (one hundred years after Jerusalem was reacquired by the Jewish people). With Hosea's passage as a second confirmation, we arrive again at the same time frame, since a generation could be anywhere from forty to one hundred years. So Jesus' time span would be from 2007 to 2067. Of course we're already well past 2007, so could we be in the window—the season? I'll let you determine this with the truth that's been presented. In my personal view, I'm certain we are.

The same is true for Hosea's words. Jesus returned to His "place" (Hosea 5:15) in AD 32. If we add two days—two thousand years—we come to 2032! Titus destroyed Jerusalem in AD 70. Adding the two thousand years, we arrive at 2070. So we find Hosea's window is 2032–2070. Therefore, both sources come out to roughly the same time period!

Here is what we can confidently declare: We're in the season—the generation—of His return. How can we be perfectly sure? Here are Hosea's next words:

> His going forth is established as the morning.
>
> HOSEA 6:3 NKJV

Does the sun rise at the appointed time every morning? Without a doubt. The season of Jesus' going forth is as sure as the timing of the rising sun. Again, we don't know the day or hour, but we know the season. Hosea's words confirm our interpretation of Jesus' words to be accurate.

Do we have other confirmations? Yes, indeed. Here's one more. When God brought Israel out of Egypt, which is a type of the world, He gave a glimpse to Moses of something significant:

> Then the LORD said to Moses, "Go to the people and consecrate them *today* and *tomorrow*, and let them wash their clothes. And let them be ready for the *third day*. For on the *third day* the LORD will come down upon Mount Sinai *in the sight of all the people*."
>
> EXODUS 19:10–11 NKJV

The people were to wash their clothes from the filth of Egypt (very significant; we'll discuss this in a future chapter). They were to do this for two days, prophetically representing two thousand years. Again, we see it was the third day—the third thousandth year—that the Lord manifested Himself *in the sight of all the people*. Once again, correlating to the thousand-year reign of Christ, it is indeed a privilege to be *in His sight*. An interesting note: It was at *the beginning* of the third day that He appeared (see Exodus 19:16–20), reflecting the beginning of the third thousand year after Jesus' first coming.

We are truly living in days of prophetic fulfillment! So, dear reader, how does the prophet Hosea counsel us? He urgently writes, "Oh, that we might know the LORD! Let us *press on* to know him" (6:3). A daily question each of us should ask ourselves is, *Am I pressing past the obstacles, distractions, and trials of this present life for the ultimate goal of knowing Him intimately?* If not, now is the time to set our hearts aright.

PASSAGE: He who is the faithful witness to all these things says, "Yes, I am coming soon!" (Revelation 22:20)

POINT: You must not forget one thing: A day with the Lord is one thousand of our years.

PONDER: Why did Peter say "Most importantly" regarding scoffers? What behavior opens us to the delusion of mocking the idea of His soon return? What can you do to keep a sense of awareness of the season we live in?

PRAYER: Dear heavenly Father, Jesus promised that when the Holy Spirit came, He would lead me into all truth and show me things to come (see John 16:13). I ask that You give me seeing eyes and a perceptive heart as to what to do in the season I'm living in. In Jesus' name, amen.

PROFESSION: Even so, come quickly, Lord Jesus! (See Revelation 22:20.)

"LOOK, I WILL COME AS UNEXPECTEDLY AS A THIEF! BLESSED ARE ALL WHO ARE WATCHING FOR ME."

REVELATION 16:15

CHAPTER 13

WATCH!

Before diving into the specifics of the second coming, let's address a frequent rebuttal of those who question its nearness. The first-century church, even those who wrote the New Testament, believed Jesus would return very soon, and a good number believed it would happen in their lifetime.

I'll actually strengthen this argument. In reading the Gospels, we see that even Jesus made statements that could be interpreted to point to His return in the first century. One being that He revealed to Peter after the resurrection that he would die a martyr's death. Peter retorted, "What about him, Lord?" (referring to the apostle John, who was standing right beside him).

> Jesus replied, "If I want him to remain alive *until I return*, what is that to you? As for you, follow me." So the rumor spread among the community of believers that this disciple wouldn't die. But that isn't what Jesus said at all.
>
> John 21:22–23

It's easy to see how this statement could imply a first-century return. Years later, when the very same John received the book of Revelation, Jesus declared three different times:

> "Behold, I am coming quickly!"
>
> Revelation 3:11; 22:7; 22:12 NKJV

Other similarly puzzling statements found in the epistles include the following: "Take courage, for the coming of the Lord is near" (James 5:8). The apostle Paul wrote: "Remember, the Lord is coming soon" (Philippians 4:5). The apostle Peter wrote: "The end of the world is coming soon" (1 Peter 4:7). The writer of Hebrews continued to strengthen the belief: "For in just a little while, the Coming One will come and not delay" (10:37). There are more, but you get the point.

How do we reconcile that it's now two thousand years later and Jesus still hasn't returned? Were the apostles in error? Was God deceiving us? Both answers are the same: Definitely not! What's the explanation? Without one, it's easy to see how these statements could fuel the fire of scoffers or skeptics. Yet there's a simple answer.

Allow me to illustrate by revisiting a personal story shared in an earlier chapter. For two months Lisa and I were away from each other during our engagement; she was in Lafayette, Indiana, preparing for our wedding, while I was in Dallas, Texas, working. A week before the wedding I was scheduled to fly into Indianapolis. Two days before the flight, we were on the phone together. I don't remember the exact words I used, but something to this effect: "We'll be together *soon*, sweetheart!"

Compared to the two months apart, which seemed like two years, two days was indeed *soon*, or *quick*! Jesus and the apostles are accurate in their statements. Two days (in divine timing) isn't a long time, especially in light of eternity past to eternity future.

For some, this answer still may not suffice, because for us it's still a long time. So let's seek out the divine wisdom for presenting it this way. Could it be that God did it to protect us? Would stressing an imminent return, which it is in divine timing, keep every generation alert, sober, and godly, and create a sense of urgency to advance the kingdom? Most definitely yes!

Jesus, after speaking of the signs of His return in Matthew 24, shares a very interesting parable. He begins by speaking of a faithful and wise servant who is looking for and is thus prepared for his master's return. But then He contrasts the faithful one with an unwise, or evil, servant:

> "If that evil servant *says in his heart*, 'My master is *delaying his coming*,' and begins to beat his fellow servants, and to eat and drink with the drunkards, the master of that servant will come on a day when he is not looking for him and at an hour that he is not aware of, and will cut him in two and appoint him his portion with the hypocrites. There shall be weeping and gnashing of teeth."
>
> MATTHEW 24:48–51 NKJV

It's interesting, not only does Peter identify as "wicked" the one who makes light of the soon return of the King, but so does Jesus. Notice the *evil* servant "says in his heart." It seems this inward posture easily leads to ungodly living. He ends up becoming adversarial to fellow servants and finds more comfort befriending those who indulge in fleshly appetites.

How would this servant beat his fellow servants? The simple answer is by taking advantage of others for his personal gain. It could manifest in the form of gossip, slander, betrayal, rudeness, heartless speech, cold behavior, and so forth. In fact, there is a long list of self-indulging mannerisms found in 2 Timothy 3:1–5. This evil servant knows his master's will yet refrains from doing it. In essence, he treats faithful, godly behavior lightly and lives for the moment. This is not a representation of the bride that Jesus is returning for.

Let's again pose our question: Could God, out of His deep love for His people, in each generation since the resurrection, devise this wisdom so we don't stray to ungodly, indulgent behavior? Could this be why we hear so much in the New Testament of the theme "a thief in the night"? In fact, once Jesus finishes answering the disciples' three questions, He follows up with a few parables, the first being:

> "Watch therefore, for you do not know what hour your Lord is coming. But know this, that if the master of the house had known what hour the thief would come, he would have watched and not allowed his house to be broken into. Therefore you also be ready, for the Son of Man is coming at an hour you do not expect."
>
> MATTHEW 24:42–44 NKJV

I remember years ago Lisa and I were ministering at a conference in Canada. Two of our sons were with us, while our other two stayed at home. Our oldest, in his early twenties at the time, was home alone because his younger brother was spending the night at a close friend's house just down the street.

On one of those evenings, late at night, some thieves broke into our house and stole a considerable number of valuables. They must have been casing our home and thought we were all away on a trip, because they weren't quiet in rummaging through our belongings. In the process, they woke our oldest son, who got out of bed, half asleep, thinking his brother had come home to get something. He called out his brother's name, didn't hear a response, and returned to his bedroom upstairs and fell back asleep. Fortunately, when the thieves downstairs heard Addison's voice, they immediately fled. The police were able to detect this by their trail of theft, which stopped abruptly with several valuable items left untouched.

Our family was caught unaware. We weren't prepared to catch or stop them. If we had known, things would have turned out completely different and we wouldn't have lost thousands of dollars' worth of items. We would have taken preventative measures to either deter or catch them. With this story in mind, let me highlight verses 42–44 again:

> *Watch* therefore, for you do not know what hour your Lord is coming. . . . Therefore you also be *ready*.

We were not *ready*, because we were not *watching*. We'd lived in that house for years and never experienced a break-in. We didn't consider it important to be on the alert and watch. People not as naïve as we were will hire a security guard to do the watching. If he falls asleep, the family is unprotected. If he's awake, the thieves are deterred.

What is the gist of what I'm saying? God desires to protect His people with a sense of alertness and urgency by keeping His Son's return both imminent and a mystery. Since Scripture reveals we're in the season of His coming, how much more should we be sober and alert, no different from the ancient bride having a higher sense of alertness a year after separating from her groom, rather than a week or two afterward.

Heeding Jesus' warning opens two areas to discuss. What does it mean to *watch*, and how do we make ourselves *ready*? We'll address the *watch* in this chapter; then later, after discussing the second coming in more detail, we'll speak to the *ready* aspect.

With both Jesus and the apostles' admonishments on end times, we constantly hear the word *watch*. Let's observe the frequency. In Mark's gospel we read:

> "Take heed, *watch* and pray; for you do not know when the time is. . . . *Watch* therefore, for you do not know when the master of the house is coming—in the evening, at midnight, at the crowing of the rooster, or in the morning. . . . And what I say to you, I say to all: *Watch*!"
>
> 13:33, 35, 37 NKJV

There are a few things to highlight in Mark's account. First, in just three verses Jesus commands us to "watch" three separate times! This alone should get our attention in a huge way.

Second, He adds the word "pray" in verse 33. We keep watch by staying in prayer. Paul instructs the Thessalonian church, immediately after writing of the Lord's imminent return, to "never stop praying" (1 Thessalonians 5:17). How can we do this?

If prayer is limited to going into a closet, shutting the door, and making requests, then this command is impossible. We must remember, prayer is not a monologue; rather, it is a dialogue. It's communion with God. Sometimes there are words, but not always.

Here's a way to illustrate the command that seems impossible. I love spending days with Lisa. Her favorite activity is working in the garden together. It's not mine, but I'm willing to do it just to be with her.

Historically, on the days we work together we get a lot accomplished, and it strengthens our close bond. Do we actually talk the entire time? No. We can speak to each other at any time during the day. The lines of communication are open, and our ears are sensitive to hearing each other's voices at all times. There may be intervals we carry on a conversation as we work. There may be moments she'll make a request of me, such as lifting a heavy bag of soil, pulling some weeds, or discussing where to plant. None of this communication could be accomplished if I had my noise-canceling earbuds in. I need to stay alert to her voice.

Communication isn't just words; it's sensitivity to what's being spoken nonverbally: a look, a gesture, or body posture. There may be times I glance over to see if Lisa needs something, or if perhaps she is giving me one of her classic "looks." After being married to her for over forty years, I can be in a room, with many others present, and she can give me one of those looks. I could write a couple of pages of what she's just communicated, whereas anyone else in the room couldn't write a paragraph.

This illustrates nonstop praying. I'll never forget when we were a young married couple, and I would go out to an isolated place and pray for an hour or two every morning. I never once saw her do this, but it seemed she was more in tune with God than I was. I complained to the Lord and He said, "John, can you imagine Lisa giving you a two-hour window each day to communicate? Perhaps the hours are set for 4–6 p.m. Imagine having a time-sensitive issue to communicate to her outside of the 'set time.' In your attempt to bring the urgent matter, she immediately puts her hand up and says, 'Not now, John, our time has not arrived. It's only 10 a.m. We can discuss this at 4 p.m.' How frustrated would you feel?"

"I wouldn't like it!" I retorted.

He then said, "Son, you have your 'set time' with Me in the mornings, but then you say 'amen' and go about your day without listening to or communicating with Me. I'd like the other twenty-two hours of the day!"

This encounter riveted me and changed my life. What about you? How does this impact you? The Lord's loving correction caused the scripture below to take on a much greater meaning:

> I will stand my watch and set myself on the rampart, and *watch* to see what He will *say* to me, and what I will answer when I am corrected.
>
> HABAKKUK 2:1 NKJV

Notice he says "*watch* to *see* what He will say." Interestingly, he didn't write "*hear* and *listen* to what He'll say." There is a *watching*—looking continuously while on a "watchtower," so to speak. In doing this we remain sensitive to what He is saying.

The third important key of Jesus' words in Mark's account is "what I say to you, I say to all: Watch!" This point is made very clear: His warning is not just for the apostles and early church; it is for us today!

In Luke's account we find another very interesting clue with Jesus' command to watch. Look closely at His words:

> "Watch therefore, and pray always that you may be counted worthy to *escape* all these things that will come to pass, and to stand before the Son of Man."
>
> LUKE 21:36 NKJV

Hold on, He uses the word *escape*! We are instructed to watch and pray without ceasing (always), for the purpose of being worthy to *escape* what He's previously discussed. Okay, now we are heading in the right direction, the direction I want to take you in the next chapter. Apologies, but I'm going to leave you hanging on this one until the proper time comes to discuss this important word *escape*.

Let's look at a few more important commands to watch in regard to His coming.

> Let us not sleep, as others do, but let us watch and be *sober*.
>
> 1 THESSALONIANS 5:6 NKJV

We are instructed to not only watch but to be sober, especially refraining from slipping into a state of sleep. The word *sober* is defined as "to be in control of one's thought processes and thus not be in danger of irrational thinking."[1] When Jesus warns, "People will be terrified at what they see coming upon the earth" (Luke 21:26), he makes clear the importance of staying in control of our thought processes.

Along the same lines, Peter writes:

> But the end of all things is at hand; therefore be serious and watchful in your prayers.
>
> 1 PETER 4:7 NKJV

The New Living Translation states that "the end of the world is coming soon," therefore we are to be "disciplined" in our prayers. Our instincts don't usually trend toward discipline; rather, it must be developed purposefully. In an earlier chapter we discussed Barna's research revealing that millions have fallen away from the faith. It's not surprising, but it was also discovered that forty-five million people in the United States stopped praying from the years 2010 to 2020. Why aren't we more frequently warning the church that the end of all things is at hand? It would help drive the desire to be disciplined in our prayers.

There are numerous other scriptures regarding the discipline of watching and praying. It's a strong emphasis. Hopefully you'll do a search yourself, but even if all that existed were those listed, we still see God has much to say about it!

PASSAGE: "Watch and pray, lest you enter into temptation." (Matthew 26:41 NKJV)

POINT: We are to stay alert and watch in continual prayer because we don't know the hour of His return.

PONDER: How can you form a discipline of praying continuously? Do you live with an awareness of the Lord being your constant companion? Think of and list ways He can speak to you without uttering words.

PRAYER: Father in heaven, You gave me the Holy Spirit as insurance for Jesus' return for me. Please help me to become more sensitive to what You are saying by watching and not just listening for articulated words. In Jesus' name, amen.

PROFESSION: I will watch and pray today and every day.

BUT LET ME REVEAL TO YOU A WONDERFUL SECRET. WE WILL NOT ALL DIE, BUT WE WILL ALL BE TRANSFORMED! IT WILL HAPPEN IN A MOMENT, IN THE BLINK OF AN EYE, WHEN THE LAST TRUMPET IS BLOWN.

1 CORINTHIANS 15:51-52

CHAPTER 14

THE CATCHING AWAY

The great and joyful hope of our miraculous transformation will occur at the return of Jesus. When a person repents of their disobedience to God and receives Jesus Christ as their Lord, three wonderful transformations take place, but not all at the same time.

The first occurs the moment we receive Jesus Christ as our Lord, and it involves who we really are—our spirits. We actually die and instantaneously are reborn. It's utterly miraculous, as we are still the same person physically, emotionally, and mentally, but we are a brand-new person spiritually (see 2 Corinthians 5:17). God places His divine nature within us and a brand-new life begins as a child of the Almighty.

At the moment of conversion, our soul—intellect, emotions, and will—begins its journey of transformation. This is a process that requires the implanted Word of God. Paul writes, "Let God transform you into a new person by changing the way you think" (Romans 12:2), and James writes to people already in the faith, "Humbly accept the word God has planted in your hearts, for it has the power to save your souls" (James 1:21). This transformation is the only one of the three in which our cooperation is required. We can speed or hinder the process, even stop or reverse it. It all depends upon our hearing and obeying God's Word. Volumes have been written, and volumes more could be, on this transformation process, but that is not the focus of this message.

The third transformation is the one all true believers crave: our new bodies. Paul writes:

> We grow weary in our present bodies, and we long to put on our heavenly bodies like new clothing. For we will put on heavenly bodies; we will not be spirits without bodies.
>
> 2 CORINTHIANS 5:2–3

Receiving our heavenly bodies will be the final transformation. Interestingly, in the letter to the church in Corinth, Paul calls it a "wonderful secret"; other translations call it "a mystery." This is not something that is spooky; rather, it is something that was hidden from God's people until after the Holy Spirit came upon the church. Jesus referred to the disciples' inability to understand certain truths by stating, "There is so much more I want to tell you, but you can't bear it now. When the Spirit of truth comes, he will guide you into all truth" (John 16:12–13).

Several mysteries have now been uncovered, most by the apostle Paul. These previously veiled truths are readily available to all who seek to know and are taught by the Spirit from the New Testament. They still aren't openly obvious, and for this reason Peter writes, "This is what our beloved brother Paul also wrote to you with the wisdom God gave him—speaking of these things in all of his letters. Some of his comments are hard to understand" (2 Peter 3:15–16).

For this specific mystery of our opening verse, what truth was previously hidden? Simply that there is a generation of us who will not die, but our living mortal bodies will be instantaneously and miraculously transformed into immortal bodies. This will happen not only with us who are alive but also with those who died in Christ and whose bodies are in the ground. It's no different from Jesus' mortal body three days after His death being transformed into a heavenly body. Currently He is the only One in heaven or on earth with this body, but upon His return we will all be blessed with a similar one.

Even though Paul refers to it as a heavenly body, it's fully capable of functioning with humans in mortal bodies. Jesus, after being raised from the dead, interacted with others without standing out freakishly. He walked unrecognized with two disciples on the road to Emmaus. Mary mistook Him for a gardener. The disciples, at first glance, perceived Him as an ordinary man on the seashore; a short while later, He ate a fish breakfast with them. He possessed flesh and bone that seemed no different from any other human. Jesus encouraged His men to "look at my hands. Look at my feet. You can see that it's really me. Touch me and make sure that I am not a ghost, because ghosts don't have bodies, as you see that I do" (Luke 24:39).

At the same time, He could instantaneously appear and disappear, walk through locked doors, and even float up into the sky. Yet even then He still seemed no different from a normal human being. However, when John saw Him on the Isle of Patmos, His face shone like the sun in all its brilliance, His eyes were like laser beams, and His voice thundered as the roaring ocean! When He returns to earth, the strongest of humans will cower and tremble with utter fear at His appearance.

In comparing these events, it's evident this "heavenly body" can take on different forms yet remain the same body. We can only imagine its functionality at this time, but "we will someday be like the heavenly man" (1 Corinthians 15:49).

Again, our transformation will happen instantly. In fact, Paul says "in a *moment*." The Greek word is *átomos*, from which we get our word *atom*. When referring to time, "it means an indivisible point of time, an instant, a moment."[1] According to quantum physics, the marker for the "indivisible point of time" is called Planck time and is 10^{-43} seconds.[2] When we get to this point it's impossible to shorten time any further. In essence, it's unimaginable how fast this transformation will occur.

Several questions now arise, the first being, How does this process transpire? Paul writes:

> We tell you this directly from the Lord . . . the Lord himself will come down from heaven with a commanding shout, with the voice of the

> archangel, and with the trumpet call of God. First, the believers who have died will rise from their graves. Then, together with them, we who are still alive and remain on the earth will be caught up in the clouds to meet the Lord in the air. Then we will be with the Lord forever. So *encourage* each other with these words.
>
> 1 THESSALONIANS 4:15–18

Let's begin with the final statement, "*encourage* each other with these words." Not *frighten* or even *warn* each other! The root word also carries the meaning of *comfort*. Does speaking of the return of Jesus bring comfort and courage to you as a devoted follower of Jesus? Or does it bring a bit of fear? If it's scary, then it hasn't been shared with you correctly.

The next statement to highlight is the phrase "directly from the Lord." All of the Epistles are the Word of God, so for Paul to preface his statements with this phrase shows heavy emphasis that should be heeded. I believe there are two main reasons for it. First, we are warned that people will mock His imminent return. They will say, "Yeah, yeah, yeah, we've heard about this for generations, and it's not materialized. Nothing has changed since the early church fathers have passed away" (my paraphrase of 2 Peter 3:3–4).

The second reason: He writes of a truly remarkable event! This will be the first time in roughly two thousand years that the Lord Jesus will leave the great city of God—the heavenly Jerusalem. Our Bridegroom is not sending angels for us, although masses of them will accompany Him. No, He is coming personally for His bride—for the church, for you and me. It's similar to the ancient Jewish wedding; the groom comes, accompanied by his wedding party, for his bride. Shouts and blowing shofars suddenly ring through the streets at an unannounced time of evening as the groom comes by stealth to "catch away" his bride. Similarly, this is a surprise, a day and hour only our Father knows, and it will be accompanied by a shout and a very loud trumpet blast.

In an atomic moment, those who have previously died in Christ in generations past will rise out of their graves. As a sidenote, we can safely conclude these people have not been in the ground all this time, because

Paul writes that to be absent from the body is to be present with the Lord. Currently God's city consists of Himself, Jesus, the Spirit of God, an innumerable company of angels, and "the spirits of just men made perfect" (Hebrews 12:23 NKJV). These are the men and women who have gone on before us in Christ, both Old and New Testament saints, and they currently possess spiritual bodies, most likely having a visible form, translucent in nature, with similar traits to human bodies. I believe this because they are in a physical city that will one day descend to earth.

So even as Jesus' Spirit was in the underworld the three days and three nights while His physical body lay in the grave (see 1 Peter 3:19; Ephesians 4:9), even so these saints have been separated from their bodies for a season. However, just as Jesus was reunited with His physical body and instantaneously transformed into His current glorified body by the power of God's Spirit, even so these saints will experience the same. They will instantaneously be reunited with their bodies, which for the majority will be dust and bones, and by the same Spirit be glorified as Jesus was on resurrection day. This is why He is frequently referred to as "the firstborn from the dead" (Colossians 1:18; Revelation 1:5 NKJV).

The next question that should be asked is, What happens to those saints who are currently living on the earth? Let's look at Paul's words again:

> Then, *together with them*, we who are still alive and remain on the earth will be *caught up* in the clouds to meet the Lord in the air. Then we will be with the Lord forever. So encourage each other with these words.
>
> 1 THESSALONIANS 4:17–18

Paul's words *together with them* should be emphasized. In that atomic second, while the deceased saints are transformed into their heavenly bodies, the exact same thing will happen with the living. In Paul's words, "We will not all die, but we will all be transformed! It will happen in a moment, in the blink of an eye" (1 Corinthians 15:51–52).

The phrase he uses to describe this atomic second event is "caught up." In Greek the word is *harpázō*, defined as "to grab or seize by force, with the purpose of removing and/or controlling—'to seize, to snatch away, to take away.'"[3] This word is found fourteen times in the New Testament, and in all accounts, it carries a "snatching away" emphasis. Let's look at some of them translated in the New King James Version (note: italic words are translated from the Greek word *harpázō*; non-italic words are the surrounding words kept for context):

- Matthew 11:12. . . . . "*take* it *by force*"
- Matthew 13:19. . . . "*snatches*"
- John 6:15 . . . . "*take* Him *by force*"
- John 10:12 . . . . "the wolf *catches* the sheep"
- Acts 8:39 . . . . "The Spirit of the Lord *caught* Philip away"
- Acts 23:10 . . . . "*take* him *by force* from among them"
- 2 Corinthians 12:4 . . "he was *caught up* into Paradise"
- 1 Thessalonians 4:17 . "*caught up* . . . in the clouds"
- Revelation 12:5 . . . . . "her child was *caught up* to God and His Throne"

There are four other scriptures (Matthew 12:29; John 10:28–29; 2 Corinthians 12:2; Jude v. 23); I encourage you to look them up. What's the main point? The other usages of this word leave no doubt it means a sudden, rapid seizing and carrying away. Jesus will do exactly this with His bride alive on the earth. In no way does this convey a gradual or figurative process.

Many have used the word *rapture.* I hesitate to, as it seems to be a trigger word that often incites arguments or shuts people down to the importance of this scripture. Please don't form an opinion based on others' ignorant reasonings or what you've concluded without proper investigation. Admittedly, the word doesn't appear in our English Bible, but it does appear in the Latin Bible.

An early church father named Jerome took twenty-three years to convert the New Testament from Greek to Latin. He completed the project in AD 390, and the translation is widely known as the Latin Vulgate. Church fathers regarded his work so highly that it was used to translate the New Testament into several foreign languages over the next one thousand years!

The Latin word Jerome used for *harpázō* was *rapiemur*, which is related to the Latin word *raptus*, from which we get the word *rapture*. Yes, the word isn't in our English Bible, but neither is the word *Trinity*, yet it's widely accepted as an accurate description of the relationship and unity of the Father, Son, and Holy Spirit. Why isn't *Trinity* so heatedly contested as *rapture* is?

From this point on I will not use the word *rapture* but will stick with our English translation "caught away" or "caught up." The only purpose for mentioning *rapture* is to establish a connection for those who have heard other sound teachers use it in relationship to what Paul writes to the Thessalonians and Corinthians.

The next question that should be asked is, Where are we meeting Him? It's important to specify because we have two entirely different locations mentioned in regard to His second coming. One is in the air, the other is on a mountain. Eventually we need to ask: Are these one and the same or two different events? We won't skirt this important question. As an initial inquiry, let's compare Paul's words with the prophet Zechariah's. Paul writes:

> We who are still alive and remain on the earth will be caught up in the *clouds* to meet the Lord in the *air*.
>
> 1 THESSALONIANS 4:17

We have two words indicating location: *clouds* and *air*. The word *clouds* is an exact translation; the Greek word simply means "a cloud" in our atmosphere.[4] The word *air* is defined: "the celestial air surrounding the earth."[5] So it's clear, this event will happen in the atmosphere somewhere between where our planes fly and the exosphere—the outer atmosphere that rockets need to break through in exiting or reentering Earth.

Why is this important? Revelation shows that when He returns with His holy ones, He will wage war on a coalition of nations that have gathered together at Armageddon to fight (see Revelation 16:16; 19:11–21). Zechariah writes:

> Then the Lord will go out to fight against those nations, as he has fought in times past. On that day his feet will stand on the Mount of Olives, east of Jerusalem. And the Mount of Olives will split apart.
>
> Zechariah 14:3–4

Both Paul and Zechariah are quite clear on location and purpose. We must ask: Why do we meet the Lord in the clouds but we are also told His feet will land on the Mount of Olives? Are these events one and the same? Do we meet Him in the air, immediately get on our white horses, do a U-turn, and follow Him back to witness the slaying of His enemies and Him putting His feet on the mountain? Is He coming for His bride and waging war at the same time? Does He have a wedding garment on under His armor for war, or are these two different happenings? We will answer these questions in the next section.

PASSAGE: "The bridegroom came, and those who were ready went in with him to the wedding." (Matthew 25:10 NKJV)

POINT: Our Bridegroom is coming for His bride with a shout and a very loud trumpet blast.

PONDER: Read Revelation 19:11–16. Does it appear that Jesus is coming to get His bride or for war? If war, then when does He come for His bride? Are they one and the same?

PRAYER: Lord, You are not the author of confusion but the God of order. You've promised to reveal Your will when I seek You earnestly. I'm asking for understanding in regard to the prophetic scriptures of Jesus' return for His bride. In Jesus' name, amen.

PROFESSION: Hasten Your coming, Lord Jesus!

WEEK 3

THE UNITING OF THE BRIDE AND GROOM

SEEK THE LORD, ALL YOU

MEEK OF THE EARTH,

WHO HAVE UPHELD HIS JUSTICE.

SEEK RIGHTEOUSNESS,

SEEK HUMILITY.

IT MAY BE THAT YOU WILL BE HIDDEN

IN THE DAY OF THE LORD'S ANGER.

ZEPHANIAH 2:3 NKJV

CHAPTER 15

NOT APPOINTED TO WRATH

We've come to the point that we must address the inescapable discussion of eschatology: When we speak of Jesus' return, does it refer to the Bridegroom *catching away* His bride or the conquering King returning to *defeat all rebellion* and set up His thousand-year reign? The answer is not one or the other; rather, it's both! However, this leads to the unavoidable question: *If it's both, do they occur at the same time or at different times*? If the answer is "different," then how can two completely different narratives be part of the same event?

Consider a typical Western wedding. I've officiated at many of them. Most often it's in two phases: the ceremony and the reception. Each occurs at two distinct times and can be in two different locations. For my wife and me, our ceremony was at the church, and afterward we drove to a historic homesite where our reception was held. Both events—though different in function, time, and location—were a part of the same wedding.

In praying, searching Scripture, and reading trustworthy ministers and church fathers' writings, I've come to believe the second coming of Jesus is one event that occurs in two phases, each having a different function, time, and location.

Before diving in, allow me to preface what's about to be discussed with both a setup and a warning. There isn't an isolated scripture that clearly addresses our question, but rather a complex tapestry of passages, with each providing an element of what's coming. When all are viewed together, they reveal a picture of what's not otherwise obvious. I believe there's a divine purpose behind this. Why? To keep us searching, that we might find the beautiful hidden secrets of wisdom within the collage of prophetic scriptures.

I hesitate to address this topic due to the concern of possible division. Please know, dear reader, this is only for you to ponder, pray about, be encouraged by, and enjoy discussing with others. It's not intended to be dogmatic or used as ammunition for arguing with others who disagree. In fact, I'll add some humor. My own wife doesn't fully agree with my interpretation, and she is the closest person to me on this earth. We respect each other's position and often joke about it.

You may now think, *If John's concerned about addressing this, why share it at all?* A fair question, and I seriously thought of avoiding the issue altogether. I contemplated which would be greater—the potential hazard or the benefit. In the end I concluded that hope and comfort far outweigh any potential risks. I also determined it's unavoidable for a proper discussion of *The King Is Coming.*

Let me first introduce the three most common beliefs of the "catching away" of the church. First is the post-tribulation view. Those who embrace this view believe that every aspect of the second coming happens at the same time. In other words, if we return to our wedding example, the ceremony and reception are one and the same, happening in the same location, at the same time. In essence, those who hold to this belief say that Jesus will "catch away" His bride at the end of the seven-year tribulation.

If this view is correct, I have a difficult time determining why a meeting needs to occur in the clouds. Why not be "caught away" to meet Him at the Mount of Olives, upon which Jesus will place His feet (Zechariah 14:3–4)? But it can't be so, otherwise Paul's writings to the Thessalonians and Corinthians are inapplicable and untrue. This certainly isn't an option, especially with his statements being prefaced with, "We tell you this directly from the Lord."

For the post-tribulation view to be accurate, it leaves only one possible scenario: Jesus will "catch away" the church in the clouds. Once there, we'll immediately mount up on horses, do a U-turn, and follow Him back to earth to witness His defeat of the rebellious nations. This seems awkward but possible.

However, there are complications. One of the main ones being the church will still be on earth for the severe wrath of God—the seven seal judgments, the seven trumpet judgments, and finally the seven bowl judgments. There will be trouble, anguish, suffering, and death never before seen or experienced.

A quick overview of the wrath to come conflicts with the understanding of God's Fatherhood. One of the devastations of His wrath includes one-fourth of all mankind being killed during just the fourth seal judgment, not to mention the catastrophes of the other six seals.

The trumpet judgments are even worse, where one of them will see a third of the earth burned and an additional large segment of mankind die from one-third of the water being made poisonous. In another trumpet judgment people will seek death to escape unimaginable torment and will not be able to find it. The sixth trumpet will kill still another one-third of mankind (we're now at four to five billion deaths and far from finished).

The final bowl judgments include all the water on earth turning to blood, killing everything that lives in water. The sun will release blasts of fiery heat that will scorch the inhabitants of earth. There will be terrible storms with hail weighing up to seventy-five pounds each. This is just a sampling of the horrific wrath that will be poured out.

If the post-tribulation view is accurate, His bride not only will have to contend with this unimaginable wrath of God but also with the wrath of the man of sin and his loyal legions. This global ruler, who is the embodiment of Satan, is given authority to overcome the saints. (See Daniel 7:25 and Revelation 13:7; we will cover who these saints are in the next chapter.) If these saints are the bride of Christ, then it's a battered bride surviving rather than a glorious bride "caught away."

At the completion of the tribulation's fury people will be scarcer than gold. If all humanity is this sparse, then how much sparser will the saints be due to a double whammy from both heaven and the world ruler? It wouldn't be much of a uniting for the Bridegroom and bride, and it wouldn't be much of a surprise either, for the prophet Daniel gives an exact number of days (see Daniel 12:11–12).

Let's move on to the second view, mid-tribulation. This one sees the "catching away" of the bride occurring somewhere during the seven-year tribulation. I personally struggle to know what scriptures this idea is based upon, so I can't speak much to it. Those who believe this declare we will not be here during the great tribulation (the last three and a half years), only the first half. An important note: The worst of God's wrath is indeed poured out on the second half of the tribulation; however, a good portion of God's wrath judgments will be poured out on the first half as well.

The third view, pre-tribulation, sees the "catching away" occurring prior to the tribulation. Some believe it's the kickstart of the tribulation; others believe there may be a brief, unknown time gap between the catching away and the beginning of the tribulation. I personally believe this third view, without any time gap. In other words, the catching away initiates the tribulation.

Remember, I have some friends who don't agree with my position. They are still my dear friends, and we're all staying busy in the harvest fields, making disciples and eagerly looking forward to His return. One of the big advantages I see with my wife's and friends' interpretation is that it keeps our hearts and minds prepared for extreme difficulty, which is not a bad thing. We are exhorted to "arm ourselves to suffer as Christ suffered" (my paraphrase of 1 Peter 4:1). However, with that said, I still don't see it unfolding this way in Scripture, and I'll give seven reasons why in the next few chapters.

Before beginning, there's a delineation that needs clarification or our discussions will result in confusion. There are three groups of saints on earth in the general time frame of the second coming (both before and during the tribulation):

1. **The church** or **the bride of Christ**: These have received Jesus Christ as their Lord and faithfully follow Him. Most of this group will already be in heaven; however, there will still be a large segment on earth when the Lord returns to catch away His bride. This group will consist of many Gentiles and some Jewish people.

2. **The Jewish saints**: These are the Jewish people whose eyes will be opened during the tribulation to recognize and worship their Messiah, Jesus Christ. They're the people Paul references when he says that, once the full number of Gentiles comes in, all of Israel will be saved (see Romans 11:25–26).
3. **The tribulation saints**: These will include all of category 2 (the Jewish saints) but will also include the Gentiles who are saved during the tribulation. I could have made numbers 2 and 3 one category, but there will be times I need to isolate the Jewish saints.

Now let's discuss why Scripture shows that the catching away of the bride occurs prior to the seven-year tribulation. I will cover seven main topics, but they are not exhaustive, and the seventh is not from Scripture but is what the early church fathers taught. Here is the list:

1. We are not appointed to wrath.
2. We enter the heavenly chamber before the outpouring of wrath.
3. The church is absent in much of Revelation.
4. The twenty-four elders appear before God's wrath is poured out.
5. The restrainer must be removed.
6. As in the days of Noah, the righteous will be spared.
7. It is what the early church fathers taught.

It will take the next four chapters to complete this discussion, but it will be fascinating. So let's begin:

1. WE ARE NOT APPOINTED TO WRATH.

There are over twenty-five references to the wrath of God in the New Testament, and even more in the Old. Most of them identify the culmination of judgment occurring during the seven-year tribulation. Some include:

> Then I heard a loud voice from the temple saying to the seven angels, "Go and pour out the bowls of the *wrath of God* on the earth."
>
> REVELATION 16:1 NKJV

> For the great day of *His wrath* has come, and who is able to stand?
>
> REVELATION 6:17 NKJV

> The nations were angry, and *Your wrath* has come.
>
> REVELATION 11:18 NKJV

This represents just a sampling of the several references found in just the book of Revelation, and you'll also find many in the Epistles. In the New Testament, the words to describe God's wrath are *thumós* and *orgḗ*, and both are used in the book of Revelation. The first word includes "the idea of punishment or punitive judgment."[1] Even more clarifying, and attention grabbing, is this definition of *thumós*: "indignation, wrath as the outburst of a vengeful mind."[2]

The second word, *orgḗ*, which is used in most references, is defined as "divine punishment based on God's angry judgment against someone."[3] These are very strong definitions and leave no wiggle room; the tribulation is the time of His punitive judgment and punishment. In fact, another passage refers to it as *fierce*:

> He Himself treads the winepress of the *fierceness* and *wrath* of Almighty God.
>
> REVELATION 19:15 NKJV

For continuity, let's review again Isaiah's description of the day of the Lord, also known as the seven-year tribulation:

> Behold, the day of the LORD comes, *cruel*, with both *wrath* and fierce anger, to lay the land desolate; and He will destroy its sinners from it. For the stars of heaven and their constellations will not give their light;

> the sun will be darkened in its going forth, and the moon will not cause its light to shine. "I will punish the world for its evil, and the wicked for their iniquity; I will halt the arrogance of the proud, and will lay low the haughtiness of the terrible. I will make a mortal more rare than fine gold."
>
> ISAIAH 13:9–12 NKJV

His wrath is labeled as *cruel*, for it will proceed from His fierce anger and will both *punish* and *destroy*. These scriptures make quite clear that the tribulation period is without a doubt the *wrath of God* and is not intended for His Son's bride but a rebellious world.

Paul writes in perfect harmony with the above passages in his epistles. He only uses the word *orgḗ*. One example is Romans 5:9, which states: "Having now been justified by His blood, we shall be *saved from wrath* through Him" (NKJV). His most interesting use of this word is found in his first letter to the Thessalonians. Paul bookends the *catching away* of the church with the very clear message that we are not appointed to wrath. Here are the bookends:

> To wait for His Son from heaven, whom He raised from the dead, *even* Jesus who delivers us from the *wrath* to come.
>
> 1 THESSALONIANS 1:10 NKJV

He proceeds to write of the *catching away* of Jesus' bride in the fourth and fifth chapters, with the following at the end of his discussion of this profound event:

> For God *did not appoint us to wrath*, but to obtain salvation through our Lord Jesus Christ . . . Therefore comfort each other and edify one another, just as you also are doing.
>
> 1 THESSALONIANS 5:9–11 NKJV

It's clear, the bride (church) is not intended to experience the wrath of God, and for the second time in this group of passages, Paul tells believers to comfort each other with these words. No one would consider the message of going through God's wrath as bringing comfort and encouragement.

There are some who would protest, "This is an *escape* mentality! We are appointed to tribulation." That is correct, as Jesus states, "In the world you will have tribulation" (John 16:33 NKJV). However, there is a huge difference between *tribulation* and *the tribulation*. Jesus is referencing persecutions, hardships, afflictions, and suffering from the trials and testings of this world.

From our work with persecuted nations, I've learned more easily than other Western believers of the intense persecution occurring in various parts of the world. In fact, as I was writing this chapter, I was informed by our sources of over one thousand believers put to death in the past month for their faith in just one part of the world. Christians are being thrown into prisons and tortured in many places in the world. Studies show more Christians have been martyred for their faith in the past one hundred years than any other time in history.[4] These are the tribulations Jesus speaks of; however, the seven-year tribulation is God's wrath. There is a huge difference; one is the world's wrath against believers, whereas the other is God's wrath against the world.

Let's address the accusation of a pre-tribulation catching away being an *escape* mentality. If it's so cowardly and unheroic, then why does Jesus instruct believers regarding the seven-year tribulation in this way:

> "Watch therefore, and pray always that you may be counted worthy to *escape* all these things."
>
> LUKE 21:36 NKJV

It's not a cowardly thing to escape the *wrath of God*. Jesus took God's wrath upon Himself to deliver us from the divine punishment to come. However, it's indeed correct to identify as a "cowardly act" trying to escape the *wrath of the world* by denying our faith or compromising the Word of God.

NOT APPOINTED TO WRATH

PASSAGE: In accordance with your hardness and your impenitent heart you are treasuring up for yourself wrath in the day of wrath and revelation of the righteous judgment of God. (Romans 2:5 NKJV)

POINT: The bride of Christ is not appointed to God's wrath.

PONDER: What is the difference between *tribulation* and *the wrath of God*? List examples in Scripture illustrating each. On a different note, what's the difference between God's discipline and His wrath? Is discipline painful? Is it helpful? (See Hebrews 12:3–11.) How are tribulation and discipline related or not related?

PRAYER: Dear heavenly Father, please help me to distinguish between what is tribulation from the world and what is discipline from Your loving hand. Please give me strength to endure and overcome the world's tribulation and to embrace Your loving discipline. In Jesus' name I pray, amen.

PROFESSION: I will embrace God's discipline, but I'm not appointed to His wrath.

COME, MY PEOPLE, ENTER YOUR CHAMBERS, AND SHUT YOUR DOORS BEHIND YOU; HIDE YOURSELF, AS IT WERE, FOR A LITTLE MOMENT, UNTIL THE INDIGNATION IS PAST. FOR BEHOLD, THE LORD COMES OUT OF HIS PLACE TO PUNISH THE INHABITANTS OF THE EARTH FOR THEIR INIQUITY.

ISAIAH 26:20-21 NKJV

CHAPTER 16

HIDDEN IN THE CHAMBER

We've already discussed the first reason I believe the bride will not be here during the seven-year tribulation, and in the next three chapters, we'll look at the others.

2. WE ENTER THE HEAVENLY CHAMBER BEFORE THE OUTPOURING OF WRATH.

Once again, we get a glimpse of the ancient Jewish wedding in Isaiah's words, but it's not obvious. Let's briefly review what we discussed in chapter 9, how the groom would prepare a room, a *chamber*, for his wife. Upon his father's approval, he would come unexpectedly to his bride's community, with shouts and shofar horns blowing in the streets. He would catch her away and immediately bring her to the bridal chamber where they'd spend the next seven days together. Afterward, the couple would emerge from hiding, and the husband would present his unveiled wife to all in attendance.

Before making the comparison, let's take a closer look at Isaiah's words for more context. The prophetic word begins:

> But those who die in the LORD will live; their bodies will rise again!
>
> Those who sleep in the earth will rise up and sing for joy! For your life-giving light will fall like dew on your people in the place of the dead! . . . Look! The LORD is coming from heaven to punish the people of the earth for their sins.
>
> ISAIAH 26:19, 21

There's no doubt he's addressing the resurrection of the saints, which is a huge aspect of the second coming. We also see that the time frame is made clear in verse 21. In comparing Isaiah's words with our New Testament rendering of the same event, we gain a more complete picture. Paul writes:

> Christ has been raised from the dead. He is the first of a great harvest of all who have died.
>
> 1 CORINTHIANS 15:20

And using almost the exact same words as Isaiah, Paul writes:

> The believers who have died will rise from their graves.
>
> 1 THESSALONIANS 4:16

Paul then gives a more thorough description of the believer's resurrection than Isaiah by writing: "Our bodies are buried in brokenness, but they will be raised in glory. They are buried in weakness, but they will be raised in strength. They are buried as natural human bodies, but they will be raised as spiritual bodies" (1 Corinthians 15:43–44). He amplifies Isaiah's words, who wrote that God's "life-giving light will fall like dew on your people in the place of the dead!" (26:19). Paul continues:

> It will happen in a moment, in the blink of an eye. . . . For when the trumpet sounds, those who have died will be raised to live forever. And we who are living will also be transformed.
>
> 1 CORINTHIANS 15:52

This can't be any clearer; Isaiah and Paul are writing about the exact same event. It's even backed by Paul stating that this prophetic promise is "directly from the Lord" (1 Thessalonians 4:15). Make no mistake about it, a certain day is coming in which Jesus will descend into the earth's atmosphere, which just so happens to be the community where His bride resides (either in the grave or still alive), swoop up His beloved, and bring her to the *chamber* He's prepared (see John 14:1–3). Let's continue with Isaiah's *very next statement* and we will see the correlation to the Jewish wedding:

> Come, my people, *enter your chambers*, and shut your doors behind you; hide yourself, as it were, for a little moment, until the indignation is past. For behold, the LORD comes out of His place to punish the inhabitants of the earth for their iniquity.
>
> ISAIAH 26:20–21 NKJV

Now, let's think through this tapestry of scriptures carefully. The most important question to ask is: Where are these chambers for the resurrected dead in the Lord? Are they on earth or in heaven? In other words, as the indignation—the wrath of God—is being poured out, are God's people who are resurrected from the graves going to once again live on earth and hide themselves in remote places such as forests, deserts, caves, communes, and so forth to avoid the plagues of judgments? No way! This thought is so far-fetched: dead people being resurrected so they can hide on earth from the persecution of the Antichrist and the wrath of God. We can undoubtedly state that these resurrected saints will be hidden in heavenly chambers.

Now for the next important question: What happens in the same split second as these who are resurrected from the graves? The answer is found in the mystery that wasn't made known to Isaiah, or any other Old Testament prophet—the mystery that Paul received "directly from the Lord." The mystery that those who are alive in Christ will also be caught up "together with them" (1 Thessalonians 4:17)—*in the same atomic second*—to meet the Lord and forever be with Him!

What is Scripture making clear? If the dead in the Lord are raised before the wrath is poured out (*hiding in chambers*), then the alive are also "caught up" before the wrath is poured out (*and will be in the same chambers*)! Both the dead and the living are united with the Lord within the same atomic second. Zephaniah confirms this as well:

> Seek the LORD, all you meek *of the earth*, who have upheld His justice. Seek righteousness, seek humility. It may be that you will be hidden in the day of the LORD's anger.
>
> ZEPHANIAH 2:3 NKJV

Going back to the Jewish wedding, once the couple is in the bridal chamber, it's seven days of *alone time*. They are hidden away from all activities taking place outside the chamber.

This point is so important that it needs to be reiterated. Isaiah and Zephaniah clearly state that *just before* the Lord punishes the inhabitants of the world, an event called the Day of the Lord—the tribulation and great tribulation—will occur, and those who are dead in the Lord will be resurrected and hidden in chambers, and Paul will complete the picture with "the mystery" that those of us who are alive in Christ will be caught up at the exact same time!

Upon the completion of the seven years, Jesus will return with His unveiled bride, defeat all rebellion, and set up His kingdom with her reigning by His side. With this in mind, note the remarkable similarities in the following scriptures:

> Behold, the Lord comes *with* ten thousand of His saints, to execute judgment on all, to convict all who are ungodly among them of all their ungodly deeds which they have committed in an ungodly way.
>
> JUDE VV. 14–15 NKJV

Jude is not describing Jesus coming *for* His bride, as Paul did with the Thessalonians, but rather coming *with* His bride. One of the aspects of Jude's words describes *the reveal* of Jesus' bride that will occur seven years after the catching away. The following verses speak specifically of the reveal:

> Therefore the world does not know us, because it did not know Him. Beloved, now we are children of God; and it has not yet been *revealed* what we shall be, but we know that when He is revealed, we shall be like Him.
>
> 1 JOHN 3:1–2 NKJV

> When Christ who is our life appears, then you also will *appear with Him* in glory.
>
> COLOSSIANS 3:4 NKJV

> For all creation is waiting eagerly for that future day when God will *reveal* who his children really are.
>
> ROMANS 8:19

The similarities are startling between the ancient Jewish wedding and the apostles' and prophets' writings of Jesus' return. Keep in mind, these men were very well versed in the format of weddings in their culture, unlike our twenty-first-century Western comprehension.

3. THE CHURCH IS ABSENT IN MUCH OF REVELATION.

The church is mentioned nineteen times in Revelation chapters 1–3. Then we don't hear of her again until Revelation 22. Why the abrupt disappearance? To bring clarity it should be noted that approximately a half dozen times we hear the word *saints* in these in-between chapters but not *church.* Who are these people if the church is gone? They fall under category 3 listed in the previous chapter: the tribulation saints (which are comprised of both Jews and Gentiles). These are the multitudes who will be saved during the tribulation (see Revelation 7).

By keeping these groups separated and in their proper settings, we prevent confusion. In returning to the church, it's both interesting and not coincidental that after Jesus speaks to the seven churches, the very next verse is

> *After these things* I looked, and behold, a door standing open in heaven. And the first voice which I heard *was like a trumpet* speaking with me, saying, *"Come up here."*
>
> REVELATION 4:1 NKJV

After these things. After what things? Jesus has just spoken to seven historic churches. The messages to these churches wouldn't have been placed in Scripture if they did not have prophetic application. There are three main views of how these messages apply:

1. They pertain to the seven historic churches.
2. They relate to the different phases of the church's condition over the past two-thousand-year span.
3. They identify the various conditions of the global church right before His second coming.

Which one is accurate? Is it possible all three are accurate? We will answer this in the final chapters, but what's important to our discussion now is the remarkable similarity the above verse has with 1 Thessalonians 4:15–17, namely the loud trumpeting voice and the words "Come up here." They both speak of a catching away using similar terminology.

Could the reason the church isn't mentioned by name any longer be because she is in the bridal chamber with Jesus? Isn't this what Isaiah and Zephaniah prophesied above? This leads to the next scriptural reason for a pre-tribulation "catching away."

4. THE TWENTY-FOUR ELDERS APPEAR BEFORE GOD'S WRATH IS POURED OUT.

Another interesting point arises when discussing the absence of the church on earth in Revelation chapters 4–21. If we read John's vision of the throne room in chapters 4 and 5, we recognize most everyone from the numerous descriptions of God's throne contained in other books of Scripture. We see the four living creatures—seraphim, the myriad angels, Jesus (the Lamb), God Almighty, and the Spirit of God. However, there is a new group we've not seen in any other place in Scripture. That would be *the twenty-four elders.* Also, there is a group now missing: "the spirits of the righteous ones . . . made perfect" (Hebrews 12:23). Who are "the elders"? Why do they suddenly appear? Why are they not found in the visions of the throne room received by Ezekiel, Isaiah, the book of Hebrews, and the psalmist? Also, where did the "spirits of the ones made perfect" go? Did they receive new resurrected bodies at the catching away of the bride?

I believe the twenty-four elders represent the Old Testament saints and New Testament saints combined into one group. What I'm about to write is conjecture, and not to be assimilated as firm truth, but could the number twenty-four come from the twelve tribes of Israel and the twelve apostles that were chosen by the Lord as founders of the church? Again, it's only a thought that I can't firmly support from Scripture, but the reason I strongly lean this way is found in their song:

> They sang a new song, saying: "You are worthy to take the scroll, and to open its seals; for You were slain, and have *redeemed us to God* by Your blood out of *every tribe and tongue and people and nation*, and have made us *kings and priests* to our God. And *we shall reign on the earth.*"
>
> REVELATION 5:9–10 NKJV

There are four indicators in these verses that show that this group is most likely the Old Testament saints and the New Testament church. Look at the words "redeemed us to God." Let me begin by stating some translations have for some reason taken the liberty to change this quote to "ransomed people to God" (see the ESV). However, the Greek word used for *us* is *hēmás*, which is defined as: "Our, us, we. To be distinguished from *humás*, your, you."[1] There is no doubt they are identifying themselves, not others.

The church has been redeemed by the blood of Jesus, and this good news was also preached to those who waited patiently in Abraham's bosom for the Messiah to come and sprinkle His blood on the mercy seat of God (see Luke 16:22–23; Ephesians 4:9–10; 1 Peter 3:18–19). These elders are clearly stating they have been redeemed by the blood of Jesus.

Second, notice they were redeemed from "every tribe and tongue and people and nation." This shows these elders are not angelic beings. They were purchased back to God by the blood of His Son from *every* tribe, tongue, people, and nation.

Some may question, Could these twenty-four elders be individuals who led exceptional lives and therefore were selected to be in this elite group? Again, this is impossible. There are 195 nations on earth. Regarding tribes, sources tell us that there are some five thousand distinct indigenous peoples spread across every inhabited climate zone and inhabited continent of the world.[2] If each elder is one person, then we would only have twenty-four nations or tribes represented, not *every* tribe, tongue, people, and nation.

Third, notice they have been made "kings and priests" to our God. There are only two individuals and only one group identified as such in Scripture: Melchizedek (see Hebrews 7:1), Jesus Christ (see Hebrews 3:1; Revelation 19:16), and those ransomed by the blood of Jesus:

> To Him who loved us and washed us from our sins in His own blood, and has made us *kings and priests* to His God and Father.
>
> REVELATION 1:5–6 NKJV

The fourth identifier is found in their words, "We shall reign on the earth." Paul writes, "If we endure, we shall also reign with Him" (2 Timothy 2:12 NKJV; see also Revelation 20:6). Angels are not promised to rule with Christ, nor are even the seraphim. Scripture is clear on this, as it states, "It is not angels who will control the future world we are talking about" (Hebrews 2:5). The only ones promised to rule with Jesus Christ are His faithful saints.

These are the four compelling reasons to believe these elders are indeed a representation of the church and Old Testament saints! But there's more. One of the first things John notices after being caught up to the throne room other than the Lord Himself is these elders. Listen to his description:

> Instantly I was in the Spirit, and I saw the throne in heaven and someone sitting on it. . . . Twenty-four thrones surrounded him, and twenty-four elders sat on them. They were all clothed in white and had gold crowns on their heads.
>
> REVELATION 4:2–4

These elders were clothed in white and had gold crowns. Who wears white and has crowns? We are told: "For the time has come for the wedding feast of the Lamb, and his bride has prepared herself. She has been given the finest of *pure white* linen to wear" (Revelation 19:7–8).

Secondly, their crowns. Paul writes, "And now the prize awaits me—the *crown* of righteousness, which the Lord, the righteous Judge, will give me on the day of his return. And the prize is not just for me but for all who eagerly look forward to his appearing" (2 Timothy 4:8). Paul connects crowns being given on the day of Christ's return to all who eagerly look for His appearing. That is all of His beloved saints, His bride!

Now comes the amazing aspect: These elders appear before any of the wrath of God is poured out. Not one seal has been broken as of yet. It's just as the prophet Isaiah declares; we are hidden in the wedding chamber before the indignation is poured out!

The most compelling reasons are yet to come.

PASSAGE: We tell you this directly from the Lord. (1 Thessalonians 4:15)

POINT: The resurrection of the saints occurs before the indignation is poured out, not during or at the end.

PONDER: Why do you think Paul uses the words "directly from the Lord" in his writing about the resurrection and catching away? Did the Spirit of God see the controversy that would surround this great event? How can you use what you've seen in this chapter to encourage and comfort your loved ones? How can you avoid disputes?

PRAYER: Father, I ask that You help me to abide in Your Word, that I may be found faithful and ready for either my resurrection or my catching away that is soon to come. In Jesus' name, amen.

PROFESSION: Jesus has prepared a chamber to protect me and His beloved saints from the indignation that is to come.

THE MYSTERY OF LAWLESSNESS IS ALREADY AT WORK; ONLY HE WHO NOW RESTRAINS WILL DO SO UNTIL HE IS TAKEN OUT OF THE WAY.

2 THESSALONIANS 2:7 NKJV

CHAPTER 17

THE RESTRAINER

What if our society, or any society, existed without the church's influence? What would our communities look like? Imagine if the force of godliness was completely removed from all spheres of life—our systems of education, the marketplaces, governments, the arts . . . The list is too long to compile. Would there be any charitable or relief organizations, elder care, quality health-care providers, or any other service providers for the needy? In pondering this, it can easily be concluded, we'd end up in a narcissistic and dark world.

Consider generations of old; what happened when godly people became scarce? The most obvious occurred during Noah's day: "The LORD observed the extent of human wickedness on the earth, and he saw that everything they thought or imagined was consistently and totally evil" (Genesis 6:5). Other civilizations that quickly come to mind are Sodom and Gomorrah, Egypt in the days of Rameses II, Israel in the days when "all the people did whatever seemed right in their own eyes" (Judges 17:6), and we can easily identify numerous others.

Humanity's natural tendency is, and always has been, to sink into corruption. Without the force of righteousness, civilizations drift further and further away from wholesome living. Why is this? Why does humanity, void of God's Word, move away from what is true and right, steadily gravitating toward perverse thinking? Why do people so easily drift into believing what is good is evil and what is evil is good? It's due to the "course of this world." Paul writes:

> You once walked according to *the course of this world*, according to the prince of the power of the air, the spirit who now works in the sons of disobedience.
>
> EPHESIANS 2:2 NKJV

Civilization is controlled by an undercurrent of dark forces—a flow, a force—which draws humanity away from what is truly best and leads to self-destruction. This current is so powerful and deceptive that it's identified in Scripture as "the mystery of *lawlessness*" (2 Thessalonians 2:7 NKJV). This phrase alone carries great insight, but only if understood. If we don't recognize it, we are sure to be affected by it.

Imagine being in a rowboat on the Niagara River and ignorant of where it leads. If you just relax, the current will steadily take you along its path. Eventually you'll end up being another of hundreds who have plummeted to their death by going over the famous Niagara Falls. But if you understand where it leads, you can take precautionary measures to avoid certain death.

What is *lawlessness*? In Greek the word is *anomia* and carries the fundamental meaning of living outside of the law. This could span from complete ignorance of the law all the way to blatant rebellion against it.[1] The best illustration of lawlessness—in fact, where it originated—occurred in the garden of Eden. In the garden's midst we find two highlighted trees: the Tree of Life and the Tree of Knowledge of Good and Evil. We've already discussed this subject in measure, now we will drill down further.

The Tree of Life can be easily defined as finding our life in God. More clearly stated: He is my perfect and loving Creator; therefore, whatever He wills for me is best. I compare this to when our four sons were toddlers. In my role as dad, Christmas Day was a "workday." To put it simply, they would open their gifts and afterward Dad would assemble them. Now, I'm a typical man. I usually open the box, pour out the pieces on the floor, toss the box and the instruction manual aside, and start building. After an hour or so I'm finished, but there are still a few pieces on the floor. Thinking the pieces are extras, I proceed to flip the On switch, and to my great displeasure, the toy doesn't work! Now I'm upset. It's defective and this company has just wasted an hour of my time on Christmas day!

Since it's a holiday, I can't call the toll-free number to complain. What do I do? I grab the instruction manual written by the guy who designed the toy, deconstruct it, then rebuild it the way he outlines in the manual, and behold, this time no pieces are left on the floor. I then hit the On switch and the toy works! This perfectly illustrates the Tree of Life: If we just do what God instructs, we will flourish.

In contrast, what behavior identifies the Tree of Knowledge of Good and Evil? It's quite clear in Scripture: "When the woman saw that the tree was *good* . . . and a tree desirable to make one *wise* . . ." (Genesis 3:6 NKJV). Notice it doesn't say, "When she saw it was *evil* and would make her *wicked*." The devastating consequences of her choice were camouflaged by *what was good for her*. Highlighting this fact gives us clear insight into what this tree truly represented. In essence, "I choose what is *good* for me *outside* of what God says. I remove myself from His law of liberty (see James 1:25), law of life (see Romans 8:2), law of love (see James 2:8), and other life-giving laws. I've brought myself under the mystery or *secret power* of lawlessness." This leads us to yet another reason I believe Scripture shows the catching away will occur before the seven-year tribulation.

5. THE RESTRAINER MUST BE REMOVED.

The apostle Paul found it necessary to write a second letter to the church in Thessalonica. They needed comforting, as some "teachers" had troubled them. The young church was told the catching away had already occurred, and the Day of the Lord—the tribulation—had already begun. Paul counters with these words:

> Let no one deceive you by any means; for that Day will not come unless the falling away comes first, and *the man of sin* is *revealed*, the son of

> perdition, who opposes and exalts himself above all that is called God or that is worshiped, so that he sits as God in the temple of God, showing himself that he is God.
>
> 2 THESSALONIANS 2:3–4 NKJV

Two things must take place before the tribulation begins. The first is the apostasy—the falling away from faith of many professing believers. The second is the identity of the *man of sin.* Many refer to him as the *Antichrist.* However, this term is only used once in the New Testament (1 John 2:18). Other names given to him are *the beast, the son of perdition, the wicked one, the lawless one,* and a few others. For the sake of ease, I'll refer to him as the Antichrist.

He is the perfect antithesis of Jesus Christ and is the full embodiment of lawless Satan himself. His reveal will occur at the beginning of the seven years when a covenant of peace is made with the Jewish nation, but halfway through:

> The ruler will make a treaty with the people for a period of one set of seven, but after half this time, he will put an end to the sacrifices and offerings. And as a climax to all his terrible deeds, he will set up a sacrilegious object that causes desecration, until the fate decreed for this defiler is finally poured out on him.
>
> DANIEL 9:27

How will such a wicked man fool the Jewish people at the onset of the seven-year tribulation? If lawlessness is masked as "what is good for me" and is already at work "secretly" in society, then, no different from what happened in the garden with Eve, this man's initial appearance will seem good and wise.

At the midpoint of the final seven years, he will claim himself to be God and above all that is called God. Horrifying! Listen carefully to what Paul goes on to say:

> And now you know what is *restraining*, that he may be revealed in his own time. For the mystery of lawlessness is already at work; only He who now

> *restrains* will do so until He is taken out of the way. And then the lawless one will be revealed, whom the Lord will consume with the breath of His mouth and destroy with the brightness of His coming.
>
> 2 THESSALONIANS 2:6–8 NKJV

In these verses we see there is a *restrainer* that is doing *two things*: first, holding back the secret power of lawlessness; and second, keeping the Antichrist from being revealed. Who is this restrainer? Rick Renner, a friend and Greek scholar, writes:

> The Greek words to describe this restrainer in verses 6 and 7 are both neuter and masculine in the original text. This implies that the identity of the restrainer may be a thing, a person (persons), or both.[2]

In order for the restrainer to hold back the secret power of lawlessness, he or it would have to be in all the areas of our social construct. There have been four of five theories on the restrainer's identity, but only two stand out as plausible. The first is the Holy Spirit, and many believe it's Him, even the New King James Version translators, as they capitalized the pronoun. However, I have a difficult time with this interpretation, for we know there will be a tremendous harvest of souls in the tribulation, and "no one can say that Jesus is Lord, except by the Holy Spirit" (1 Corinthians 12:3). He is the One who opens a person's heart to recognize Jesus as the Christ. Therefore Holy Spirit must be here during the tribulation.

The other possibility is the body of Christ or the church. I like this choice. Let's recall our question at the beginning of the chapter: What would society be like if all of a sudden the church's influence was completely removed? Jesus states:

> "I will build my church, and all the powers of hell will not *conquer* it. And I will give you the keys of the Kingdom of Heaven. Whatever you forbid on earth will be forbidden in heaven, and whatever you permit on earth will be permitted in heaven."
>
> MATTHEW 16:18–19

The church cannot be *conquered*; therefore, it's a restraining force against the mystery of lawlessness. In the New King James Version it is translated, "I will build My church, and the gates of Hades shall not prevail against it." Gates are not offensive; rather, they are defensive. The church is told to advance the kingdom by making disciples of all nations (see Matthew 28:19). The Greek word for *nations* is *ethnos*, which is defined as "a body of persons united by kinship, culture, and common traditions."[3] This certainly includes actual nations, tribes, territories, and ethnic groups. However, it also encompasses persons with a commonality, such as body-builders, entertainers, pilots, hairstylists, salespeople, stay-at-home moms, and so forth.

The church is to continuously advance. It's a force of light, and the gates of darkness cannot stop it. Just as darkness doesn't overcome light but is always overcome by light, even so the church has been not only a restraining force but an advancing force. In fact, Jesus clearly communicates in a parable that the church is to "occupy till I come" (Luke 19:13 KJV).

The church has been sorely persecuted throughout its entire existence. Many Christians have been brutally martyred, but the church continues to occupy, advance, and tear down the strongholds of hell. No force has been able to overcome it all through the two-thousand-year Age of Grace.

However, during the tribulation, the Antichrist will be given power over the saints. He will succeed and conquer anything he desires. Heaven will allow this:

> He was given authority to do whatever he wanted for forty-two months. . . . And the beast was allowed to wage war against God's *holy people* and to *conquer them*.
>
> REVELATION 13:5, 7

Once again, let's ask, Who are the *holy people*? They are the tribulation saints—all of Israel and many converted Gentiles. They are not given Jesus' promise to the church that "all the powers of hell will *not conquer it*"

(Matthew 16:18). During these seven years, the Antichrist will be permitted to *conquer* the believers. Daniel prophesies the saints will be placed under his *control* the final three and a half years.

> He will defy the Most High and oppress the holy people of the Most High. He will try to change their sacred festivals and laws, and they will be placed under his *control* for a time, times, and half a time.
>
> DANIEL 7:25

Again, Daniel prophesies of the man of lawlessness:

> He will become very strong, but not by his own power. He will cause a shocking amount of destruction and succeed in everything he does. He will destroy powerful leaders and *devastate* the holy people.
>
> DANIEL 8:24

He will *devastate* the holy people! Daniel is later told by the angel Gabriel they will be "completely shattered" (Daniel 12:7 NKJV). Heartbreaking! This prophet was being shown what would happen to his nation. Jesus, along the same lines, foretells that once the Antichrist pronounces himself to be God, a great slaughter will begin. He gives the key indicator of who is being discussed:

> "The day is coming when you will see what Daniel the prophet spoke about—the sacrilegious object that causes desecration standing in the Holy Place." (Reader, pay attention!) "Then those in Judea must flee to the hills. . . . And pray that your flight will not be in winter or *on the Sabbath*. For there will be greater anguish than at any time since the world began. And it will never be so great again. In fact, unless that time of calamity is shortened, not a single person will survive. But it will be shortened for the sake of God's chosen ones."
>
> MATTHEW 24:15–22

Jesus references what we just read in Daniel 9:27—what will occur three and a half years into the tribulation—the moment the Antichrist declares himself to be God. If Jesus' message is directed toward the church, why does He say, "Pray that your flight will not be . . . on the Sabbath"? This clarifies who He's addressing: the Jewish people who've now embraced their Messiah.

Zechariah gives dreadful insight into what will transpire: The Antichrist will murder two-thirds of the people in Israel; the one-third who survive will be purified as silver and gold (see Zechariah 13:7–9). This undoubtedly will mark it as the greatest anguish of all time.

As badly as the church has been persecuted over the past two thousand years, it has never been overcome or conquered. Regarding the church, Jesus' words clearly state, "All the powers of hell will not conquer it" (Matthew 16:18). However, Scripture clearly states the Antichrist will *oppress*, *devastate*, *conquer*, and *completely shatter* the saints. Without the understanding that we've just discussed this would appear to be a contradiction, but now we know each of these descriptive words is drawn from multiple scriptures that all apply to the tribulation saints (see category 3 from chapter 15), not to the church. The church, or bride, will have already been taken up and hidden away in the wedding chamber of heaven.

PASSAGE: "You are the light of the world." (Matthew 5:14)

POINT: The church is the light of the world and restrains the secret power of lawlessness and the identity of the man of sin.

PONDER: Does light conquer darkness? Can darkness overcome light? Is there such thing as a "flashdark"? What does it mean that Antichrist will oppress, devastate, conquer, and completely shatter the saints? Will heaven allow mankind to descend unchecked into total depravity during the tribulation?

PRAYER: Father in heaven, I pray that I may not be weighed down by the lusts and cares of this life and the Day come on me unexpectedly. May I remain a restraining force against lawlessness that would seek to permeate my sphere of influence. In Jesus' name, amen.

PROFESSION: I am a part of the restraining force against lawlessness.

"WHEN THE SON OF MAN RETURNS, IT WILL BE LIKE IT WAS IN NOAH'S DAY."

MATTHEW 24:37

CHAPTER 18

LIKE NOAH'S DAY

Our Creator is wonderfully patient, kind, long-suffering, and merciful. His unfathomable love is everlasting! However, eventually mankind's disobedience reaches the point of no return, and the ensuing divine fury is quite serious. Sadly, too many are unaware of the sternness of God's wrath. I believe it's from not acknowledging how offensive sin is to our holy God.

Isaiah was one of the godliest men on earth during his generation. He declared the righteousness of God and exposed the sinfulness of men, at one point crying out, "Woe to those who take advantage of the weakness of others, to drunkards, to those who tempt and mock God, to those who call evil good and good evil, to the proud, and other sins that are seemingly insignificant to our Western mindset" (my paraphrase of Isaiah 5:8–22).

But in the very next chapter Isaiah was "caught up" to the throne of God and saw with his own eyes the glory of God, and his reaction wasn't "Hello, God, it's me, Isaiah. I've been busy doing Your work!" Nor was it "Wow, there He is! I've looked forward to this my whole life!" Quite the contrary; it was "Woe is me! It's all over! I am doomed, for I am a sinful man" (Isaiah 6:5 NKJV/NLT). What brought on such a response? For the first time in his life, he realizes who this holy God really is, and also who he is before this holy God.

Job was identified as "the finest man in all the earth. He is blameless—a man of complete integrity. He fears God and stays away from evil" (Job 1:8). Who made this remarkable comment? It wasn't Job's pastor exaggerating his favorite church member's character, nor was it a civil leader bragging on Job's community service; it was almighty God! And please note, he wasn't just compared to the members of his community but to every person on earth, and God doesn't exaggerate. Wouldn't you love to have the Lord make this comment about you? I know I would!

Yet later when Job sees the Lord, he cries out, "I have heard of You by the hearing of the ear, but now my eye sees You. Therefore I *abhor* myself" (Job 42:5–6 NKJV). Keep in mind, *abhor* means hate, despise, loathe! What happened? Job had heard about God from his parents, in his fellowship meetings, and discovered Him in prayer, but he'd never been in His glorious presence. In beholding the Lord God for the first time in his life, Job comes to the startling revelation of who this holy God is that he's been serving, and also who he is before this holy God.

Moses was the godliest man in his generation. God declared that he was the humblest man on planet Earth (see Numbers 12:3). Wouldn't you love to have that said about you? But again, it's not just anyone commenting, it's God Almighty. This is Moses, who's been revered for generations. However, when he saw the Lord he said, "I am terrified and trembling" (Hebrews 12:21).

John the apostle was the disciple who followed Jesus most closely. He was the one the Master "loved." Yet when he saw Jesus on the mountain in His glory, along with Peter and James, they were all "terrified and fell face down on the ground" (Matthew 17:6). Later, on the Isle of Patmos, he saw Jesus and fell at His feet as if he were dead.

Humanity, in comparison to God, is so depraved that it's too wide of a breach to articulate. The more we comprehend this reality, the more in awe we are of His salvation, but at the same time, our realization of His wrath grows more terrifying. Could this be why the psalmist writes, "Who can comprehend the power of your anger?" (Psalm 90:11).

God's love is beyond comprehension, but equally so is His wrath. Listen to this warning given to believers: "It is a fearful thing to fall into the hands of the living God" (Hebrews 10:31 NKJV). And again, could this be why Peter writes to the church, "If the righteous are *barely* saved, what will happen to godless sinners?" (1 Peter 4:18). The word *barely* here is defined as "with difficulty, hardly, scarcely."[1] No different from Isaiah, Job, Moses, or John, even the godliest person on earth is *scarcely* saved from His wrath.

In contemplating our common present-day teachings, this great deliverance has lost its due weight; we've dumbed it down and made it commonplace. Could this marginalization be from our living in, being affected by, and adapting to a very sick world? With little conviction, why do we entertain ourselves with the very things that are offensive to God? A recent poll shows over 50 percent of professing and practicing (those who attend church and pray regularly) Christian men frequently view pornography, but what's most alarming is that 47 percent of those men have no problem with it![2] People marry, divorce for no biblical reason, and remarry thinking nothing of it. Unmarried women and men live together and attend their evangelical churches believing they are right with God. People call themselves "gay Christians." A young girl boasts on Instagram that she experienced Jesus' presence the entire time her baby was being murdered in her womb! How can we drift so far from that which is holy and godly, while still professing faith?

Have we become desensitized to the behavior separating mankind from God? Is our standard "Western Christian culture" grossly sick compared to heaven's? If you're physically and mentally sick, and live among people who share your condition, the longer you abide in that atmosphere, the more you'll believe everyone's normal. It's not until an outsider, one with a sound mind and a healthy, strong body, enters your community that you grasp the reality of your and everyone else's true condition. Could this be why such godly men responded with such utter terror when coming in contact with our holy God? Isaiah first cried out over his own condition, but his next agonizing cry was for those who were in his community. He wailed, "I live among a people with filthy lips" (Isaiah 6:5).

Apart from God, we are not normal! We are depraved, sick, and utterly evil. We deserve wrath to the uttermost for our corrupt condition and behavior. The more we grasp this, the more we comprehend how great His mercy is. We must never drift toward an attitude of entitlement. The magnitude of God's wrath is unspeakably great, and that's what we deserve. This brings us to the next reason I believe the church will not be here for the seven-year tribulation.

6. AS IN THE DAYS OF NOAH, THE RIGHTEOUS WILL BE SPARED.

Scripture records three terrifying accounts of God's wrath being poured out on Gentile people. First, the entire human race in the days of Noah. The Lord opened the fountains of the deep and caused a heavy rain to fall nonstop for forty days and nights. He covered the earth with water, drowning every living thing that breathed air. However, one man walked with God; not one drop of water affected him or his family. God waited until Noah was safely in the ark—*the chamber of safety*—before pouring out His wrath.

The second is Sodom and Gomorrah. We read that "the LORD rained down fire and burning sulfur from the sky on Sodom and Gomorrah. He utterly destroyed them, along with the other cities and villages of the plain, wiping out all the people" (Genesis 19:24–25).

In 2021 a scientific journal published a sixty-four-page article that points to a horrific fireball explosion that occurred in the same geographic area as these two cities over thirty-five hundred years ago. The investigation was conducted by an international team of scientists. They determined all eight thousand inhabitants of a one-hundred-acre city (believed to be Sodom) were incinerated by a fireball with a temperature of over 3,600 degrees Fahrenheit! These experts estimate a meteor exploded approximately 2.5 miles aboveground, creating a 740-mile-per-hour shock wave that was one thousand times more powerful than the atomic bomb that blew up Hiroshima, Japan.[3]

The book of Genesis tells us, "God had listened to Abraham's request and kept Lot safe, removing him from the disaster that engulfed the cities on the plain" (Genesis 19:29). Again, as with Noah, the righteous were put in a place of safety before God's wrath was poured out. The angels made sure

Lot and his family were far enough away from the incineration that they didn't feel its effects.

The third account of God's wrath being poured out was upon the Egyptians. However, this one is different in two ways. First, in both of the previous judgments, the unbelievers were given no warning as to what was coming; they were taken by surprise. Whereas with Egypt, the people were warned of each act of judgment and, in some cases, were made aware of the timing.

Second, God's people were not removed from the land that came under judgment. The Israelites had to endure the first three plagues that were brought against Egypt: all the water being turned to blood and the unimaginable invasion of frogs and gnats. However, God did protect Goshen, the home of His people, from the final seven plagues.

How do these acts of judgment relate to our discussion? Interestingly, in the New Testament writings of the coming outpouring of wrath, only two of the three are used as comparisons, and done so frequently: the great flood and Sodom and Gomorrah. Egypt is not used once as an example of God's wrath to come. Here are the listings for your personal study:

The days of Noah: Matthew 24:37–38; Luke 17:26–27; 2 Peter 2:5
Sodom and Gomorrah: Luke 17:28–30; 2 Peter 2:6–7; Jude v. 7

Let's briefly look at one passage about each. We'll begin with Noah:

> "When the Son of Man returns, it will be like it was in Noah's day. In those days, the people enjoyed banquets and parties and weddings right up to the time Noah entered his boat and the flood came and destroyed them all."
>
> LUKE 17:26–27

There's a recurring comparison both Jesus and the apostles make. They highlight that unbelievers were in a state of peace, prosperity, and safety prior to judgment. There were no indicators of what was coming. Similarly, with the ancient twin cities:

> "And the world will be as it was in the days of Lot. People went about their daily business—eating and drinking, buying and selling, farming and building—until the morning Lot left Sodom. Then fire and burning sulfur rained down from heaven and destroyed them all."
>
> LUKE 17:28–29

When the wrath of God is being poured out in the tribulation, it will not be "life as usual" for those who inhabit the earth. Many will suffer so greatly that they will seek death for months, but it will escape them. Water will be turned to blood and seventy-five-pound hailstones will fall, just to name a few of the specific disastrous events. Destruction and death will be so abundant that in the end people will be as scarce as gold. Along the same lines Paul writes:

> For you yourselves know perfectly that the day of the Lord [the seven-year tribulation] so comes as a thief in the night. For when they say, "Peace and safety!" then sudden destruction comes upon them, as labor pains upon a pregnant woman. And they shall not escape. But you, brethren, are not in darkness, so that this Day should overtake you as a thief. You are all sons of light and sons of the day.
>
> 1 THESSALONIANS 5:2–5 NKJV

Two things to note. First, unbelievers will all say, "Peace and safety." This will not be what people say as the seal, trumpet, and bowl judgments are being poured out. However, unbelievers could say this prior to the Bridegroom coming by stealth to catch away His bride. Second, Paul states this day will not overtake us as a thief because as *children of light,* we will have been caught away prior to the Day of the Lord—the outpouring of destruction.

As a final note, we can only imagine the horrifying experience of the three Old Testament judgments. Yet repeatedly we are told in Scripture that the suffering that will occur in the tribulation will be far greater than any of these, or any other cataclysmic chaos in history. There will *never* have been such anguish and death.

7. IT IS WHAT THE EARLY CHURCH FATHERS TAUGHT

For this final reason, my text will not come from Scripture, but rather from the words of the early church fathers. How should we view their writings? No different from how we would view the writings of Billy Graham, A. W. Tozer, C. S. Lewis, or any other great church father or theologian of more recent days. With great caution I firmly warn: Their words are not to be taken as absolute truth, but we should consider they were anointed, spent much time in prayer, and were not too far removed from John the apostle who wrote Revelation.

Many today argue that the concept of a rapture originated in the 1800s with a man named John Nelson Darby, a noted Bible scholar who was a respected leader in the church. Yet this is not accurate; several early church fathers wrote about it. Here are a few:

Irenaeus (AD 130–203): a well-known bishop of Lyons in Gaul. He wrote that Enoch was an example of the catching away of the church:

> And therefore, when in the end the Church will be suddenly caught up from this, then it is said, "There will be tribulation such as not been since the beginning, nor will be."
>
> *Against Heresies*, 5.29

Victorinus: a bishop of Poetovio (Eastern Europe). He authored a commentary in AD 240 and was eventually martyred for his faith. He wrote:

> The wrath of God always strikes the obstinate people . . . and these shall be in the last time, when the Church shall have gone out of the midst.
>
> *Commentary on the Apocalypse*, 15.1

Ephraem (AD 306–373): a renowned scholar and theologian. He founded the School of Nisibis, which became the center of learning for the Eastern church. He wrote:

> For all the saints and elect of God are gathered prior to the tribulation that is to come, and are taken to the Lord lest they see the confusion and the great tribulation coming upon the unrighteous world.[4]

Others who wrote in alignment with these three church fathers are Shepherd of Hermas (AD 150), Hippolytus (AD 210), and Cyprian (AD 250). It is important to note that, no different from today, it appears the early church fathers didn't unanimously agree on a pre-tribulation "catching away" of the church.

Dear reader, I've provided seven reasons giving evidence to the church being caught away before the tribulation. Once again—and I cannot emphasize this enough—it's my hope that these reasons create an urgency in your labor for His kingdom and move you to be prepared at all times. It's also my earnest hope that what's been shared will bring encouragement and comfort to you who are diligently and wholeheartedly serving our Lord and Bridegroom, Jesus Christ.

PASSAGE: The day of the Lord so comes as a thief in the night. . . . But you, brethren, are not in darkness, so that this Day should overtake you as a thief. You are all *sons of light* and *sons of the day*. (1 Thessalonians 5:2, 4–5 NKJV)

POINT: The Day of the Lord will impact the children of darkness and the children of light differently.

PONDER: How can the Day of the Lord come by surprise to some but not to others? Describe what it looks like to be in darkness; alternately, describe what it looks like to *not* be in darkness. Describe what it looks like to be *sons (and daughters) of light* and *of the day* (see Ephesians 5:8 and 1 John 1:6–7; 2:9–11).

PRAYER: Father, in Jesus' name, teach me to walk and abide in the light as Jesus is in the light. I ask that the Day will not overtake me as a thief. Amen.

PROFESSION: I will abide in the light so the Day will not overtake me as a thief.

"THE TIME HAS COME FOR THE
WEDDING FEAST OF THE LAMB,
AND HIS BRIDE HAS
PREPARED HERSELF."

REVELATION 19:7

CHAPTER 19

PREPARING OURSELVES

Most university students are very familiar with finals week. As an engineering student at Purdue University, I and others who took our education seriously knew it was the academic climax of the semester. After months of instruction, the final exams would reveal how much we had learned. The tests would go well if we had paid attention in class, done the homework, and studied. If we neglected these responsibilities, we'd regret it, especially once our final grades were posted.

At Purdue, exams were held in lecture halls or classrooms in various buildings on campus. It was each student's obligation to acquire the location, date, and time at which the final would take place. On average, this took all of ten minutes, but the bulk of time and energy was spent *preparing* for the actual test.

We've spent a few chapters discussing the specifics of Jesus' soon return, and this is important. However, no different from obtaining details *about* the final exam, the bulk of our focus should be the *preparation* for Christ's return.

I had foolish fraternity brothers who spent the majority of their semester frequenting parties, chasing girls, and pursuing fun and pleasure. They skipped classes, neglected homework, and didn't give attention to study.

Without exception they found themselves in panic mode during finals week, usually loading up on caffeine or other stimulants to pull all-nighters before their exams. They had lost their focus as to why they were at the university—to be educated. Most fell far short of their potential, didn't fully learn what was being taught, and had little to show for their time at school.

The wise students stayed focused on their education. Their prep for finals started the first day of the semester. It consisted of regular class attendance, asking good questions, completing their homework assignments, and seeking out friends who would encourage good study habits. For all the students, finals week merely reflected their choices during the semester.

In light of this, consider our opening passage: "His bride has prepared herself." Another translation reads: "His wife has made herself ready" (NKJV). Once again, we are responsible for the preparation. Just as our teachers gave us what we needed for the final exam but didn't take us by the hand to get it done, the Lord has provided what's needed to be prepared for what's coming in these last days.

Going back to our illustration of an ancient Jewish wedding, can you imagine the bride spending all her time and energy trying to figure out which night the groom was coming, and in the process neglecting to make her wedding dress, pull together her needed items, and pack her bags for the big day? Even worse, what if she grew weary of his absence and didn't stay faithful, lived carelessly for the moment, and lost her virginity while waiting for his return?

Both the university and wedding analogies convey a similar message: We determine by our ongoing decisions and actions whether we will be prepared or unprepared. The outcomes of both metaphors are similar; if the student or bride is prepared, the end result is abundant joy, satisfaction, and fulfillment. However, what are the results of not being prepared? I'll use my example to answer this question. Even though it was over forty years ago, I still remember the anticipation of my report card coming in the mail at the end of each semester. If I hadn't been diligent, I found myself feeling nervous and even trembling. If I had maintained focus, my attitude was one of confidence. I distinctly remember the one semester I didn't fully apply myself; I felt *ashamed* once my parents saw my grades. Similarly, if the bride isn't prepared, once the groom shows up, she feels a sense of *shame*. Look closely at what the apostle John writes:

> Little children, *abide* in Him, that when He appears, we may have confidence and not be *ashamed* before Him at His coming.
>
> 1 JOHN 2:28 NKJV

The word *abide* is from the Greek word *ménō*, which means "to remain, abide, dwell . . . remaining steadfast"; and regarding relationship, "to be and remain united with him, one with him in heart, mind, and will."[1] This definition clearly communicates consistency and closeness in our walk. Another way of saying *abide* in the context of John's message is to *remain in fellowship* with Jesus.

This passage is clearly written to children of God—believers, not unbelievers. If we don't *remain in fellowship* with Him, we'll be like my foolish fraternity brothers or the foolish bride. This passage also says we'll experience *shame*. The Greek word is *aischúnō*, meaning "to feel shame or disgrace because of having done something wrong or something beneath one's dignity."[2] This is sobering, but it's a reality.

There were countless times I didn't want to open my thermodynamics or physics book to study or do homework. But knowing that my dad and mom, whom I deeply loved and who graciously paid my full tuition, would see my grades, there was a healthy fear in me. I dreaded their disappointment; I didn't want to feel *shame* before them. I experienced it once, and it was painful. I was determined not to let it happen again, so my motivation to avoid saddening them made it easier to not follow my foolish fraternity brothers in living for the moment. It strengthened the discipline needed to open my textbooks when I didn't feel like it.

Knowing the price our Father and Jesus paid for our redemption and how deeply They love us should stimulate us to remain steadfast. The awareness that we can be *ashamed* when Jesus appears should put a healthy fear in us. This holy fear develops the spiritual discipline to obey Him when we don't feel like obeying Him. Paul writes,

> My beloved, as you have always obeyed, not as in *my presence* only, but now much more in *my absence*, work out your own salvation with *fear* and *trembling*.
>
> PHILIPPIANS 2:12 NKJV

Paul is writing to the Philippian believers. However, it's the Word of God and should be read as if He is speaking these words to us personally. It's easier to obey God when you sense His tangible *presence* in services, prayer meetings, rich fellowship with others, manifested blessings, and answered prayer. However, what about in *His absence*—when you don't sense His tangible presence, and distractions and temptations are pulling on you? When you are feeling a little lonely, surfing the web, and run across pornography late at night? When your wife has been critical and one of your female associates comes on to you during a business trip? When someone hurts you deeply and you want revenge? Will you obey in these times? The healthy fear of disappointing your Lord will protect you from these traps. It safeguards you from experiencing shame at His return.

So how do we "remain in fellowship" with Him? A few verses earlier John writes:

> So you must remain faithful to what you have been taught from the beginning. If you do, you will *remain in fellowship* with the Son and with the Father.
>
> 1 JOHN 2:24

This couldn't be clearer; staying consistently obedient to what we were taught from the *beginning* keeps us in fellowship with Him. What does John mean by "from the beginning"? Is he referencing our first introduction to Christianity, no matter what was taught? Absolutely not! This is not our sure foundation. We are told, "In the *beginning* the Word already existed . . . and the Word was God . . . [and] the Word became human" (John 1:1, 14). Jesus is the beginning, the truth, the eternal Word revealed. To remain faithful to what we have been taught from the beginning is simply this: an ongoing relationship of intimacy founded in and guided by what Jesus, through His Spirit, speaks to us from the overall counsel of Scripture.

Our first introduction to Christianity could have been slightly off or even steeped in error in regard to the truth. Our foundation must be firm, for John's next statement is:

> I am writing these things to warn you about those who want to lead you astray.
>
> 1 JOHN 2:26

According to Scripture, there is an abundance of false teachers in these last days. These wolves claim to represent God and appear well meaning, but they will isolate strategic portions of Scripture and shrewdly omit others to change the core message of truth. Their skewed teachings will bring false hope and comfort and subtly pull people away from *abiding in fellowship* with the Lord of glory. Or on the opposite end of the spectrum and in more rare cases, they will be legalistic, which will also pull us away from His presence. Paul strongly encourages us to stay founded in the Word of God so "we will not be influenced when people try to trick us with lies so clever they sound like the truth" (Ephesians 4:14). He was quite serious about this and wrote in a different letter:

> There are some who trouble you and want to *pervert* the gospel of Christ. But even if we, or an angel from heaven, preach any other gospel to you than what we have preached to you, let him be accursed.
>
> GALATIANS 1:7–8 NKJV

Paul included himself in this stern warning and went so far as to say even if it was an angel from heaven—and not even a fallen angel! I'll also include myself in this mix. If anyone says anything different from the overall counsel of God's Word, do not allow the words to corrupt your life by pulling you out of fellowship with Jesus. Be like the noble and wise Berean believers, who "listened eagerly to Paul's message. They searched the Scriptures day after day to see if Paul and Silas were teaching the truth" (Acts 17:11).

Notice the word *pervert.* It's from the Greek word *metastréphō*, which is defined as "to cause a change of state, with emphasis upon the difference in the resulting state."[3] To put it simply, the teaching sounds logical and true, but its emphasis causes the core message to shift away from what it was originally intended to mean. It sounds like the truth, but it's a lie that will corrupt us.

I'll give two examples. In Paul's letter above, he targeted teachers who subtly twisted the grace of God. They shifted the emphasis away from grace being a gift that can only be received by faith to obtaining it by keeping the law—working to earn it. Even though Jesus was still preached, their message didn't represent the truth of who He is; they presented "a different Jesus" (2 Corinthians 11:4; the Corinthians experienced the same battle). Their message was cleverly presented and even sounded like the truth, but careful search of the overall counsel of the Word of God ("taught from the beginning") uncovered its deceptive error.

In our day, it's largely the opposite. False teachers have crept in and distorted grace in a different way. Interestingly, the early church also had to address this serious problem. Jude writes: "Some ungodly people have wormed their way into your churches, saying that God's marvelous grace allows us to live immoral lives" (Jude v. 4). Once again, as in the above example, the emphasis shift is very subtle. It teaches correctly that grace is a gift of forgiveness and salvation but omits the scriptural truth that it *empowers us* to obey what we couldn't before in our own ability. Peter writes, "By his divine power [*the gift of grace*] God has given us everything we need for living a godly life" (2 Peter 1:3). James brings the balance by writing, "I will show you my faith by my actions" (James 2:18 GNT).

The foundation of the counsel of the Scripture ("taught from the beginning") is corrupted, and due to the emphasis shift, its subtlety implies that living in sin is insignificant. Now we dangerously excuse habitual sin by taking comfort in a distorted grace.

But this is not what was taught from the beginning! Our nature was to sin before being transformed, but the old man died, and God placed His divine nature within us the moment we became one with Christ. Now we are no longer slaves of sin but are empowered to choose whether we will submit to righteousness or yield to our flesh by submitting to the bondage of sin. This is why John writes:

> So we are lying if we say we have *fellowship* with God but go on living in spiritual darkness [*habitual sin*].
>
> 1 JOHN 1:6

The emphasis shift of the false teaching of grace opens the door for sin to become much easier to submit to, which in turn draws us away from abiding in fellowship with Jesus. John is not addressing someone who periodically sins and quickly repents, but rather one who habitually sins (see 1 John 3:6).

In either of the previous two examples, the shift of emphasis away from the foundational message of grace (what was taught from the beginning) is quite dangerous. It draws us away from the truth that protects us from being ashamed at His appearing—abiding in Him. If we don't abide in Him, we lose fellowship with Him! Notice I didn't say *relationship* with Him, but rather *fellowship.* Fellowship speaks of intimacy, and without it, we grow further and further from God's heart. Sin hardens our heart and keeps us disconnected from the fellowship that strengthens us.

If we lack fellowship with Him, we can easily miss what He is directing us to do. It's like being a part of a football team and you're one of the eleven guys on the field. However, you're unable to get into the huddle to hear the play called by the quarterback, your leader. Once the ball is snapped you can only guess what you are supposed to do. You're out of fellowship with your leader and team. The other players know exactly what their role is, but you're clueless. When the play is over, you will be *ashamed* before your leader and other team members. This is what sin does to our heart: It keeps us out of Jesus' huddle, and if that continues, we will inevitably be ashamed when He appears.

It's important to keep a healthy fear of not drifting away from His fellowship. I'm sure many of my fraternity brothers, once out in the working world, wished they'd been consistent with their learning and not so easily drawn away by what wasn't important. On a much larger scale, many at Jesus' coming will experience profound regret due to not abiding in Him.

PASSAGE: Dear children, remain in fellowship with Christ so that when he returns, you will be full of courage and not shrink back from him in shame. (1 John 2:28)

POINT: We will either have confidence or be ashamed when Jesus returns.

PONDER: Am I allowing sin to linger in my life? What belief has caused me to do so? What is the meaning of this statement: "God has given me everything I need for living a godly life"?

PRAYER: Dear Father, may I remain in fellowship with You. I renounce all belief that I could be intimate with You while living in habitual sin. I renounce by the power of Your grace the sins I've tolerated. In Jesus' name, amen.

PROFESSION: I am no longer a slave to sin! (See Romans 6:5–7.)

“LET US BE GLAD AND REJOICE AND GIVE HIM GLORY, FOR THE MARRIAGE OF THE LAMB HAS COME, AND HIS WIFE HAS MADE HERSELF READY.” AND TO HER IT WAS GRANTED TO BE ARRAYED IN FINE LINEN, CLEAN AND BRIGHT, FOR THE FINE LINEN IS THE RIGHTEOUS ACTS OF THE SAINTS.

REVELATION 19:7–8 NKJV

CHAPTER 20

OUR WEDDING GARMENT

The marriage of the Lamb—how glorious an occasion this will be! No words can properly describe the grandeur, wonder, and celebration of this joyous event. In reflecting on my own experience, it's not hard to recall the excitement I felt once Lisa's and my wedding day finally arrived. However, it didn't just happen. A significant amount of preparation was required to make it our most memorable day.

I didn't fully comprehend the enormous amount of work Lisa put into the wedding until I arrived in town a week beforehand. There was much to do with the details of planning, setting schedules, and coordinating people, not to mention the work of transforming a Presbyterian church and historic home into beautiful environments suitable for the occasion.

Yet what gave me the greatest joy and pleasure wasn't the décor, flowers, food, spectacular cake, or decorations. None of them remotely compared to the magnificent beauty I beheld when Lisa appeared at the back of the church with her father. The surroundings only enhanced the focus of the day—my glorious bride. Her splendor intensified with each step she took toward me; her soft, tender smile and the deep love I beheld in her longing eyes only magnified her attractiveness. I was overwhelmed; her countenance was breathtaking, and a significant part of it was her gorgeous white dress that accentuated her beauty.

But consider a different scenario, one in which the bride, in her big moment, appeared at the back of a church unkempt and wearing a soiled, filthy, and wrinkled white dress. The groom would be utterly shocked! His first thought would most likely be, *How inappropriate!* He would barely notice his bride because his attention would be fixated on the dirt, grime, and stains covering his bride's garment. He would be disappointed, to say the least, and perhaps angry.

What would her lack of planning and inaction communicate to him? Was this just another event, was it insignificant, did she even care? It might be important to her in that moment, but her lack of preparation would reflect her overall view of the marriage; it would communicate a trivial attitude regarding the union.

We are responsible to prepare for our marriage with the King, for we're explicitly told Jesus' wife "has made herself ready." To restate the words of the apostle John, Christ's bride is "to be arrayed in *fine linen*, *clean* and *bright*, for the fine linen is the *righteous acts* of the saints" (Revelation 19:8 NKJV). Three specific items are highlighted: First, the garment is made of *fine linen*, second, it's *clean*, and third, it's *bright*. Keep all three in mind as we continue our discussion.

The Greek word for *righteous acts* is *dikaíōma*, defined as "an act which is in accordance with what God requires."[1] Another Greek dictionary defines it as "an action that meets expectations as to what is right or just."[2] This speaks to what we do, not only to what we believe. Grace and faith are most important, but the evidence we truly possess both is our corresponding *actions*. Jesus says to all seven churches in the book of Revelation one of two statements. Depending on the translation, He says either, "I know all the things *you do*" (2:2, 19; 3:1, 8, 15) or "I know your works" (2:9, 13 NKJV). Interestingly, He does not say to one church, "I know all the things *you believe*." The emphasis falls on our corresponding *works*, not merely what we *believe*.

Additionally, the fact that this garment is clean and bright tells us it's not just our labor, works, and actions but our thoughts, motives, and the intentions behind them that matter. Are they pure? In other words, does our behavior flow out of a heart that is abiding, remaining in fellowship, or in union with the Lord? Do we love what He loves, hate what He hates? Are we holy as He is holy, engaged as He is always engaged?

Let's take a step back and look at the overarching view of the bride. In the New Testament, there is only one clear description of the church Jesus is returning for. It is not a *relevant church*. Please don't misunderstand; relevance is important, as we will win far fewer lost souls without it. Paul emphasizes, "I try to find common ground with everyone, doing everything I can to save some" (1 Corinthians 9:22).

The bride is not identified as a *community church*. Again, *community* is very important. God is the One who said, "It is not good that man should be alone" (Genesis 2:18 NKJV). If we look at what the early church focused on, it was prayer, doctrine, and *fellowship* (see Acts 2:42). Fellowship is very important!

She's not described as a *leadership church*. Yes, leadership is critical to the success of the body of Christ. We wouldn't accomplish much on a large scale without good leadership. It's identified as one of God's gifts to the church (see Romans 12:8).

Even more important is serving. Jesus amplified its significance by washing the apostles' feet in His last illustrated message. In another incident He boldly stated, "I am among you as the One who serves" (Luke 22:27 NKJV). Yet the church isn't identified as a *serving bride*.

The only description of the church that Jesus is returning for is found in Paul's words to the Ephesians:

> Christ loved the church. He gave up his life for her to make her *holy* and clean, washed by the cleansing of God's word. He did this to present her to himself as a glorious church without a spot or wrinkle or any other blemish. Instead, *she will be holy*.
>
> EPHESIANS 5:25–27

The single and overall description of the bride He's returning for is *a holy church*. This is what makes her garments clean and bright; it's what makes her glorious. This cannot be stressed enough!

To help emphasize this important point, let's look at it from a different approach. It's interesting to note, when Isaiah sees the Lord upon His throne, the mighty seraphim are crying out so loud they are shaking heaven's massive throne room arena to its foundations. This is a structure that probably holds over a billion beings. Can you imagine the volume and intensity of their shouts? They are not singing a song to make God feel special or appreciated; they are responding to what they behold. Every moment another facet of His glory is revealed, and one shouts to the other three living creatures: "Holy, holy, holy is the Lord of Heaven's Armies!" (Isaiah 6:3; see also Revelation 4:5–8).

No different from Isaiah, who cried out, "Woe is me," these angels are overwhelmed by God's glory. They are not thinking, *Come on, we've been doing this for ten trillion years, we'd like to take a break and explore other parts of the universe.* No, they don't want to be anywhere else, as there's nothing more spectacular, beautiful, and awesome in all creation than the Creator Himself.

What's noteworthy is they are not crying out, "Faithful, faithful, faithful . . ." Is God faithful? Yes, no one in the universe is more so; He's perfectly dependable! But this is not His characteristic that stands out the most. They are not even crying out "Love, love, love . . ." Is God love? Yes! He doesn't have love, He *is* love; it's His very essence (see 1 John 4:8). Yet once again this characteristic is not what stands out. What stands out above all other traits is His *holiness*! Oswald Chambers wrote:

> When we preach the love of God there is a danger of forgetting that the Bible reveals not first the love of God but the intense, blazing holiness of God, with His love at the center of that holiness.[3]

Here is the interesting correlation. The predominant characteristic of God is His *holiness*, and the same is true for His bride! This isn't a coincidence. With this in mind, we need to pay very close attention to *holiness*. This is confirmed in Peter's words:

> But the day of the Lord will come as unexpectedly as a thief. Then the heavens will pass away with a terrible noise, and the very elements

> themselves will disappear in fire, and the earth and everything on it will be found to deserve judgment. Since everything around us is going to be destroyed like this, *what holy and godly lives you should live.*
>
> 2 PETER 3:10–11

These are strong words! Again, we get a picture of the wrath of God from yet another writer of Scripture. Let's be brutally honest, it's a terrifying description of what the world is going to face! In light of this, does Peter accentuate our success, leadership, relevance, fellowship, or any other important aspect of our Christian walk? No, the behavior he stresses is to live *a holy and godly life*, which certainly is identified by our *righteous acts*, the very material our clean and bright garment is made of.

I know that there are many who see holiness as dull, boring, or even suppressive. Sadly, due to legalism or ignorance, they have a warped view of what it truly is. C. S. Lewis wrote, "How little people know who think that holiness is dull. When one meets the real thing . . . it is irresistible."[4]

One reason it seems so dull is the way it's been presented. Many teachers have made it an end unto itself. When we do this, we easily slip over into legalism, which draws the life out of us. It's actually a doorway or a bridge to something that every heart longs for who truly wants a relationship with Jesus. But allow me to first elaborate on holiness, then we can address what it leads to.

The root word *holy* is the Greek word *hagios*, which means "set apart for God, to be, as it were, exclusively his."[5] I love this definition, and it's beautifully articulated in these words from God to us: "Don't link up with those who will pollute you. I want you all for myself" (2 Corinthians 6:17 MSG).

Imagine a young man, we'll call him Matt, who has been dating a girl named Sarah for a couple of years. He's deeply in love and wants to marry her. He's methodically planned out his proposal and once the big moment arrives, he gets down on one knee and endearingly entreats her with these heartfelt words: "Sarah, I love you with all my heart. I want to spend the rest of my life with you. Will you marry me?"

She squeals with an excited "Yes, yes, yes!" She immediately pulls him up, jumps into his arms with both her feet wrapped around his waist and her arms around his neck, almost choking him, and exuberantly and joyously celebrates. After passionately kissing, holding each other and together staring at the beautiful engagement ring for a minute or two, she begins to speak dreamily of what's ahead for them.

Matt happily listens as Sarah dreams aloud of their wonderful life ahead, the children they will have, how they will spend their time together, and many other facets of married life. But then he's shocked by what comes next. Without breaking stride and just as sincerely, she continues, "Now Matt, as you know, I dated Tim for two years in high school. I would love to have a couple nights alone with him each year. Also, Aaron was my college beau, and I would like the same arrangement with him. But you will be my favorite, Matt. I will love you much more than Tim and Aaron, and we will have at least 360 nights a year alone together."

What do you think Matt's response would be? It's not hard to guess. Is there any young man you've ever met who would agree to this arrangement in married life? Most men would be shocked, followed by enraged, and finally out of exasperation would demand the engagement ring back, breaking the relationship.

Do we think Jesus is coming back for a bride who communicates by her actions, "Jesus, You are my favorite, I love You more than my old sins, but I still would like to date them. When they flirt with me it helps my self-esteem and brings me pleasure. I'll only sleep with them a few nights a year."

If you believe this, you are as naïve and out of touch with reality as Sarah is. Yet somehow we've not made it abundantly clear that in order to receive Jesus we must break up with our sins. This is identified in the New Testament as *repentance* and is mandatory to enter and maintain a relationship with Jesus. It means we will not flirt or engage with those behaviors that drove nails into Jesus' hands and feet.

When we think back to our earlier discussion of the "bride price" He paid for us (the terrible suffering He endured), how can we even remotely flirt with what the world pursues and loves? James writes to professing believers:

> You want only what will give you pleasure. You adulterers! Don't you realize that friendship with the world makes you an enemy of God? I say it again: If you want to be a friend of the world, you make yourself an enemy of God. Do you think the Scriptures have no meaning? They say that God is passionate that the spirit he has placed within us should be faithful to him.
>
> JAMES 4:3–5

The world seeks pleasure and self-gratification and takes pride in its achievements. It doesn't deny itself, take up its cross, and follow Jesus' words. Yet authentic believers are given grace and truth to do so.

In our modern Western church, there are numerous professing "believers" who still desire what unbelievers pursue while having a "relationship" with Jesus. It's utterly impossible; those who think like this are as deceived as Sarah and are viewed by heaven as adulterers. They are breaking their covenant with God!

A holy life involves living a separate life. Just as a faithful engaged or married woman doesn't flirt with other men, even so we live separated lives because we are betrothed to One, and just as Jesus gave Himself completely to us, even so we give ourselves completely to Him. This is the recipe for a successful eternal marriage.

Holiness is not an option; it's the only way to have a pure, bright, and spotless relationship with our Groom. In the coming chapter we'll see just how we can keep our wedding garment from getting stained. We will then show what holiness leads us into. It's truly the most exciting aspect of our relationship with God.

PASSAGE: "You have a few names even in Sardis who have not defiled their garments; and they shall walk with Me in white, for they are worthy." (Revelation 3:4 NKJV)

POINT: We are to prepare by keeping our wedding garment clean.

PONDER: What does it practically look like to prepare for Jesus' coming? What would soil or stain my garment? Is there any behavior that I flirt with that is offensive to Jesus?

PRAYER: Lord God, I choose to be all in with Jesus the way a bride commits her heart and life to her groom. I will no longer live for myself but for Jesus Christ. Jesus, You are my supreme Lord and Bridegroom! Amen.

PROFESSION: I am all in. No flirting with what is offensive to my Bridegroom.

LET YOUR GARMENTS ALWAYS BE WHITE, AND LET YOUR HEAD LACK NO OIL.

ECCLESIASTES 9:8 NKJV

CHAPTER 21

KEEPING YOUR GARMENT CLEAN

Most of us enjoy a good pasta dish. My wife is Sicilian, and when she makes one of her specialties, it's a treat. Lisa normally makes lighter sauces with an olive oil base, but periodically she'll make a red tomato sauce. If she does, and I come to the table wearing a white shirt, she'll encourage me to change to prevent staining it. My normal response is "No, it's fine, I'll be careful." But almost every time, I regret not taking her advice, as the sauce spattering on my shirt seems unavoidable. Ignoring her warning, I end up with stains on my white shirt.

All of us know not to walk through mud with white tennis shoes or to paint, garden, or work on a vehicle while wearing a white shirt unless we don't mind staining it. We have to be careful with white furniture, bed-covers, curtains, walls, and an array of other white articles. Why? White doesn't conceal dirt, grime, or any other stains.

A very similar principle is true in the spiritual realm. There are attractive environments, practices, and lifestyles deemed normal by the people of the world that, if engaged in or even flirted with, will stain a believer's white garment. Only by staying strong in our spirit through prayer and a steady intake of God's Word are we able to recognize and resist the alluring draw (see Matthew 26:41; Acts 20:32; Jude v. 20). If we don't strengthen ourselves in this way, it's easy to fall prey to corruption, no different from easily staining my white shirt with Lisa's pasta sauce. A major aspect of authentic Christianity is to "keep oneself unspotted from the world" (James 1:27 NKJV).

To state it bluntly, we stain our white wedding garment when we seek a relationship with the world, living no different from the lost. I most certainly am not referring to going into the various sectors of society for the purpose of bringing His light; we're commanded to do this! Rather, I'm referring to embracing behavior that's contrary to God's Word with the assumption there will be no consequences. We are told, "Can a man scoop a flame into his lap and not have his clothes catch on fire? Can he walk on hot coals and not blister his feet?" (Proverbs 6:27–28). Bottom line: Your garment will end up stained!

Allow me to give some specifics to help avoid confusion. I'm speaking of behavior such as going to a porn site assuming we won't damage our soul. Another would be refusing to forgive one who has hurt us, planning revenge, gossiping, or slandering to get even with them. We stain our garments by these types of behaviors.

Another example would be divorcing for unscriptural reasons (see Matthew 19:9): splitting the union because of irreconcilable differences, not getting along, developing different interests, lost love, or the numerous other nonbiblical reasons people sever the sacred covenant in our times. Have we forgotten the Lord God is specific in addressing this? He declares:

> "For the man who does not love his wife but divorces her . . . covers his garment with violence."
>
> MALACHI 2:16 ESV

The stain isn't red sauce; it's much worse—it's violence. Just as stains of red sauce on a white garment require deep cleaning to eliminate, so also the violence to our souls by unscriptural divorce is not easily removed. God's forgiveness through the blood of Jesus immediately cleanses us once we genuinely repent. However, it takes intentional humility, the washing of

God's Word, forgiveness, and sometimes deliverance to clear the stain from our soul.

We risk staining our garment when we form friendship bonds with unbelievers who show no interest in leaving this world's system. They possess no desire to honor God; instead, they persist in immorality, adultery, sexual perversions, greed, and other ungodly behavior, some even while claiming to be Christians. To intertwine your life with them is dangerous and, if continued, will inevitably stain your garments and affect your ability to abide in fellowship with Jesus. It's no accident we are told:

> Don't team up with those who are unbelievers. How can righteousness be a partner with wickedness? How can light live with darkness? What harmony can there be between Christ and the devil? How can a believer be a partner with an unbeliever?
>
> 2 CORINTHIANS 6:14–15

There's no wiggle room here. So often people ignore these specific words of God by claiming the literal interpretation is legalistic and creates bondage. The rebuttal to dismiss this command is that Jesus was called the "friend of sinners." This is indeed what He was accused of. However, He was bringing the kingdom of God to the lost who were hungry and open to hear.

Zacchaeus was the most notorious of sinners in his community. Yet he climbed a tree just to see Jesus. That's hunger! Once the Master acknowledged him, he showed immediate signs of repentance by stating he would give back fourfold to those he'd stolen from and half his goods to the poor. The people were very displeased and complained that Jesus chose a "renowned sinner" to hang out with, yet what they missed is Zacchaeus's deep desire to receive truth and change (see Luke 19:1–9).

There is another huge aspect to consider. Jesus controlled the narrative and atmosphere in the midst of these "notorious sinners." The focus of conversation was not off-color jokes, empty stories, or foolish talk. No, it stayed focused on conveying the truth of the kingdom. So often when professing believers ignore the command to live separated lives and subsequently develop relationships with unbelievers, they blend in rather than controlling the narrative, keeping it in line with the kingdom. If they're honest, they discover they're flirting with the world, not reaching it.

Have we forgotten Paul's warning:

> Do not be so deceived and misled! Evil companionships (communion, associations) corrupt and deprave good manners and morals and character.
>
> 1 CORINTHIANS 15:33 AMPC

Consider a marriage. Would a husband be okay with his wife spending an evening with a single man? Would he be okay with his wife going on a vacation with another married man, even if they promised to stay in separate hotel rooms? No, it's putting his spouse in an environment that will almost surely foster compromise and damage their covenant and relationship.

God is a jealous God. He's not jealous *of* us; He's jealous *for* us! He wants our entire hearts and lives, not just a fake alignment that includes lovers outside of Him. This is why we are told, "Pursue . . . holiness, without which no one will see the Lord" (Hebrews 12:14 NKJV).

The Greek word for *pursue* is *diṓkō* and is defined as "to do something with intense effort and with definite purpose or goal."[1] This word carries the idea of strong determination coupled with great effort to arrive at the target. There's not a hint of being casual in attitude; rather, it indicates a chasing after with urgency. This is how we are to chase after living a pure and separated life.

At this point it's important to clarify the two different aspects of holiness found in the New Testament. If we lump all holiness into one bucket, many scriptures become confusing.

The first aspect is *positional holiness*. We are told in several New Testament scriptures that Jesus' sacrifice made us holy. It's something we never could have done on our own. Two examples include:

> God chose you to be the holy people he loves.
>
> COLOSSIANS 3:12

> God loved us and chose us in Christ to be holy and without fault in his eyes.
>
> EPHESIANS 1:4

We didn't merit this privilege. Out of His great love for us, we were *positionally* declared holy in Christ the moment we gave our lives to His lordship.

Again, I'll refer to my own marriage to exemplify. On October 2, 1982, Lisa and I were married. She took the *position* of my wife. Today, forty-three years later, she's not *more* my wife, nor will she ever be more my wife *positionally* than the day we were married.

The same is true for our relationship with God. We became Jesus' bride, separated unto Him, declared to be holy, the day we gave our lives to His lordship. I've now been walking with Jesus for more than forty-five years; I am living a godlier life now than the first year of my walk with Him. However, *positionally*, I am not "more holy" now than the day I became His, nor will I ever be more holy.

In returning to our marriage, since we are discussing a bride, I will use Lisa as an example. Before we were married, she hung out with other guys, gave them her phone number, and dated them. However, once we were wed, she stopped all of these practices. In fact, she stayed clear of all environments not suitable for a married woman. Her behavior *reflected* her position. Along the same lines Peter writes:

> You must live as God's obedient children. Don't slip back into your old ways of living to satisfy your own desires. You didn't know any better then. But now you *must be holy in everything you do.*
>
> 1 PETER 1:14–15

It's clear, Peter is discussing our *behavior*, not our *position*. The Amplified version brings this out clearly by stating: "in all your conduct and manner of living." Peter is charging us to do what any faithful wife does. We are to take on a behavior that *reflects* our position. This is not optional; rather, it is a "must be" command. We will encounter "should be" statements in Scripture, and we're wise to heed these charges. But it's another thing entirely when we find a "must be" command. To ignore it or treat it lightly is foolish and often carries severe consequences.

Peter's is just one of the many *behavioral* holiness commands in the New Testament. Interestingly, another is found just prior to Paul's most in-depth writings of the catching away of the bride of Christ:

> God did not call us to live in immorality, but in holiness. So then, whoever rejects this teaching is not rejecting a human being, but God.
>
> 1 THESSALONIANS 4:7–8 GNT

To violate this command to live holy is not a trivial thing and is quite costly. However, to heed it brings one of the greatest promises in Scripture. This brings us to C. S. Lewis's description of the "irresistible" aspect of holiness—what it leads to. To elaborate, let's look again at the key verse:

> Pursue . . . holiness, without which no one will *see the Lord.*
>
> HEBREWS 12:14 NKJV

Is this addressing *positional* or *behavioral* holiness? Let's answer by using another example. Can you imagine if my wife was in a ladies prayer group and said to her friends, "Girls, please pray that I would be John's wife."

Everyone in the room would be confused by her request and question, "Lisa, you became his wife over forty years ago. Why pray for this?"

However, if Lisa asked, "Girls, please pray I'd be a better wife to John," they would understand she is talking about her behavior, not her position. The same is true regarding the above verse. We're to pursue *behavioral* holiness, because without it, we will not "see the Lord." But this is a perplexing comment. What does Scripture mean by declaring we will not see the Lord? We are clearly told in another place:

> Look! He comes with the clouds of heaven. And *everyone* will see him—even those who pierced him.
>
> REVELATION 1:7

Everyone, even those who drove the nails into His hands, will see Jesus when He returns. All nations will behold Him, the living and dead alike, and all who have ever lived will see Jesus at the judgment. What is the writer of Hebrews referring to?

Consider this. In my sixty-six years of being a citizen of the USA, I've been under the leadership of eleven presidents. I've been under their authority; their decisions have affected my life and shaped my community's way of living. However, I've never *seen one* or, more clearly stated, not been in the *presence* of one of our presidents. On the other hand, there are citizens who are in the president's presence; they work with him or are his friends.

In the same way, there are people who are under the leadership of Jesus Christ. His decisions affect their lives, but they are not *in His presence—not seeing Him*. Jesus clearly states:

> The person who has My commands and keeps them is the one who [really] loves Me; and whoever [really] loves Me will be loved by My Father, and I [too] will love him and will show (reveal, manifest) Myself to him. [I will let Myself be clearly *seen* by him and make Myself real to him.]
>
> JOHN 14:21 AMPC

The person who *sees* Jesus, experiencing His *manifested presence*, is loyal in action and not merely in word. People like that prioritize being set apart for Him, which means they will not flirt with the offensive things unbelievers chase after and are in love with. This person's priority is to obey Jesus, even if it's difficult, fosters hardship, or incites persecution.

Again, let's look at a marriage. I don't desire to flirt with, date, or sleep with other women. What's my motivation? First and foremost, I fear God and don't want to break His heart. But the other reason, which is also quite strong, is that I don't want to lose the many times Lisa shares with me the intimate secrets of her heart. I love being close with her!

A husband who's committing adultery with other women may be able to hold his marriage license in his wife's face and declare they're married. It may be technically true, but what he forfeits is intimacy with her. She will have no desire for him to be in her presence. Furthermore, that marriage is not going to last long if he continues.

As a Western church, have we committed adultery with the world but taken our marriage license—the grace of God and the promised new birth—and held it up, declaring we are technically saved and belong to Him? We then wonder why we're not experiencing intimacy with Him. The number one reason I don't want to commit adultery with the world is because I don't want to ever lose the moments when God whispers a secret, a promise, an unobvious truth or hidden way from His Word that I've never known before. Or best of all, when He reveals a deep longing of His heart. This is more valuable than all the riches this world could ever offer!

This is the irresistible aspect of holiness. When you pursue it, you live in communion with Him and thus will be confident at His return. However, if you flirt with darkness, you are pulled out of fellowship with Him and can easily stain your wedding garment. You will be ashamed by your garment stains at the grand reunion of the bride and Groom.

When you understand the motive behind pursuing holiness, it becomes a delight, not a religious command. It's all dependent on your perspective. So dear one, chase after holiness. You will not be disappointed, and ten thousand years from now, you will not fret missing out on something. Instead, you will be forever glad you remained loyal to our heavenly Groom in this dark world.

PASSAGE: "Behold, I am coming as a thief. Blessed is he who watches, and keeps his garments." (Revelation 16:15 NKJV)

POINT: Pursuing holiness keeps us in fellowship with Jesus.

PONDER: What keeps you from pursuing holiness? Make a list. In light of what you've learned, are these behaviors worth what you lose—intimacy with God? If not, what steps will you take to cut them off?

PRAYER: Lord God, I choose to pursue holiness. Please give me the humility, strength, and grace to do so. Lead me in the way to keep my garment free from being spotted. In Jesus' name, amen.

PROFESSION: I will make pursuing holiness a priority!

WEEK 4

PREPARE FOR HIS RETURN

THIS LETTER IS FROM JOHN TO THE SEVEN CHURCHES IN THE PROVINCE OF ASIA.

REVELATION 1:4

CHAPTER 22

REVELATION'S SEVEN CHURCHES

Can you imagine opening your email inbox and seeing a message to you straight from Jesus? This is in essence what happened for seven Asian church leaders at the end of the first century. I'll briefly set the stage before elaborating.

John the apostle, in the latter years of his life, lived in Ephesus for almost three decades. He was the last of the original twelve apostles to pass away and lived approximately one hundred years.[1]

In the year AD 93, John was arrested at the age of ninety as a political offender and stood trial before Emperor Domitian. He was ordered to burn pagan incense but refused. This infuriated the emperor, who sentenced him to be immersed in a boiling vat of oil. John came out unscathed.

This frightened the emperor, who immediately banished John to the Isle of Patmos,[2] which was twenty-four miles off the coast of Asia Minor. This was a rocky, deserted island where Rome sent its worst prisoners. He spent eighteen months on this island until Domitian's death. Shortly after, the new emperor, Nerva, granted amnesty to John.

It was on this island that John was given the book of Revelation. One of its main purposes is to show Jesus' servants future events, especially at the very end of time up to the inauguration of the new heavens and earth, and most importantly how to prepare.

In the second and third chapters, we find these seven letters to the church leaders. There are different views as to why the messages to these churches are in this canonized book of the Bible, but we'll only consider the main three:

1. The *historical view* states they apply to the historic churches only. However, this cannot be true, for God would never put messages in the canonized Scripture if they didn't have prophetic application.
2. The *dispensational view* states that each represents seven distinct conditions of the church from the day of Pentecost until today.
3. The *timeless view* states that each embodies various characteristics that can be found in any church worldwide at any given time during the church age. I like this view because all seven apply in the present, which aligns with Scripture being the timeless, living Word of God. I'll adopt this view, though I'm not ruling out the second view.

Each letter is directed to the "angel" of the churches.[3] The Greek word is *ággelos* and carries the meaning of "a messenger." *The Complete Word Study Dictionary: New Testament* states: "The angels of the seven churches are probably the bishops or pastors of those churches."[4] I agree, as Jesus states they are in His right hand, which speaks to the entrustment of His authority (see Revelation 1:20). For the most part, each message follows a pattern:

1. Church identified
2. Description of the One speaking—Jesus
3. Present condition of the church
4. Praise for the church's strengths
5. Exposure of their faults
6. Corrective action they must take
7. The promise attached to heeding His instructions

What I've written is not intended to be an in-depth examination but to highlight what's important to our discussion in each message. Some will be brief, while others will be more in-depth.

Some of my most intimate and impactful times with Jesus have occurred when prayerfully reading these seven messages. On these memorable occasions, I've experienced the chastening of the Lord in my personal life, and heeding His correction has brought strength and godliness in areas I was lacking. I hope the same will happen for you as we highlight the strengths, faults, needed correction, and instructions given by the Chief Shepherd of the church.

One other important detail: I will not quote the entirety of the message but will list important points for our discussion, keeping it succinct. For this reason, I recommend having your Bible open to these chapters in Revelation as a reference, although it's not mandatory. I will also paraphrase some of the statements to modernize them for relevance.

THE CHURCH AT EPHESUS (REVELATION 2:1–7)

Jesus opens this letter with the words, "I know your works" (2:2 NKJV). He is addressing *what they do*, not what they believe, and this occurs with all of the seven churches. Here is a list of what He likes about this church:

1. They work hard for the kingdom. They're quite active in church, in outreach, and most likely in financially supporting these efforts.
2. They are patient, consistently bearing up under difficult circumstances.
3. They don't tolerate evil people. They are not unequally yoked—creating friendship bonds with unbelievers, a danger we discussed in the previous chapter.
4. They don't fall for self-appointed leaders who assume authority that has not been divinely commissioned.
5. They have suffered but refused to quit.

This is a phenomenal report card! If Jesus said this to our team at Messenger International, I would be elated. However, what comes next is shocking: "But I have this complaint against you. You don't love me or each other as you did at first!" (2:4).

Wow! How is this so, and in what way can this happen to any of us? How can we possess such a great report card but at the same time have this devastating fault? There is only one explanation: We become strong in *truth* and *mission* but lack genuine *love*. We are told that what truly brings edification to the church is to speak the *truth* in *love* (see Ephesians 4:15). When we possess truth apart from love, we become dogmatic. This narrows our vision, creating this mentality: We perceive anyone who aligns and operates exactly as we do as true believers and anyone who doesn't as wolves.

We are quick to accuse others of being false teachers or false prophets when in reality we're more concerned about different ministry methods or slight variations in our interpretation of the minor aspects of Scripture. (Recall Jesus says there are weightier matters of the Word of God.) In other words, we divide over minors and carefully look for others' faults. We depart from love's command to be "ever ready to believe the best of every person" (1 Corinthians 13:7 AMPC). It's as if people who are not in "our camp" are guilty until proven innocent.

We see this with the leaders who criticized Jesus. Repeatedly we're told that these men watched Jesus closely that they might find an accusation against Him (see Mark 3:2; Luke 6:7; 14:1). They possessed a critical eye and not true discernment rooted in love (see Philippians 1:9). Let me give an illustration to bring absolute clarity.

We see religious leaders finding fault with Jesus' disciples for breaking the letter of the command in plucking heads of grain to provide nourishment for their bodies on the Sabbath. But when we have a critical eye, we miss the overall counsel of the Word of God and tunnel focus on what matches our viewpoint. This is exactly what Jesus was up against with these experts in the Torah.

Jesus responds with what appears as a perplexing historical account found in Scripture. It would indirectly challenge their narrow interpretation. He cites that David entered the temple and ate "the showbread, and also gave some to those with him, which is not lawful for any but the priests to eat"

(Luke 6:4 NKJV). David, in essence, did something that was contrary to the law of Moses, and Jesus used this historical event to justify His disciples' act.

Let's compare the above scenario with another I hear often. It seems there are many critics who match the description of this Ephesus church, who say that women are not allowed to preach due to three statements of the apostle Paul (see 1 Corinthians 11:2–16; 14:33–38; 1 Timothy 2:8–15). Have they forgotten that God also states that our daughters and women would prophesy—proclaim His messages (see Acts 2:17–18)—that Philip had four daughters "who proclaimed God's message" (Acts 21:9 GNT); or that "the Lord announces the word, and the women who proclaim it are a mighty throng" (Psalm 68:11 NIV)? These critics have a narrow interpretation, rather than the overarching interpretation of Scripture.

Let me cite a different perplexing situation of the New Testament that is similar to how Jesus counters the leaders' criticism. Paul talks about people preaching with the motives of selfish ambition, jealousy, and rivalry; these "ministers" hoped their preaching would add to Paul's afflictions of torture in prison. Yet hear what Paul writes:

> They preach with selfish ambition, not sincerely, intending to make my chains more painful to me. But that doesn't matter. Whether their motives are false or genuine, the message about Christ is being preached either way, so I rejoice.
>
> PHILIPPIANS 1:17–18

The greater truth in Paul's eyes was Christ being preached, whether the motives were pure or not. How amazing! If Paul rejoices over the gospel being preached out of wicked motives, do you think he would get bent out of shape by a woman who has pure motives preaching the gospel? Never! Paul wasn't a legalist without love; he recognized the higher aspects of truth out of his discerning heart.

Why aren't these leaders of our modern "Ephesus church" carrying the same heart as Paul? Why aren't they saying, "Whether it's a woman or a man teaching, praise God that the gospel is being communicated"?

And yet, I've witnessed firsthand the condemnation of women and organizations who encourage women to minister by these people who have left their first love. We see a similar criticism in other areas: end time events, healing, the infilling of the Holy Spirit, and a slew of other truths. Why can't we realize there are the majors—such as the deity of Jesus, His blood shed for the remission of sins, sanctification, the virgin birth, and many other pivotal aspects of our redemption—that we should address and strongly correct but not divide over the minors?

There is another aspect of "false discernment" to point out. If some people are teaching something that is not 100 percent accurate to the entire counsel of God's Word, it doesn't necessarily make them false teachers. Perhaps they have tender hearts and when gently corrected with the truth in love will change once they see the way of God more accurately. We see this with Apollos, who was genuine but needed further instruction. Aquila and Priscilla "took him aside and explained the way of God even more accurately" (Acts 18:26). Apollos made the change!

But the sad thing is, these ministers who align with the Ephesus church will use their pulpits, podcasts, YouTube channels, or other platforms to condemn ministers without first approaching them. Why not gently instruct so they can see the way more clearly? (See 2 Timothy 2:24–26.) Perhaps after sitting together, the one poised to pounce may see things differently. Those who love Jesus grow humbler and more teachable as time passes.

These who align with the Ephesus church have left their "first love." When they were saved, they loved Jesus deeply and, consequently, His people. They didn't care about who brought the gospel—a man, a woman, or even the methods used—as much as they cared about the foundational teaching and presence of God.

When we leave our first love, it manifests in the way we treat others, especially believers who are not in our circles or people we view as beneath us. Jesus says, "When you did it to one of the least of these my brothers and sisters, you were doing it to me!" (Matthew 25:40). Let's not be quick to criticize and cut off others and call them out by name. Those who align with the Ephesus church's plight seem to look for and draw strength from the fight more than the pursuit of peace. If you find yourself quickly critical, ready to rebuke and fight over your interpretations of the peripheral matters of Scripture, ask yourself honestly, *Have I left my first love? Are my works now done out of the motive of being right and accurate more than administering God's eternal Word from a heart filled with compassion and love?*

Jesus tells this church that if they don't repent of their labor that is void of love, "I will come to you quickly and remove your lampstand from its place" (Revelation 2:5 NKJV). In other words, they will lose their influence in the body of Christ. I think you can look at churches, ministries, and movements in the past couple of decades that once had great influence but today have lost it.

A final note: There are rewards promised to each of the seven churches that overcome by heeding the correction Jesus gives. I will list them in our final chapter.

THE CHURCH AT SMYRNA (REVELATION 2:8–11)

Once again, Jesus opens with this church's works—what they do rather than what they believe. He states His full awareness of the tribulation or persecution they're enduring. Also, that they are poor, but He is quick to add that they are really rich. (James 2:5 states, "Has God not chosen the poor of this world to be rich in faith and heirs of the kingdom which He promised to those who love Him?" [NKJV]).

This is not to say that the financially well off can't be rich in faith. King David, who was very wealthy financially, called himself "this poor man" (Psalm 34:6 NKJV). It's hard for a rich man to enter the kingdom, not impossible. Joseph of Arimathea was identified in Scripture as a rich disciple of Jesus and was also rich in faith, as he was the only one who had the courage to approach Pilate and ask for Jesus' body (see Matthew 27:57–60). That's stunning faith!

Unhealthy rich people are those who trust in their riches rather than God. We will soon see a church full of people nothing like Joseph and King

David. This upcoming church we will examine saw their financial wealth as their security, and it caused them to be indifferent and not rely on their relationship with God. But that's for another chapter.

The Smyrna church didn't receive any correction from the Master, only instructions for handling what they were up against and what was coming. He recognized how looked down upon they were by those who claimed to be in covenant relationship with God but were really a part of the congregation of Satan. Jesus warned they would be sorely persecuted, even thrown into prison. His instruction was for them to be faithful to the Word of God even to death.

In traveling globally to minister the gospel, I have spent time with and know many who are persecuted in their communities or nations for their faith. What an honor it is to call them brothers or sisters. Their godly character and passion for the kingdom stand out. Along the same lines, Jesus points out to the Smyrna church that testing brings purification. By obeying God's Word in the midst of persecution, we will grow in godly character. It's His promise (see 1 Peter 1:6–9; 4:1–2). Remember, God will not allow anything to come our way that He doesn't give us the grace to victoriously endure.

> God is faithful, who will not allow you to be tempted beyond what you are able, but with the temptation will also make the way of escape, that you may be able to bear it.
>
> 1 CORINTHIANS 10:13 NKJV

Dear reader, hold on to this promise, which is both sure and steadfast.

PASSAGE: "You don't love me or each other as you did at first!" (Revelation 2:4)

POINT: Truth apart from love will lead us to legalism.

PONDER: Have I become dogmatic? Do I look for the fight more than seek peace and pursue it? Have I majored in minors and minored in majors in Scripture? How can this change?

PRAYER: Father, I ask You to pour Your compassion and love into my heart. You promised it would be shed abroad in my heart by the Holy Spirit (see Romans 5:5). In Jesus' name, amen.

PROFESSION: I will seek both truth and love, and not one at the expense of the other.

TOLERANCE IS THE VIRTUE OF THE MAN WITHOUT CONVICTIONS.

G. K. CHESTERTON

CHAPTER 23

DESTRUCTIVE TOLERANCE

Imagine a formerly convicted pedophile wooing a young girl away from her yard into his car. He's cheerful, charming, and speaks tenderly to her. Because the girl's father doesn't want to create a scene, he says nothing and doesn't try to stop this predator. Her dad, due to his inaction and silence, allows his child's life to be destroyed. Very few fathers would turn their heads to such an assault, and if they did, they would be condemned by most in society. Most fathers' behavior would be similar to a mother bear robbed of her cubs. Yet we are about to learn of church leaders who tolerated behavior that was destroying their people's lives.

In the previous chapter we discussed the dogmatic church of Ephesus. They were zealots, and Jesus commended them for confronting what was life-threatening; in His words: "This is in your favor: You hate the evil deeds of the Nicolaitans, just as I do" (Revelation 2:6). However, from a lack of fervent love, the Ephesus church's zeal surpassed the foundational tenets of the faith and gravitated toward *legalism*, which is "strict, literal, or excessive conformity to the law or to a religious or moral code."[1] In the Ephesus church, those who eagerly confronted issues void of fervent love most likely majored in the minors, causing their fruit to be detrimental rather than life-giving.

In this chapter, it may seem I'm contradicting myself, but I'm not. I'll point to how the pendulum can swing easily to the opposite extreme. In our present times, both in church and society, we've run up against an unscriptural love that lacks truth, and this is a recipe that quickly leads to deception.

THE CHURCH AT PERGAMUM AND THYATIRA (REVELATION 2:12–29)

I'm choosing to address these two churches together since there are overlapping themes. Again, it is not my intent to make this an exhaustive study of the seven Asian churches, because that would require an entire book.

Jesus opens the message to the Pergamum church by identifying Himself as "one with the sharp two-edged sword" (2:12) and to Thyatira as "the Son of God, whose eyes are like flames of fire" (2:18). Today, Jesus might have used the term *laser beams* to describe His eyes. There is a good chance He chose these identifiers due to what He's about to address, as His words will perform a needed surgery.

To both churches He opens with, "I know your works" (2:13, 19 NKJV). Once again, He addresses what they do rather than what they believe, but with these two churches, it's more about what they are *not* doing.

Let's begin with Pergamum, Rome's capital of Asia Minor. The church most likely faced significant challenges, as the city was steeped in pagan worship and other cultic practices. In fact, Jesus declared that Satan had his throne in this city. It was clearly a dark place. Here are His praises:

1. They've remained loyal to Jesus amid utter corruption in the city.
2. They've refused to deny Jesus even when one of their own was martyred.

It appears this church was strong in standing up against occult practices outside the church, but it caved when it should have been addressing ungodly behavior inside the church. This is no light matter in the eyes of our Lord.

Thyatira was the smallest of the cities to receive a direct message from

Jesus. It was a commercial town on the Lycus River and was well-known for its guilds in trades such as cloth, bronze, leatherworking, and pottery. The city possessed a special temple to Apollo, the "sun god," which possibly explains why the Lord introduced Himself as "the Son of God."[2]

Jesus praises this church's many strengths. They were loaded with

1. Love
2. Faith
3. Service
4. Patient endurance

Once again, this is a fabulous report card coming from the Master Himself. And His next words bring it to another level: "And I can see your constant improvement in all these things" (Revelation 2:19). Just the kind of encouragement you would love to receive, right? This is a remarkable list, and how incredible it is that this church was "constantly improving" in all four of these fundamental virtues of discipleship. *Maintaining* is not the word that identifies this church, but rather *advancing*. Just as with Ephesus's initial report, I would be delighted if He said this about our team at Messenger International.

Yet Jesus' complaints—two against Pergamum and one against Thyatira—are stern, and so important to emphasize. His rebukes don't center around their actions but rather their *inactions*. They were tolerating practices that were destroying people's spiritual lives. To Pergamum Jesus states:

> "But I have a few complaints against you. You *tolerate* some among you whose teaching is like that of Balaam, who showed Balak how to trip up the people of Israel. He taught them to sin by eating food offered to idols and by committing sexual sin. In a similar way, you have some Nicolaitans among you who follow the same teaching." (2:14–15)

Tolerate is the key word, as it is the root of the problem. We see a similar rebuke with Thyatira's leadership. In their case it was a woman whom He compares to Jezebel of the Old Testament.

> "But I have this complaint against you. You are *permitting* that woman—that Jezebel who calls herself a prophet—to lead my servants astray. She teaches them to commit sexual sin and to eat food offered to idols." (2:20)

Balaam, the Nicolaitans, and Jezebel all operated under a similar motive: to subtly pull people away from devotion and faithfulness to God and woo them over to what the world chases after. Another key word for this church is *permitting*, which is synonymous with *tolerating*. The two churches' errors are quite similar—they overlook what should be confronted.

Let's put all the cards on the table: In essence, *silence is nonverbal communication*. Not saying a word conveys agreement and grants permission by communicating, "What you're doing is fine." There is an old Latin proverb that states, "Silence gives consent; he ought to have spoken when he was able to." It's clear these church leaders' sins were not what they were doing or saying but what they were *not doing* and *not saying*.

Lisa and I took scuba diving lessons when we were first married. We both became Open Water Certified Divers. Something that stood out to us in our few weeks of intense training was how many times we heard our dive master call out, "Never stop breathing!" Then he would tell a story to emphasize his repeated command. One true story was about a beauty pageant winner who died because she panicked and stopped breathing due to fear and quickly swam to the surface from eighty feet down. Her lungs rapidly expanded to the point that they both ruptured. After telling the story, he would firmly say another five times before class was over, "Never stop breathing!" Next class he'd hit it from another angle, such as giving the science behind it or sharing a different story, while constantly repeating, "Never stop breathing!"

After a few weeks of classroom training, when we got into the water for our first dive, the foremost thought in Lisa's and my mind was, *Keep a constant flow of air moving in and out of my lungs*. He had put such a healthy fear in us that we didn't dare stop breathing. His repeated warnings protected us from being another statistic of needless death underwater.

In a similar way, the apostle Paul highly stresses something with church leaders in Miletus:

> I never *shrank back* from telling you what you needed to hear, either publicly or in your homes. . . . I declare today that I have been faithful. If anyone suffers eternal death, it's not my fault, for I didn't *shrink from* declaring all that God wants you to know.
>
> ACTS 20:20, 26–27

"If anyone suffers eternal death, it's not my fault"—what a statement! The New King James Version brings this out stronger by translating his words, "I am innocent of the blood of all men." Let's reverse what he says: *Their blood would be on his hands if he withheld what was needed!*

The Amplified Version also gives the description of *shrink from* as "kept back or fell short from declaring." If this was applied to our dive master, to *fall short from declaring* would have been for him to casually mention in a single class, "Hey, guys, keep breathing when you're diving." To *withhold* goes further; it's to "*keep back* from declaring." This would imply that he didn't say anything at all about maintaining breathing and just hoped we'd figure it out. If he did either one, a host of us likely would have died, especially on the latter negligence.

The huge question now becomes: What *necessary information* did Paul not withhold? He continues in the very next verse:

> So guard yourselves and God's people. . . . I know that *false teachers*, like vicious wolves, will come *in among you* after I leave, not sparing the flock. Even some men from *your own group* will rise up and *distort the truth* in order to draw a following.
>
> ACTS 20:28–30

The needed warning was to *beware of false teachers*! They would come in *among* the people. Pergamum was great at standing against the blatant pagan worship of the city, but what both churches were not warning their people of were those who came in by stealth, or were already within, and were perverting the foundational tenets of the faith. In the same way Jude, the Lord's half brother and an apostle, warns by writing:

> Dear friends, I had been eagerly planning to write to you about the salvation we all share. But now I find that I must write about something else, urging you to defend the faith that God has entrusted once for all time to his holy people. I say this because some ungodly people have wormed their way into your churches, saying that God's marvelous grace *allows us* to live immoral lives.
>
> JUDE VV. 3–4

He wanted to write regarding all the great aspects of salvation, but there was an urgent matter—more pressing, imperative, serious, crucial—for exposing deception. Notice these false believers or teachers don't come in wearing wolves' clothing. They come in secretly, knowing the language, culture, and customs but twisting the grace of God to be a permissive grace rather than an empowering grace. This counterfeit grace promises eternal life yet permits us to pursue the idolatry and sexual immorality the world pursues. To put it in an earlier chapter's terms, it pulls us away from chasing after genuine holiness.

In the same way, Peter warns: "Many will follow their evil teaching and *shameful immorality*" (2 Peter 2:2). These false leaders and counterfeit believers are not going to mislead a *few*, but rather *many*! If unconfronted, they will pull masses away from a sanctified life into one with an appearance of Christianity that in reality separates the hearers from living in fellowship with Jesus. Paul warns of them: "Such people claim they know God, but they *deny him* by the way they live" (Titus 1:16). Their denial of Jesus is not verbal; no church today or in the first century would tolerate that. Rather they deny Him by the lifestyle they model and by subtly twisting the Word of God to accommodate it.

Paul reminds the leaders in Miletus of how adamant he is in his warning: "Remember that for three years I did not cease to *warn everyone night and day with tears*" (Acts 20:31 NKJV).

Everyone! Night and day! He was nothing like the leaders of Pergamum or Thyatira. He was more like our dive instructor, whose greatest care was that none of his students would die on his watch. He and Paul carried a similar resolve.

We have pastors and leaders today who say little to nothing about the death trap of sexual immorality, homosexuality, greed, gender ideology, killing human beings in mothers' wombs, and our society's other idolatrous practices. Recently, at his private ranch, a friend cried out to me, "Why aren't ministers addressing the relevant issues of today? Why are they silent? How are people supposed to know if the preacher doesn't say anything?"

I had no answer. I can't figure out why so many leaders are silent, tolerating and permitting what pulls people out of fellowship with Jesus. Have we forgotten that *what we don't confront will not change*? We are *commanded* to

> Preach the word of God. Be prepared, whether the time is favorable or not. Patiently correct, rebuke, and encourage your people with good teaching. For a time is coming when people will no longer listen to sound and wholesome teaching. They will follow their own desires and will look for teachers who will tell them whatever their itching ears want to hear.
>
> 2 TIMOTHY 4:2–3

When is it not favorable? It's when you might lose friends, followers, church members, tithers, supporters, or anyone of influence. Even if it may cost a longtime friendship, we're *commanded* to preach the Word of God that confronts, but to do it with love. We are to correct and rebuke, as well as encourage. It seems in the Western church we only encourage—that's one-third of our responsibility. The Amplified Version states: "You as preacher of the Word are to show people in what way their lives are wrong." We are leaving out two-thirds of the message!

Not heeding Jesus' correction of inaction carries great consequences. To Pergamum He warns: "Repent of your sin, or I will come to you suddenly and fight against them with the sword of my mouth" (Revelation 2:16). What sin? The sin of tolerance! Please keep in mind, He's not addressing the false teachers; He's addressing the *tolerance*. It's a sin! View "permitting" or "withholding what is necessary" as you would view murder, adultery, or any other obvious sin.

To Thyatira He declares: "I will throw her on a bed of suffering, and those who commit adultery with her will suffer greatly unless they repent and turn away from her evil deeds. I will strike her children dead" (Revelation 2:22–23). What adultery is He speaking of? Were all the people hopping in bed with this woman? No. This is the adultery:

> You want only what will give you pleasure. You adulterers! Don't you realize that friendship with the world makes you an enemy of God? I say it again: If you want to be a friend of the world, you make yourself an enemy of God.
>
> JAMES 4:3–4

James highlights his repetition by saying, "I say it again . . ." Like our dive instructor, he, too, is much different from the leaders and believers of Thyatira and Pergamum. Here is the takeaway: If we church leaders are silent on these major issues, the people's blood will be on our hands.

Yet it's not just leaders who tolerate; it's any of us who allow idolatry or sexual immorality to go on in our personal lives. Are we overlooking it or are we delaying addressing it? The first person to correct is not others, it's ourselves. Then we can help others with compassion. We are told:

> Put to death your members which are on the earth: fornication, uncleanness, passion, evil desire, and *covetousness, which is idolatry.* Because of these things the wrath of God is coming upon the sons of disobedience.
>
> COLOSSIANS 3:5–6 NKJV

We think of an idol worshipper as one who bows down to a statue, which is true in some civilizations. However, these man-made images are only used as a front to truly get what the worshipper covets, whether it's sexual immorality or some other vice. The true root of idolatry is when we put *anything* of this life as a higher priority than our love, devotion, and obedience to God. We give our strength, time, energy, and love—that which should be directed to our Bridegroom—to the pursuit of other things.

Please don't misunderstand. We are told that God "richly gives us all we need for our enjoyment" (1 Timothy 6:17). There are so many beautiful things in this life that are given as gifts of blessing to enjoy, recreate with, be refreshed by, and experience true rest. However, when these things crowd in and start capturing our hearts to the point that we no longer prioritize our love, service, and obedience to Jesus, they become idols. An idol can be food, social media, popularity, a celebrity, a sport, making money, a relationship . . . and the list would include millions of others. An idol isn't anything of itself; we are the ones who make it an idol. What may be an idol to one may not be an idol to another.

In over forty years of ministry, I've discovered that what is frequently intermingled with idolatry is some form of sexual immorality. The two are closely connected; the origins of sexual vices often point to idolatry. I was bound to pornography at age eleven. I gave my life to Jesus when I was nineteen, and many ungodly behaviors immediately broke off my life the moment I was saved, such as drunkenness, cursing, and other inappropriate, sinful behaviors. However, pornography persisted. I didn't realize it initially, but it was an idol. It was the giant I needed to slay by God's might, by His grace.

It didn't happen overnight. The true battle wasn't breaking the power—that was easy. It was the struggle to get my heart to the right place that I truly wanted it gone. I believed I sincerely wanted it destroyed for a few years, but it took God showing me the error of my sorrow, which was self-focused, not godly. I was more afraid of judgment than I was of breaking my Bridegroom's heart.

Once it became more about His heart than my fear of what I'd suffer or miss out on, it became easy. On May 6, 1985, it was broken, and I'm still free to this day. I knew that *tolerating* this sexual vice would eventually bring horrible consequences. It's a battle that I share in depth in my book *Killing Kryptonite.*

Whether you are leading others or just leading yourself, to leave idolatry and sexual sin unconfronted will cost you dearly. The great news is this: God's power is more than enough to overcome and break any bondage of this world.

In the next chapter we will address the core messages to the final three churches. They are, in my opinion, the most confrontational and challenging messages to the seven churches.

PASSAGE: "I, the Lord your God, am a jealous God who will not tolerate your affection for any other gods." (Deuteronomy 5:9)

POINT: What we tolerate and do not confront will not change.

PONDER: What idols am I tolerating in my life, or in those I lead, that are deteriorating true faith and causing me to drift back to the world? What is causing me to permit this? How can this change?

PRAYER: Father, forgive me for tolerating what You paid such a high price to free me from. I repent of ________ and choose to forsake it, not for the fear of judgment but out of the desire to delight Your heart. In Jesus' name, amen.

PROFESSION: I will not tolerate that which God hates.

WAKE UP, WAKE UP, O ZION! CLOTHE YOURSELF WITH STRENGTH. PUT ON YOUR BEAUTIFUL CLOTHES.

ISAIAH 52:1

CHAPTER 24

WAKE UP!

Consider an American tourist traveling for the first time to Australia. He knows nothing about its sea life, assumes it's no different from coastal Florida, and heads straight to the beach at Cairns. It just so happens there are an unusual number of box jellyfish in the water, one of the deadliest creatures in the ocean. Just one sting can kill a man in roughly five minutes.

The locals, all sitting on the beach, not daring to venture into the water, see our tourist happily running toward the shore to dive in for his inaugural swim in the Coral Sea. What would they do? Would they just sit and watch? No, they'd forcefully yell, "Stop! Don't go in!" Or perhaps they'd even tackle him. Bottom line, if they care at all, they'll stop at nothing to keep him from plunging to his death. One of the most *unloving* things these locals could do is not warn this man. Furthermore, one of the most *hateful* things they could do is say nothing.

Jesus performs a similar rescue attempt with two of our last three churches, which happen to look a lot like a large portion of modern Western churches. If you think His previous messages are stern and intense, you'll discover these reach another level. But remember, He's attempting to save their lives!

THE CHURCH AT SARDIS (REVELATION 3:1–6)

The city of Sardis fell under Roman control in 189 BC. By the first century AD, it was known for its emperor worship and an impressive temple dedicated to Artemis.[1] Sardis was one of the most pleasant places to live in the ancient world. It was a center of worldwide trade and one of the most affluent cities at the time. Life was easy in Sardis. Even in the pagan world, it had a reputation for materialism and decadence. The pagans there were extremely accepting and didn't care if you worshiped their gods or not—they just wanted to make money and have a good time.[2]

The society of Sardis rubbed off on these believers in a negative way. Rather than taking advantage of the lack of persecution and abundant resources to be more effective in building the kingdom, the church became more worldly. Jesus opens again by stating, "I know all the things you do" (3:1). Are you seeing a pattern? It's not what we believe but what we do that He examines. The apostle James's words sound similar: "So you see, we are shown to be right with God by *what we do*, not by faith alone" (James 2:24).

You can repeatedly tell me there's power in an outlet, but if every appliance I plug in doesn't work, it doesn't matter what you believe and strongly declare; the fact is, there is no power in the outlet. You can declare over and over you believe in Jesus and strongly proclaim your faith, but is your life different from before you said you believe? Do you stand out in a lost world? Are you advancing the kingdom? If not, you have a faith that is not real by heaven's standards. Grace is not at work in you, for true grace is effective.

Thus, in the introduction to this church, there are no praises or compliments from Jesus up front. Right out of the gate, He attempts to keep these people from plunging to their eternal death, bluntly stating:

> "You have a reputation for being alive—but you are dead. *Wake up*! Strengthen what little remains, for even what is left is almost dead. I find that your actions do not meet the requirements of my God."
>
> REVELATION 3:1–2

Their reputation among Christians in other communities is they are a blessed and cutting-edge church. In our day this would mean they are relevant, progressive, not lacking resources, producing popular and widely used worship songs, seeing many "conversions," and all the rest you'd find in most "alive" churches.

What's the measuring stick? It's that their *actions* do not meet the requirements of God! For Jesus to say this means they're not pursuing holiness and godliness. Most likely, they're offended easily; they gossip, slander, quarrel; and are competitive. They enjoy inspiring and entertaining ministers who encourage with their teachings but shy away from confronting their love of materialism, pleasure, and lack of virtue.

If they do any outreach, such as holiday feedings, helping those who've faced natural disasters, or supporting missionaries, it might be done to compensate for a lack of godliness; it quiets the voice of conviction. What are Jesus' next words?

> "Go back to what you heard and believed at first; hold to it firmly. Repent and turn to me again. If you don't *wake up*, I will come to you suddenly, as *unexpected as a thief*."
>
> REVELATION 3:3

He uses the phrase "wake up" for the second time! A good part of this church has clearly departed from the way of life. Their doctrine has been influenced and reshaped by society and by immersing themselves in the Sardis culture rather than the Word of God. They live more as citizens of this world than heaven. Jesus says if they don't *wake up* and *repent*, they will be left behind in the catching away of the church.

You may question what I just wrote. However, we know that those who are walking in fellowship with Jesus will not be caught unaware; they will not experience His coming as "unexpected as a thief." Recall Paul's words to the church:

> The day of the Lord [*seven-year tribulation*] so comes as a thief in the night. . . . But you, brethren, *are not in darkness, so that this Day should overtake you as a thief.* You are all sons of light and sons of the day. We are

> not of the night nor of darkness. Therefore let us not sleep, as others do, but let us watch and be sober.
>
> 1 THESSALONIANS 5:2–6 NKJV

Those who pursue godliness and holiness and give their talents and energy to His kingdom are "awake," and the "time of wrath" will not overtake them as a thief. Paul then says, "Let us not sleep, as others do." This wake-up call is Jesus' attempt to stop them from diving into the Coral Sea, so to speak. He deeply loves them and passionately doesn't want them to plunge to their death.

He then turns His attention to the few in the church who have not been compromised by their affluent society, but at the same time He continues speaking to the majority by warning of the horrific consequences of not "waking up":

> "Yet there are some in the church in Sardis who have not *soiled their clothes* with evil. They will walk with me in white, for they are worthy. All who are victorious will be clothed in white. I will never *erase* their names from the Book of Life, but I will announce before my Father and his angels that they are mine."
>
> REVELATION 3:4–5

Soiled their clothes! Recall that one definition of true Christianity is to keep oneself unspotted from the world. We are told by the apostle Jude that we are to hate "the garment *stained* by the flesh" (Jude v. 23 ESV). Revelation 16:15 states: "Blessed is he who watches, and keeps his garments, lest he walk naked and they see his shame" (NKJV).

We have not emphasized the seriousness of this in our Western church. To neglect holiness, when God has empowered us by His grace to pursue it, is not a trifling thing. In Matthew 22 Jesus tells a parable of a wedding feast; we just don't hear a lot of preaching on it because it's radical. It doesn't fit our narrative of Western Christianity. The final part of the story goes like this:

> "But when the king came in to see the guests, he saw a man there who did not have on a wedding garment. So he said to him, 'Friend, how did you come in here without a wedding garment?' And he was speechless. Then the king said to the servants, 'Bind him hand and foot, take him away, and cast him into outer darkness; there will be weeping and gnashing of teeth.'"
>
> MATTHEW 22:11–13 NKJV

Let's rewind this sobering story a little. The king encouraged his servants to go to the highways and byways and bring all who were willing to come to the wedding so that his house would be filled. This speechless man represents the segment of those who say yes to the invitation but don't highly esteem it. Did he think he could come in with the same attire he wore on the streets—in the world?

Let's imagine we are invited to a royal wedding as an honored guest. Up front we'd be blown away by the kindness of the monarch. When he sends his servant to invite us, because we are utterly poor, we are granted money to purchase a proper outfit. However, we soon forget the enormity of the event and become distracted by using the money to purchase tickets for a few NBA games, concerts, video games, and other pleasurable experiences. Once the wedding day arrives, we enter the building without proper attire. Our actions clearly reveal our trivial view of the king's gracious invitation. It wouldn't end well for us. This, in essence, is what Jesus is communicating.

Again, we are told that we've been "given the finest of pure white linen to wear. For the fine linen represents the good deeds of God's holy people" (Revelation 19:8). We can never, and I repeat, *never*, save ourselves! Salvation is an unmerited gift, just like the invitation of the monarch and the money he provides in my example above. Yet we show by our actions whether we view it as commonplace or the greatest privilege of our life. It's sobering when you really think about it.

We need to address the difficult word *erase*. Remember, Jesus is speaking to a church, not a city or a cultic church. Let's restate His exact words: "I will never *erase* their names from the Book of Life" (Revelation 3:5). The

Greek word is *exaleíphō*, which means "to eliminate, to do away with, to wipe out."[3] By inserting this definition, He is saying, "I will not eliminate or wipe out their names from the Book of Life." Jesus wouldn't mention this if it weren't possible but only if it could happen!

Let's return to our opening example but change it up a little. If an Australian tourist came to Florida and started running to the beach and the locals yelled out, "Stop, there's box jellyfish in the water!" they'd be lying. Box jellyfish don't exist in Florida. Jesus would never lie or deceive like this! He is trying to prevent this church, or any of us, from making life-destroying choices. Which is better: that we are sternly warned now or that we experience the sting of death later?

Let's be frank, our names were not written in the Book of Life until we received Jesus Christ as Lord. Paul writes of his "fellow workers, whose names are in the Book of Life" (Philippians 4:3 NKJV). Jesus' passionate love is manifesting through calling any wayward child back to His heart. This is true love! We are told:

> A man who *wanders* from the way of understanding will *rest* in the assembly of the dead.
>
> PROVERBS 21:16 NKJV

The word *wanders* describes what many are doing in the twenty-first century, and His Word predicts that many more will do so before He returns. Along the same lines, James writes:

> Brethren, if anyone among you *wanders* from the truth, and someone turns him back, let him know that he who turns a sinner from the error of his way will save a soul from death and cover a multitude of sins.
>
> JAMES 5:19–20 NKJV

James isn't speaking to unbelievers wandering away, for an unconverted person can't meander; he or she is already lost. No, he addresses "brethren"—those whose names are written in the Book of Life. To turn this person back is one of the most loving things we can do. To lie and say, "You're okay," when in fact, he or she is not, is one of the cruelest things we can do.

The apostle Peter, in the same way, warns of the strong forces that attempt to pull believers away from the path of life. He writes:

> And when people escape from the wickedness of the world by knowing our Lord and Savior Jesus Christ and then get tangled up and enslaved by sin again, they are worse off than before. It would be better if they had never known the way to righteousness than to know it and then reject the command they were given to live a holy life.
>
> 2 PETER 2:20–21

Let's ask questions. Are these people saved? First major point: They've escaped the wickedness of the world by coming to know our Lord Jesus. Second, he says they know "the way to righteousness." Twice Peter affirms their salvation. Yet notice they revert to sin and the world, and they are not just entangled but remain in the state of wandering away. Peter makes it clear that it would have been better to have never known the Christian life than to walk away and stay away. However, this is important: Anyone can come back at any time if they've wandered away! This is exactly what Jesus is doing with the Sardis church that He loves so deeply. James and Peter are doing the same.

My fellow believer, we can no longer treat lightly living an ungodly or worldly life when God has given us His divine nature and empowered us to live godly. What we could never do before in our own strength is provided by His grace once we're born again.

> He has given us great and precious promises. These are the promises that enable you to share his divine nature and escape the world's corruption caused by human desires.
>
> 2 PETER 1:4

He's given us what we never had in our possession or by our own merit—what we need to *purchase* a proper garment for the grand day of being united with our King. His divine nature and precious promises have "given us everything we need for living a godly life" (2 Peter 1:3).

We have now ventured into the truth of "purchasing." This is something we will see clearly in Scripture in the next chapter with the final church as well as the parable of the ten virgins.

The next time you encounter someone who tells you it's impossible to walk away from the faith, it may be one of two things: They're a local who also doesn't know what's in the water or, much worse, a local who doesn't care if you plunge into the sea with a large contingent of box jellyfish. I'd rather be informed and warned now by the Word of God before it is too late.

PASSAGE: We are citizens of heaven, where the Lord Jesus Christ lives. And we are eagerly waiting for him to return as our Savior. (Philippians 3:20)

POINT: We are called to live as citizens of heaven.

PONDER: Do I live like a citizen of heaven or a citizen of this world? Are there aspects of my society's culture that are influencing me away from what I see in Scripture? How am I living like a citizen of heaven? Do I need to "wake up"?

PRAYER: Dear Father, in Jesus' name, strengthen me by Your grace to live in my society as an ambassador of the kingdom of my Lord Jesus Christ. Amen.

PROFESSION: I am not of this world, but I am called to reach this world!

BUT DON'T JUST LISTEN TO GOD'S WORD. YOU MUST DO WHAT IT SAYS. OTHERWISE, YOU ARE ONLY FOOLING YOURSELVES.

JAMES 1:22

CHAPTER 25

EXPOSING INDIFFERENCE

I've been color challenged for as long as I can remember. Once, when taking an examination, I was presented with twelve large mosaics consisting of hundreds of tiny circles of various colors. Within the mosaic the matching colors would reveal a clear image. Well, to most it was clear. The image could be a shape, number, or letter of the alphabet. We were asked to identify the image within each of the mosaics. I thought I did great, but my score reflected one out of twelve were correct!

One St. Patrick's Day, my wife was out of town. I enthusiastically picked out my green shirt to wear and join in the fun. At the office there was a lot of discussion about the creative ways team members sported their green outfits, but nobody was saying anything about my shirt. I finally asked a group of team members, "Why hasn't anyone mentioned anything about my green shirt?" My son was the first to speak up. "Dad, you don't have any green on." It turned out my shirt was gray. We all had a great laugh.

How awkward it is to wholeheartedly believe you're doing something well, only to find out you're not. Much worse, how terrible to believe you're well off spiritually, when according to God's standards you're on the verge of being rejected. If the term *rejected* sounds a little strong, look at Jesus' choice of words!

THE CHURCH IN LAODICEA (REVELATION 3:14–22)

This brings us to the final two churches, but I'm skipping over Philadelphia temporarily to focus on the last church Jesus addresses. The past couple chapters have been hard pills to swallow, and Laodicea won't be any easier. I would love to end on a positive note, which is why I've chosen to keep Philadelphia's report for last. The second reason points to our previous chapter, where I snuck in a preview of "buying" something from Jesus, and I want to elaborate while the thought is fresh.

Laodicea was well-known in the ancient world for its wealth. The extent of its resources was so deep that the city was rebuilt without Rome's financial aid after the devastating earthquake of AD 60. Laodicea was strong in the textile industry and in banking. It was renowned for its medical school that produced treatments of a spice nard for ears and an eye salve. Laodicea lacked a good water supply, so it was forced to bring water in through a system of stone pipes from Denizli, which was six miles north.[1]

Jesus opens His message to the church by identifying Himself as "the faithful and true witness" (Revelation 3:14). In essence, He tells us the truth every time, even when it is uncomfortable to hear. He will never flatter or deceive. Again, He opens with:

> "I know all the things you do, that you are neither *hot* nor *cold*. I wish that you were one or the other! But since you are like *lukewarm* water, neither hot nor cold, I will spit you out of my mouth!"
>
> REVELATION 3:15–16

Is it abundantly clear that He is examining how we steward our lives by what we *do*? One day in prayer the Lord asked me, "John, did I say to any of the seven churches, 'I know what you believe'?" His question in that moment riveted me. I immediately opened my Bible and read the opening statements to all seven churches and discovered actions, not belief or intentions, were the focus of Jesus' examination.

Before going any further, we need to highlight some key words. Jesus uses the city's external supply of water to illustrate their relationship with Him. There are three temperatures identified: *hot*, *cold*, and *lukewarm*. What do they represent? To make it simple, *hot* is the disciple who is on fire for Him. Their love burns and is evidenced by their godly life and obedient works. *Cold* is the person who wants nothing to do with Jesus; he or she thinks Christianity is a waste of time and has no interest in serving their Creator.

What is *lukewarm*? It describes a chameleon, someone who easily adapts to the atmosphere they find themselves in. This person possesses enough hot to blend in with the on-fire believer and enough cold to not stand out to the unbeliever. They rarely make a difference for the kingdom and only find themselves involved if it doesn't conflict with their mood, personal interests, or agenda.

Here is the shocker. Jesus says, "I wish you were either hot or cold!" To make this plain, Jesus is saying to this church that He would rather they be on fire for God; that's the easy one. The harder pill to swallow is the word "cold." He's stating they'd be better off by being completely outside of the church with no interest in it. Why? It's simple: The person who is cold knows they are lost and therefore is easier to reach. The person who is lukewarm thinks they are right with God, when in reality they're not. We know this to be true because of what Jesus proceeds to say:

> "I could wish you were cold or hot. So then, because you are lukewarm, and neither cold nor hot, I will *vomit* you out of My mouth."
>
> REVELATION 3:15–16 NKJV

Vomit! Let's go to the original to make sure this is an accurate translation. The Greek word is *eméō* and is defined as "to vomit. . . . It is also possible to interpret 'to vomit out of the mouth' as an idiom meaning 'to reject.'"[2] I hesitate to put this image before you, but can you recall a time when you vomited? The flu bug went through our house recently and I was the last to get infected. I vomited. I can still close my eyes and see the forcefulness with which the contents inside my body came out into the toilet that I was hugging.

Please keep in mind, Jesus is speaking to a church, not a "supposed church." Why don't we hear this warning more frequently? I can only assume it is due to how our Western church mentality embraces "lukewarm" behavior as actual "Christian" behavior. We call people Christians who identify with Jesus but in essence live mostly for themselves. Yet why don't we pay closer attention to Jesus' repeated words:

> Then he said to the crowd, "If any of you wants to be my follower, you must give up your own way, take up your cross daily, and follow me. If you try to hang on to your life, you will lose it. But if you give up your life for my sake, you will save it."
>
> LUKE 9:23–24

If we really listen to His words, we cannot call someone a Christian who regularly views pornography, tells off-color jokes, lies, gossips, refuses to forgive, lives sexually immorally, is greedy, lives for pleasure, is self-promoting, self-seeking, or any other behavior that is commonly practiced by unbelievers.

Jesus continues:

> "You say, 'I am rich. I have everything I want. I don't need a thing!' And you don't realize that you are wretched and miserable and poor and blind and naked."
>
> REVELATION 3:17

Let me list His comparison for greater clarity. The left will consist of how they saw themselves; the right is how God saw them:

rich, not lacking, without need . . . miserable, poor, blind, naked

They were completely unaware of their true state! Could this be true with many in the Western church? Are we unaware of our true state? There's a reason Paul said to a church whose behavior was similar to unbelievers, "Examine yourselves to see if your faith is genuine" (2 Corinthians 13:5). We are not to examine ourselves by our group standards; the majority may be in error. The only criteria we're to use is the Word of God! We should read our Bibles and ask the Holy Spirit to expose areas of compromise, indifference, or idolatry.

Jesus continues:

> "So I advise you to buy gold from me—gold that has been purified by fire. Then you will be rich. Also buy white garments from me so you will not be shamed by your nakedness, and ointment for your eyes so you will be able to see."
>
> REVELATION 3:18

Now we run into the idea of buying something from Jesus. How do we do this? Salvation is a free gift; it's clear we can never earn it. How can we buy something that prevents us from being "rejected violently" by Him?

We see the same mystery with the parable of the ten virgins. (Please read Matthew 25:1–13.) All of them were familiar with the bridegroom, all of them had lights, and they all were in a state of expectancy of his return. Keep in mind, those who are cold are not looking for the Bridegroom, but the lukewarm are. Jesus is identifying those who *profess* belonging to Him.

Five were wise and five were foolish. Immediately our attention should be arrested by the fact that it wasn't eight wise and two foolish. No, half were unwise. Let's not forget, just as this church, who thinks they are fine, end up being vomited if no change occurs, even so these unwise virgins who are looking for Him are rejected. Jesus says, "They stood outside, calling, 'Lord! Lord! Open the door for us!' But he called back, 'Believe me, I don't know you!'" (Matthew 25:11–12).

What was the difference between the wise and the foolish? The separating factor doesn't manifest until just before the bridegroom comes. Each had lamps, but the wise had extra oil and the foolish lacked enough to endure to the end. For years I struggled to understand this parable. One morning

I yelled out at the top of my voice, "Lord, please show me what I'm missing here!" That day He showed me. The key to the entire parable is found in the words of the wise virgins addressing the foolish regarding what they should do:

> "We don't have enough for all of us. Go to a shop and *buy* some for yourselves."
>
> MATTHEW 25:9

We meet up with *buy* once again, and it's the key. Picture ten girls walking into a Bass Pro Shop to purchase a lamp and oil. The foolish step up to the counter and give their money and get what they think is required. The wise, on the other hand, pool all their resources together—all their savings, bonds, treasury notes, retirement funds, and so on. They step up to the same counter, pile all the money in front of the clerk, and say, "I'll take the lamp plus all the extra oil this money can buy."

The wise gave their entire lives; the foolish only gave what they thought was required to be saved. They kept back part of their life, whereas the wise held nothing back. Thus, we discover how to "buy" from Jesus. Salvation is free; we could never earn it, but to endure to the end takes doing what's required: "You must give up your own way, take up your cross daily, and follow me. If you try to hang on to *any aspect of* your life, you will lose it. But if you give up your *entire* life for my sake, you will save it" (Luke 9:23–24).

Three things to purchase by laying down our lives:

1. *Fine gold*—representing obedience to His Word in the face of trials and persecution. We refuse to compromise to avoid the personal disadvantage.
2. *White garments*—recall from the last chapter the man who showed up to the wedding without the proper garment. It speaks of righteous acts—godly living (see Revelation 19:7–8).
3. *Eye salve*—so that we can see. We pursue genuine humility by not

constantly seeking our own interests but striving first and foremost for whatever is important to Jesus.

Jesus then says to the Laodicean church: "I correct and discipline everyone I love. So be diligent and turn from your indifference" (Revelation 3:19). He loves them! Thus, the motive behind His bluntness. He's calling them away from self-destruction. He doesn't want them to miss the catching away. Dear reader, if perhaps you feel the chastening of the Lord, it's because He loves you and always gives a way out—repentance! The greatest reward is offered to this church: to reign with Jesus (see Revelation 3:21)!

THE CHURCH IN PHILADELPHIA (REVELATION 3:7-13)

Philadelphia was founded around 140 BC. Its founder was Attalus Philadelphus of Pergamum, from whom the city derived its name. It was intended to be a center of missionary activity for the Greek way of life. The city was prosperous, partly from its flourishing vineyards. It was a center of worship of the god Dionysus and contained temples to many other gods.

The church's enemies came from outside, not from inside, for there is no mention of heresy or dissent. It had a good deal in common with Smyrna. Both receive no criticism, only praise. Both suffered from those who called themselves Jews and were not, and both were persecuted by the Romans.[3]

Jesus says to this church:

> "I know all the things you do, and I have opened a door for you that no one can close. You have little strength, yet you obeyed my word and did not deny me. Look, I will force those who belong to Satan's synagogue—those liars who say they are Jews but are not—to come and bow down at your feet. They will acknowledge that you are the ones I love."
>
> REVELATION 3:8–9

Once again, Jesus opens with "I know all the things you do." Amazing consistency!

They had little strength, possibly from being a small congregation, yet they obeyed Him in all things. Therefore, He opened a door for them that He declared no one could shut! We sometimes use this statement loosely, yet it's meant for those who love and fear Him—who obey even when it takes every bit of strength to do so. As Pergamum and Thyatira were similar to each other, so this church is similar to the Smyrna church. What He says to Philadelphia and Smyrna He says to any others who heed His correction and endure in obedience:

> "Because you have obeyed my command to persevere, I will protect you from the great time of testing that will come upon the whole world to test those who belong to this world."
>
> REVELATION 3:10

It appears from Jesus' words and other portions of Scripture we've reviewed that all loyal believers will be caught up before the seven-year tribulation. However, not all who classify themselves as believers are necessarily true Christ followers. From the parable of the virgins, it could be said that only 50 percent of those who are looking for His return are truly His. I've heard a few leaders over the past decade make a statement along the lines of, "In prayer the Holy Spirit showed me half of the church isn't in a true relationship with Jesus." I think the parable of the virgins confirms this.

It's easy to surrender all to Him but so difficult if you're still enamored with this world. God will give you the grace if your heart is sincere. Your opportunity is right now if you haven't totally surrendered your life to His lordship. It's not too late, and a wonderful life awaits you!

PASSAGE: Examine and test and evaluate your own selves to see whether you are holding to your faith and showing the proper fruits of it. (2 Corinthians 13:5 AMPC)

POINT: We do not want to find ourselves in a lukewarm state in our walk with Jesus.

PONDER: Do you believe after reading Jesus' words that it's possible to be a lukewarm Christian? Would Jesus ever vomit out those who are truly His? What are we to buy from Him? What does this look like practically?

PRAYER: Dear God, I don't ever want to believe I am in good standing with You and yet be lukewarm. I humble myself, repent of willful disobedience to Your Word, and turn to Jesus Christ as my supreme Lord with all my heart. I'm all in from this moment forward! Thank You for filling my heart with Your Spirit. In Jesus' name, amen.

PROFESSION: I am hot for Jesus and His kingdom!

"BE DRESSED FOR SERVICE AND KEEP YOUR LAMPS BURNING, AS THOUGH YOU WERE WAITING FOR YOUR MASTER TO RETURN."

LUKE 12:35-36

CHAPTER 26

BE DRESSED FOR SERVICE

The King is coming, and we are one day closer to His return than we were yesterday, "for our salvation *is* nearer now than when we *first* believed" (Romans 13:11). Time continues to move forward, and our window of opportunity to reach lost humanity and disciple the nations is rapidly closing. For this reason, we are exhorted to make "the best use of the time, because the days are evil" (Ephesians 5:16 ESV). This summarizes one of our major responsibilities—to steward the gift of time well.

Jesus briefs us on how to best manage time as we anticipate His soon arrival. His words found in Luke's gospel consolidate His three most emphasized instructions for the end times. We've covered two but still need to address one. They are as follows:

1. Be dressed for service.
2. Keep our lamps burning.
3. Wait (or watch).

We've discussed what it means to "keep our lamps burning." It's living a sanctified life as if we know He's returning today. We do this by staying in fellowship with His Spirit and keeping ourselves unspotted from the world.

It speaks of pursuing holiness and refusing to flirt with or engage in the things of this world that He suffered to set us free from. This can only be accomplished by His grace, which is freely made available to those who lay down their lives for Him, as illustrated in the story of the wise virgins.

We've discussed *watching.* We are to live with an eager expectation of His coming. In doing so we live humbly, in holy fear, and remain in constant prayer—staying in His "huddle," so to speak. We abide in Him and make it a priority to have His words abide in us. This means that we approach His Word with humility on a regular basis, not with the attitude of showing others how much we know about the Bible, but rather to meet with Him, see Him, and be transformed into His image as our mind is renewed. This keeps us washed with the water of His Word, which is our defense against being soiled or spotted by the world.

The subject that we have not yet addressed specifically is being "dressed for service," or to say it more clearly, "to remain engaged in kingdom service." Let's amplify this charge by turning to Matthew's gospel, which also highlights the "big three." After writing down Jesus' discourse about the end of the age and His imminent return, Matthew records the Master's parables intended to keep us ready. The first, which is actually two short ones, covers the *watching* aspect (see Matthew 24:42–51). The second, the parable of the ten virgins (see Matthew 25:1–13), addresses the sanctified or holy life. The third, the parable of the talents (see Matthew 25:14–30), speaks to being *engaged in kingdom service.*

Before discussing this parable, let's look at Paul's words. He writes that every believer is

> His workmanship, created in Christ Jesus for good works, which God prepared *beforehand* that we *should* walk in them.
>
> EPHESIANS 2:10 ESV

There are two words to highlight: The first is *beforehand*, and the second is *should.* Notice it doesn't say we *would*, but rather *should*; this highlights our free will. It is imperative that we know God has called every one of His children to do specific works for His kingdom. David writes:

> You saw me before I was born. Every day of my life was recorded in your book. Every moment was laid out before a single day had passed.
>
> Psalm 139:16

Our assigned "good works" were prepared prior to our birth. In fact, I believe Scripture shows them before the earth was formed, but that's for another study. The important fact: God wrote your intended magnificent biography before your parents ever knew you. In essence, *you were created on purpose for a purpose.*

When you hear the statement, "He (or she) has a calling on his (or her) life," does your mind go to the limited few—a pastor, worship leader, missionary, or other full-time vocational ministry position? If so, this is far from the full picture. Every child of God has a calling. It may be in the realm of education, health care, government, the arts, the marketplace . . . The possibilities are too numerous to list.

In my more than four decades of traveling and ministering, I've met many people who, out of deep devotion to Jesus, pursued vocational ministry with the belief that it was the most effective way to serve Him. After struggling for a few years, they discovered—usually after deep prayer fueled by their misery—that they were called to a different realm than vocational ministry. Their lives ended up being extremely fruitful once they moved into the arena of life God had created them for. I've written a book devoted to this very important aspect of our Christian life entitled *You Are Called.* I strongly recommend reading it, as I can only give the big picture in this chapter.

In order for us to accomplish our divine works, God has given us supernatural abilities. They are identified in Scripture as *gifts*, for which the Greek word is *charisma*. Its root word is *charis*, which is translated "grace." The root word enlightens us that our gifts are unearned and undeserved. In essence, they are God-given abilities enabling us to accomplish our divine assignments. We could never fulfill these assignments in our own ability. One of my gifts would be writing, which just so happened to be my worst subject in high school. It wasn't until God spoke to me in prayer "to write" that this *charisma* was imparted.

If our assigned tasks were capable of being accomplished in our own ability, then He would have to share the glory with us. In divine wisdom He called us to do things that are beyond our natural abilities so that we would have to depend on His grace to accomplish them. This results in Him getting *all* the glory.

The only way we can impact eternity with these abilities is to believe and obey. It's similar to "saving grace": Even though grace is available to all, only those who "believe" receive its saving benefit. Romans 5:2 gives us the divine law of receiving from heaven: "We have access by faith into this grace in which we stand" (NKJV). In applying this law to *charisma*, we discover if we don't believe, we don't receive and, consequently, can't adequately aid others by impacting them on an eternal level. It's imperative that we be established in this, and it should be one of the first things we teach new believers in their journey of discipleship. For Jesus says:

> "My nourishment comes from doing the will of God, who sent me, and from finishing his work."
>
> JOHN 4:34

Jesus' nourishment came from doing and finishing what He was sent to do. The New King James Version uses the word "food." Can you imagine going a month without eating and then trying to do a week's worth of hard labor? You'd faint! The same truth applies to us, for Jesus says:

> "As the Father has sent Me, I also send you."
>
> JOHN 20:21 NKJV

Over the years, I've observed that a root issue of Christians falling into gross habitual sin and eventually falling away from the faith is that they disengaged from what God created them to do. Their departure may have been earmarked by sexual immorality, substance abuse, pleasure seeking, idolatry, apathy, and so forth, but the core issue was a lack of strength to continue the fight against the world's flow of lawlessness. Our strength for the battle to continue pressing on into the high calling is sustained by doing what we are called to do; it's our food—our nourishment.

This brings us to the parable of the talents. Jesus informs us the kingdom of God is like

> "A man going on a journey, who called his servants and entrusted to them his property. To one he gave five talents, to another two, to another one, to each according to his ability."
>
> Matthew 25:14–15 ESV

A talent is a measure of weight, especially used for money; it's approximately seventy-five pounds of silver. In parables, Jesus usually isn't talking about what He's talking about. In other words, He's not talking about money here, but rather what God entrusts to each of us—gifts (*charisma*). They are His property. My ability to lead, speak, and write is not my own, it's His. A businesswoman's entrepreneurial skills to flourish in the marketplace are not hers but God's. A skilled Navy SEAL's abilities to defend our nation are not his but the Lord's.

In the parable, the first two servants engage in labor using what was given to them. In essence, they multiply what ultimately belongs to the master. The interpretation is that they used their entrusted abilities to build God's kingdom, not their own enterprises.

The third servant, though, doesn't use what was committed to him to build what belongs to the master. There's a good chance he does use them, however, for his selfish desires—what would benefit only him or his family. Even though they're used, in the owner's eyes, it's as if he buried them. We must remember that Jesus paid a very high price for the kingdom, yet He committed the responsibility of building it to us. If we refrain from engaging in His greatest interest, it communicates an apathetic attitude toward what is valuable to Him.

Jesus is giving us a key ingredient for two very important things: first, an opportunity to avoid being shipwrecked by staying the course; and second, an opportunity to receive a great reward at the judgment seat for believers.

When we use our God-given abilities to build His kingdom, it affects others in a magnificent way and ultimately rewards us eternally. If we don't, we can easily slip into a lethargic, indifferent life—a comfortable life, like the Laodicean church, or even into idolatry, like some of the other churches. Our fading strength is the consequence of disengaging from our divine calling.

Jesus wraps up this riveting parable by sharing the outcome of those who heed His instructions and those who don't. The ones who use what is entrusted to them to multiply the kingdom will be given more responsibility, but the ones who don't, like the third servant, will suffer great loss at the judgment. Listen to Jesus' words:

> "Then he ordered, 'Take the money from this servant, and give it to the one with the ten bags of silver. To those who use well what they are given, even more will be given, and they will have an abundance. But from those who do nothing, even what little they have will be taken away. Now throw this useless servant into outer darkness, where there will be weeping and gnashing of teeth.'"
>
> MATTHEW 25:28–30

There is another equally riveting parable Jesus shares that parallels this third servant:

> "A man planted a fig tree in his garden and came again and again to see if there was any fruit on it, but he was always disappointed. Finally, he said to his gardener, 'I've waited three years, and there hasn't been a single fig! Cut it down. It's just taking up space in the garden.'
>
> "The gardener answered, 'Sir, give it one more chance. Leave it another year, and I'll give it *special attention* and plenty of fertilizer. If we get figs next year, fine. If not, then you can cut it down.'"
>
> LUKE 13:6–9

Could it be that the letters to five of the seven churches were the "special attention" Jesus referred to? None of us want to find ourselves in the place of needing this special attention as a last-ditch effort of the Holy Spirit to bring us back to a place of fruitfulness. We must remember, some of Jesus' final words before His crucifixion were "You didn't choose me. I chose you. I appointed you to go and produce lasting fruit" (John 15:16).

It's a serious matter to neglect building His kingdom with what He's entrusted to us. It's quite sad that much of the Western church hasn't fully recognized and responded to this. So many people attend our churches a couple times a month or less, go about their busy lives seeking pleasure or accumulating wealth, and don't consider their responsibility to further the Lord's kingdom. There's little conviction due to numerous church leaders not wanting to put "pressure" on folks to get engaged. However, when getting engaged is presented in a healthy way, people get excited to be a part of building what lasts forever. This is what I observed in the Brazilian church that had grown from one man to over three hundred thousand in sixteen years. Their people keep focused on the eternal rather than the seventy-to-eighty-year perspective.

How do we discover what we are called to do? There are three key factors: The first is to seek God sincerely and earnestly in faith, not haphazardly or half-heartedly in wonder and doubt. We are told, "It is impossible to please God without faith. Anyone who wants to come to him must believe that God exists and that he rewards those who sincerely seek him" (Hebrews 11:6).

The second is to be planted in a local church or body of believers with a God-ordained leader. We are told, "Those who are *planted in* the house of the LORD shall flourish in the courts of our God" (Psalm 92:13 NKJV). The key here is being *planted in*, not visiting or periodically attending, a local church. Consider this: If you plant a peach seed, it won't grow into a mango tree. It will flourish into a peach tree, just as it was designed to do by the Creator. It's the same for us. If we're committed to the house of God, we will flourish into what we're called to be, whether that's in the marketplace, government, health care, or any of the other numerous fields we can be called to. God wants the church's influence in every nation—every sector of society. We are called to be both a restraining and an influencing force.

The third key is huge. It's dedicating ourselves fully to the kingdom as our priority, which should subsequently trump any of our personal desires. In essence, we die to our own interests and entrust our personal desires to the Lord to be met by Him. Jesus says:

> "I tell you the truth, unless a kernel of wheat is planted in the soil and dies, it remains alone. But its death will produce many new kernels—a plentiful harvest of new lives. Those who love their life in this world will lose it. Those who care nothing for their life in this world will keep it for eternity."
>
> JOHN 12:24–25

There is nothing that can be added to these clear words; they go to the very core of the matter. We can choose our own way, or we can submit to what God has designed for our lives and reap the reward of life, peace, and fulfillment.

You'll find deep inward satisfaction awaiting you when you heed the calling He's placed on your life. You're not too old to engage. Moses began his work when he was eighty years old. One of the great men of God in the twentieth century, Smith Wigglesworth, didn't begin walking in his calling until he was in his fifties. You are not too young either. The prophet Jeremiah and King David were both sixteen years old when they were called. Take heart: You are never too young or old to engage in your divine calling. Others are waiting for what you carry!

PASSAGE: "Well done, my good and faithful servant. You have been faithful in handling this small amount, so now I will give you many more responsibilities. Let's celebrate together!" (Matthew 25:21)

POINT: The words "well done" are what each of us long to hear from the mouth of our Savior.

PONDER: What are you doing with the life God has given you? Are you engaged in building lives for His glory? What could you do differently? In what ways have you drifted from being focused on your divine assignment? What have you been doing well?

PRAYER: Dear Lord, I ask sincerely and wholeheartedly in faith, what is my current assignment to build Your kingdom? What more do You desire of me? What do I need to do less of? Please expose any distractions, weights, or sins that are slowing me down. In Jesus' name, amen.

PROFESSION: I will fulfill my divine assignment so that I will hear the words "Well done!"

SEE HOW THE FARMER WAITS FOR THE PRECIOUS FRUIT OF THE EARTH, WAITING PATIENTLY FOR IT UNTIL IT RECEIVES THE EARLY AND LATTER RAIN. YOU ALSO BE PATIENT. ESTABLISH YOUR HEARTS, FOR THE COMING OF THE LORD IS AT HAND.

JAMES 5:7-8 NKJV

CHAPTER 27

AN ESTABLISHED HEART

We live in a time where the virtue of patience is waning. It's hard to stay steady over long periods of time when we've grown accustomed to instantaneous or quick results. It's not just one aspect of our lives but nearly all areas. Whether it's information, entertainment, food, education, purchases, loans, or countless other areas of life, what once required much more time to obtain now takes just moments.

Many innovations have fabulously improved our quality of life, but danger arises when "instantaneous results" bleed over into what needs consistency over time to obtain. One of these important qualities is the development of inner strength to *endure until the end* (see Matthew 10:22; 24:13; Mark 13:13).

In our chapter-opening passage, the word "patient" is used twice by the apostle James regarding the coming of the Lord. It speaks of consistency no matter the circumstances. This is how our hearts become *established*; the Greek word used, *stērízō*, means "to cause someone to become stronger in the sense of more firm and unchanging in attitude or belief."[1] This carries the idea of growing more resolute the longer it takes for the desired end, which only occurs through consistent prayer and studying and obeying God's Word. The darkness of this world can wear on us if we don't stay resolute in our purpose of knowing and glorifying our Bridegroom.

To *establish* our hearts speaks of remaining loyal and unchanging, and refusing to back away no matter how difficult or dark things become. It means we refuse to quit and avoid drifting into idolatry or slothfulness. This undoubtedly will be the root cause of so many walking away from the faith just before the Lord's return.

Let's reconsider the parable of the virgins. It was the midnight hour that the unwise bridesmaids ran out of oil; their hearts weren't established. Science tells us that midnight is the darkest time of night due to the sun being at the lowest point in comparison to the horizon.[2] In essence, the longer the bridegroom was delayed, the darker the world became. In the first half of Isaiah 60:2, we read:

> For behold, the darkness shall cover the earth, and deep darkness the people. (NKJV)

Sounds bleak, doesn't it? However, it isn't for those whose hearts are set, remaining consistent in their close fellowship with the Lord no matter the difficulties. The rest of the verse declares:

> But the LORD will arise over you, and His glory will be seen upon you.

This cannot be speaking of the millennial reign of Jesus Christ, for Satan and his hordes will be locked up. Their dark influence will be absent during this age. This verse addresses a very dark time in the world when God's Spirit will manifest in a powerful manner—His glory will be seen on His people. Many will be drawn into the kingdom as a result. It's often referred to as the latter rain.

In the days of Isaiah there were two primary sets of rains: the early and the latter. One arrived just after planting time; and the other, just before harvesttime. The former would germinate the seeds and aid the plants in their initial development, and the latter would mature the fruit for the ingathering. This doesn't mean there weren't rains in between planting and harvesting, as there surely were; it merely referred to focused rains needed to saturate the ground for the beginning and end of the growing season.

If we look at the book of Acts, we get insight into the early rain. Peter refers to God's Spirit being "poured out" on the day of Pentecost (see Acts 2:16–21). This outpouring resulted in the church's rapid growth and establishment. It was kick-started by a remarkable wonder resulting in three thousand souls being saved. Shortly afterward, an additional five thousand came to Jesus after a well-known crippled man was instantly healed. Eventually entire cities came into the kingdom—Samaria, Lydda, and Sharon all were saved, and everyone heard the gospel in Joppa (see Acts 8; 9:34–35, 42). The glory of God was so mighty that people were dropping dead for lying in His presence, a building shook during prayer, and people were laid in the streets—not a single street but *streets*—and one of God's servants just walked by and all the sick, crippled, and diseased were healed.

This outpouring began with the Jewish people but eventually carried over to the Gentiles (non-Jewish people). The same outpouring would occur in whatever city or country the disciples journeyed to. The church grew so rapidly that in just two years "all who dwelt in Asia heard the word of the Lord Jesus, both Jews and Greeks" (Acts 19:10 NKJV). They didn't have any modern-day forms of communication—no radios, televisions, smartphones, social media, or any other mediums of mass communication. This is remarkable! The outpouring of God's Spirit was so profound that in the Greek city of Thessalonica, civil leaders cried out: "These who have turned the world upside down have come here too" (Acts 17:6 NKJV).

I was in prayer many years ago when the Spirit of God spoke to me, "Son, what I will do before Jesus' return makes the book of Acts look like child's play; it will be *seven times* greater."

I was in shock but knew it was God's voice. I asked Him to show me at least three scriptures to support this shocking statement. That same day He gave them, the first being:

> The glory of this latter temple shall be greater than the former.
>
> HAGGAI 2:9 NKJV

In the new covenant, the church is the temple of God. The old covenant was a shadow of what God would do in the new. Just as the temple of Herod exceeded the greatness of the temple of Solomon, even so the glory of God on the church will be greater just prior to His second coming than it was in days of the early church.

The second was Ecclesiastes 7:8:

> The end of a thing is better than its beginning. (NKJV)

To solidify this one, He asked me, "Didn't I save the best wine for last?" and I remembered Jesus' first reported miracle at the Cana wedding (see John 2:10).

When I questioned the "seven times," He led me to this scripture:

> O people of Zion, who live in Jerusalem,
> you will weep no more.
> He will be gracious if you ask for help.
> He will surely respond to the sound of your cries.
> Though the Lord gave you adversity for food
> and suffering for drink,
> he will still be with you to teach you.
> You will see your teacher with your own eyes.
>
> ISAIAH 30:19–20

I do realize this passage, as well as Isaiah 60:2, is a prophetic scripture for the Jewish people and Jerusalem. However, often what God does with Israel carries over to the church, which is comprised mostly of Gentiles. Recall, the early rain began with the Jewish believers but eventually spread to all believers, especially in the Gentile nations. Similarly, the latter rain will begin with the church—predominantly the Gentiles and some Jewish believers—but will continue primarily to the Jewish people. It's marvelous when we think this through; the early and latter rains will affect both the Jewish nation and the church. Magnificent!

Notice Isaiah says that the people will *see their Teacher.* The English Standard Version translates this "your Teacher will not hide himself anymore, but your eyes shall see your Teacher." Jesus will be revealed to all His people—the church prior to the tribulation and the Jewish people in the tribulation, as also spoken by Zechariah the prophet regarding Israel: "They will look on me whom they have pierced" (Zechariah 12:10). We clearly see that this speaks of the season of Jesus' second coming—the season of the latter rain.

Isaiah then writes:

> Then you will destroy all your silver idols and your precious gold images. You will throw them out like filthy rags, saying to them, "Good riddance!"
>
> ISAIAH 30:22

Remember, idolatry is more than worshiping statues or images—it's greed or covetousness; it's putting someone or something before our relationship with Jesus; it's when we draw our strength from them rather than from God. The prophet says once we see this great wave of returning to the Lord by His people, this is what will occur:

> Then the LORD will bless you with rain. . . . In that day . . . the moon will be as bright as the sun, and the sun will be *seven times brighter*—like the light of seven days in one! So it will be when the LORD begins to heal his people and cure the wounds he gave them.
>
> ISAIAH 30:23, 25–26

Hold on! When a natural rain occurs, the sun is not seven times brighter. So He must not be speaking of natural rain but the rain of His Spirit. In that day the glory of Jesus will be seven times brighter than what has been seen before!

When I saw this scripture, I realized that what's coming will eclipse the magnificent glory we see in the book of Acts. However, tremendous opposition also accompanied the great outpouring. We may soon face a greater level of darkness and persecution, but the bride will be glorious, not defeated!

We are to establish our hearts in preparation for the outpouring of His Spirit and the coming of the Lord. I personally believe we will witness both a great falling away and a great ingathering of souls at the same time. In recent decades, we've seen many people walk away from the faith, but recent polls show an increase of faith, especially among young people.[3] Could it be the beginning of the latter rain? The former rain of God's Spirit started with a bang on the day of Pentecost; could the latter rain be just the opposite? Perhaps starting with a trickle and ending with a gusher that draws masses into the kingdom and climaxes with His return?

The true church will become increasingly glorious, but at the same time the harlot church—those who claim faith but have not laid down their lives for Him—will continue to greatly increase in size and acceptance by the world. This harlot church will go into the tribulation, as Jesus warns:

> "Indeed I will cast her into a sickbed, and those who commit adultery with her into great tribulation, unless they repent of their deeds. I will kill her children with death."
>
> REVELATION 2:22–23 NKJV

Those who are part of this harlot church are described by Paul as follows:

> I have told you often before, and I say it again with tears in my eyes, that there are many whose conduct shows they are really enemies of the cross of Christ.
>
> PHILIPPIANS 3:18

It is not what they say that gives away their true nature; it's the way they live—their conduct. They actually confess to be in relationship with Jesus, but their behavior shows otherwise (see Titus 1:16). Notice, Paul has tears in his eyes in speaking of those who deceive others as well as themselves (see 2 Timothy 3:13). He cares deeply for those who will be affected by these propagators of idolatry, lewdness, and lukewarmness. He continues:

> They are headed for destruction. Their god is their appetite, they brag about shameful things, and they think only about this life here on earth.
>
> PHILIPPIANS 3:19

The destruction they will encounter will climax in the great tribulation when the Antichrist devours them, as foretold by the apostle John:

> "The scarlet beast and his ten horns all hate the prostitute [the harlot church]. They will strip her naked, eat her flesh, and burn her remains with fire. For God has put a plan into their minds, a plan that will carry out his purposes. They will agree to give their authority to the scarlet beast, and so the words of God will be fulfilled."
>
> REVELATION 17:16–17

Most Bible commentaries agree that this is the harlot church. One writes:

> "She is also bent on imitating the true church. She is 'dressed in purple and scarlet, and . . . glittering with gold, precious stones and pearls' (Revelation 17:4 NIV; Revelation 18:16). Remarkably, her dress is almost identical to the appearance of the true church depicted in Revelation 21:18–19: 'the city of pure gold. . . . The foundations of the city walls were decorated with every kind of precious stone' (NIV). Revelation, therefore, depicts two cities as two women. The true people of God are a faithful bride, that is, the new Jerusalem, whereas the unfaithful are a prostitute, namely, Babylon."[4]

This is why we are told to be patient and establish our hearts to remain loyal no matter how dark it gets. God will give us grace; He will continually purify us as we look forward with great anticipation to the coming of our King.

> We are citizens of heaven, where the Lord Jesus Christ lives. And we are eagerly waiting for him to return as our Savior. He will take our weak

> mortal bodies and change them into glorious bodies like his own, using the same power with which he will bring everything under his control.
>
> PHILIPPIANS 3:20–21

Dear reader, I want to comfort your heart and protect you from the strategies of Satan, who desires to pull you away. If he was able to do that with Adam and Eve in a perfect environment where the presence of God was so wonderfully tangible, how much more can he do so in a corrupt environment?

I don't intend to scare you but to convince you how serious the times are. It is not the time to relax and just flow with the current of society. It's time to be sober, alert, watchful in prayer, and rooted and grounded in the Word of God. We are in a war; it's a war for our souls and the souls of those we love. God's grace is sufficient, and He will keep us strong to the end, but we must stay in fellowship with Him.

After Jude warns of the deceptive teachers and false brothers and sisters who will infiltrate the church and pervert the true grace of God, he gives the greatest encouragement:

> Now all glory to God, who is *able* to keep you from falling away and will bring you with great joy into his glorious presence without a single fault.
>
> JUDE V. 24

He is *able*; therefore we must cooperate! Stay in fellowship with Him, be patient in troubles, and have your heart established in truth.

PASSAGE: Ask the LORD for rain in the time of the latter rain. (Zechariah 10:1 NKJV)

POINT: Establish your heart for His coming and be prepared for the greatest outpouring of His Spirit any previous generation has witnessed.

PONDER: How do you establish your heart? Describe what this looks like practically. What do you think the apostle Peter means when he writes that we should be "established in the present truth" (2 Peter 1:12 NKJV)? How would you describe "present truth"? (Hint: Try looking up this verse in other translations.)

PRAYER: Dear Father, it's the time of the latter rain, and You instructed me to pray for it. Therefore, I ask You to send the latter rain of Your Holy Spirit. May I have the privilege of being a part of the greatest ingathering of souls of all time. I also ask, Holy Spirit, that You would help me to establish my heart in present truth. In Jesus' name, amen.

PROFESSION: I will establish my heart in truth.

"LOOK, I AM COMING SOON, BRINGING MY REWARD WITH ME TO REPAY ALL PEOPLE ACCORDING TO THEIR DEEDS."

REVELATION 22:12

CHAPTER 28

ETERNAL REWARDS

Have you ever attended or witnessed an awards ceremony? Perhaps you've watched three Olympians take the podium to receive their gold, silver, and bronze medals. These athletes trained diligently, excelled in their performance, and were awarded for their efforts before millions. Afterward, their lives changed significantly as doors of opportunity opened to them.

Let's make it more personal. Perhaps there was a time when you received an academic or athletic award, or you were honored by your employer for a job well done. Do you remember the joy and satisfaction you felt? Do you remember celebrating with those you love? It's probable that your hard work procured a life change—a scholarship, promotion, pay raise, or increased responsibility.

Now put yourself on the other side of that same storyline. Have you been the one who didn't receive any recognition and watched as awards or accolades were given to your peers? Was there a reason you weren't recognized? Could it be that you didn't apply yourself? Perhaps you did a sloppy job, didn't train as diligently as you should have, or neglected your studies. If any of these reasons were true of your performance, the ceremony wasn't a pleasant experience. You felt regret at the moment and even afterward for not applying yourself. Consequently, there was no promotion, increase in responsibility, or scholarship offered to you. In light of this, listen to the apostle Paul's words:

> Don't you realize that in a race everyone runs, but only one person gets the prize? So run to win! All athletes are disciplined in their training. They do it to win a prize that will fade away, but we do it for an eternal prize. So I run with purpose in every step.
>
> 1 CORINTHIANS 9:24–26

The greatest award ceremony of all time is rapidly approaching for believers. There are many eternal prizes that will be handed out. As in the above examples, the rewards will be much more than medals, plaques, or trophies; they will be accompanied by eternal positions that carry responsibility and authority. This event is referred to as the judgment seat of Christ. Paul urges a very carnal church to wake up so they don't have regrets at this ceremony. He urges them, as well as us, to diligently train and run "with purpose in every step" in order to receive the everlasting prize. We are told to win; however, we're not competing against each other, but rather against a world that's bent on hindering or even stopping us. We all should be cheering for each other!

Another wise apostle writes in similar fashion. He was faithful to Jesus since his teenage years, and penning these words in his nineties, he says:

> Look to yourselves, that we do not lose those things we worked for, but that we may receive a *full* reward.
>
> 2 JOHN V. 8 NKJV

Notice he encourages us to live in a way that we receive the *full* reward—not a *partial* one, and especially not *none* at all. He's the apostle of love who personally witnessed the events of the end times as he records them in Revelation. Both he and Paul are reminding us that Jesus is returning, and His reward is with Him! Let's look closely at Paul's writings to the carnal Corinthian church:

> We are confident, yes, well pleased rather to be absent from the body and to be present with the Lord.
>
> 2 CORINTHIANS 5:8 NKJV

We know for certain Paul is only writing to believers, for unbelievers are not in the presence of the Lord once out of their bodies; rather, they're in hell. This isn't a harsh statement but a factual one. We must remember, Jesus came to save us from our self-inflicted condemnation (see John 3:18 NKJV). Paul continues:

> Therefore we make it our aim, whether present or absent, to be *well* pleasing to Him.
>
> 2 CORINTHIANS 5:9 NKJV

We cannot do anything to make God love us any more than He already does. However, we are responsible for how pleased He is with us. For this reason, Paul makes his goal not just to be pleasing to God but *well* pleasing—and we should make this our goal too. Why?

> For we must all appear before the judgment seat of Christ, that each one may receive the things *done* in the body, according to what he has done, whether *good* or *bad*.
>
> 2 CORINTHIANS 5:10 NKJV

Scripture speaks of a number of future judgments; however, the two main ones are the *believer's judgment* and the *great white throne judgment* (the judgment of those who refused to submit to God's plan of salvation). They occur approximately a thousand years apart from each other, as the latter occurs after the thousand-year reign of Christ on earth.

The believer's judgment will most likely occur in heaven during the seven-year tribulation. We don't have firm evidence of this in Scripture, although we have a clue. The twenty-four elders, whom we've previously identified as the "resurrected" and "caught away" saints, have crowns before the throne at the time of the tribulation (see Revelation 4:4, 10). This would indicate they have already been examined and awarded.

The Greek word for "judgment seat" is *bēma* and is defined as "a raised platform mounted by steps and usually furnished with a seat, used by officials in addressing an assembly, often on judicial matters."[1] From this seat of authority Jesus will thoroughly examine our lives and we will either be rewarded or receive nothing for how we lived as believers.

We will not be judged for our sins, as they have been eradicated by the blood of Jesus. You may question, then, What does Paul mean when he says we will give an account for not only the good but also the *bad*? The Greek word *kakós* is defined as "bad, worthless . . . recede, retire, retreat in battle."[2] This word speaks of the adverse or worthless effects we've had on others by not walking in the character of Christ. It also speaks of missed opportunities due to either disobedience to a direct word from God or neglecting to act on His revealed written Word.

In essence, we will give an account of how we stewarded the life and gifts He entrusted to us to build His kingdom. We will answer for every life we impacted in either a positive or negative way, for He has said that what we did to the least of His brothers and sisters, we did to Him (see Matthew 25:40).

Not only will our words and works be examined, but our hidden thoughts and intentions will be made known to all. Paul writes:

> Don't make judgments about anyone ahead of time—before the Lord returns. For he will bring our *darkest secrets* to light and will reveal our *private motives*. Then God will give to each one whatever *praise* is due.
>
> 1 CORINTHIANS 4:5

Our first question should be, Does this refer to the unbeliever's or believer's judgment? The last sentence of the verse clarifies that it's the believer's judgment, for at the great white throne judgment no sinner will receive praise from God.

What would our "darkest secrets" and "private motives" include? Did we give, minister, pray, serve, labor, or fast to be seen by men; or were we motivated by obedience, love, and compassion? Did we serve out of obligation or with a willing attitude? Did we resent serving or did we find pleasure in it? Did we labor for the purpose of personal gain or the impact we could have on others? Did we join the worship team because we secretly desired to be noticed and celebrated or because we desired to lead people into the presence of God? When we received praise, did we allow it to puff us up or did we redirect it in our heart to the One who deserves it? Did we seek to satisfy our selfish interests and soothe our insecurities or did we truly seek to glorify Jesus? The scenarios are almost endless, but all possibilities will be carefully examined and made known to all at the judgment seat of Christ.

The word *judgment* is often associated with condemnation. However, in the verse from 1 Corinthians, and most others in the New Testament regarding believers, it's really more about a *decision* that's rendered after a thorough investigation. Jesus' decisions over our lives are called "eternal judgment" (Hebrews 6:2), more clearly understood as "eternal decisions." There will never be any changes, revisions, or amendments made to these decisions. Simply put, they will stand forever. So *what* we do with the cross of Calvary determines *where* we will spend eternity. However, *the way we live* as believers determines *how* we will spend eternity.

In Scripture, often believers are referred to as "builders," one of many references being "The stone that the *builders* rejected has now become the cornerstone" (1 Peter 2:7). And again, "Unless the Lord builds a house, the work of the *builders* is wasted" (Psalm 127:1). We could view this identification of *builders* as being *subcontractors* erecting God's home that He will live in forever. His home has a name—*Zion* (see Psalm 132:13–14), and its material consists of living stones—all His saints (see 1 Peter 2:5), with Jesus being the chief cornerstone (see Isaiah 28:16).

If we retreat from our assignments by choosing to live in a way that is motivated by selfish interests and gain, that will be judged as one of the "bad" behaviors. Paul leaves no wiggle room regarding our examination at the judgment. He writes, "Whoever is building on this foundation [the lordship of Jesus Christ] must be very careful" (1 Corinthians 3:10). It's abundantly clear: *How* we build is of the essence:

> Anyone who builds on that foundation may use a variety of materials—gold, silver, jewels, wood, hay, or straw. But on the judgment day, fire will reveal what kind of work each builder has done. The fire will show if a person's work has any value.
>
> 1 CORINTHIANS 3:12–13

As discussed in chapter 26, there are a variety of ways we can choose to spend our God-given time and use our God-given gifts. If we live for self-gain, we build using combustible material that is temporary. If we live selflessly to build His kingdom, we use material that is purified and eternal. The Word of God is the fire that examines our life and reveals what was behind our motives, words, and behavior.

Paul goes on to say, "If the work survives, that builder will receive a reward" (v. 14). Hopefully it's the *full* reward. However, the next words are riveting:

> But if the work is burned up, the builder will suffer *great* loss. The builder will be *saved*, but like someone barely escaping through a wall of flames.
>
> 1 CORINTHIANS 3:15

There is so much here. First, notice the builder is *saved*. This isn't about an unbeliever who is condemned to the lake of fire forever, but rather one who will eternally reside in God's kingdom.

Second, the loss is *great*. The Greek word used here implies a sense of profound loss. Keep in mind this intense loss will not only be felt at the judgment but will affect how we live in the millennium and on into the eternal new heavens and earth.

Third, the comparison given is like one *barely escaping through a wall of flames*. Let's modernize this. Westerners prepare for retirement (I personally don't subscribe to this mentality, as retirement speaks of retreating from assignment). However, since it is relatable, I'll use it for illustration purposes.

What if when the big day arrives for our retiree, his bank goes belly-up? Everything in his checking and savings accounts is lost. The same day,

Social Security and all the companies holding his IRAs and 401(k) plans go bankrupt. Not only that, but our retiree's home burns to the ground, and he escapes with just the shirt on his back. He's lost everything! This storyline would be considered a disaster. Yet Paul uses a similar description for how some believers will enter eternity. It is not for a period of twenty years (the average length of retirement); rather, it is forever!

Again, Paul declares the believer to be saved, yet everything is burned up and forever lost. Remember, it's an *eternal* judgment/decision. Please don't misunderstand: To be saved is far from insignificant and infinitely better than being lost in the lake of fire for all eternity. We all will rejoice beyond comprehension, but will there be a sense of what could have been?

Let's ponder this a little further. James tells us our life is a vapor—a blip on a screen or, in reality, even quicker (see James 4:14 NKJV). In simple mathematics, any finite number divided by (or compared to) infinity is equal to zero. So, if you live eighty years in this life and compare it to eternity, this life would be zero. If you make it 120 years, which all of us consider a long life, it's still zero compared to eternity. Therefore, what we do during this blip on the screen or, more accurately, in this zero time, determines how we will spend eternity.

Let's attempt to comprehend by using just the millennium as an example. Please remember, the believer's judgment affects our forever, but I'm only going to use Jesus' short thousand-year reign on earth because it's relatable. How you live in your short life determines how you will spend the next one thousand years, including the authority entrusted to you, the job you'll do, the people you'll work with, your proximity to the King, and the location of your residence.

Clearly, these are not minor issues—and a thousand years is a long time. Just think, a thousand years prior to this book's copyright date, Europe was in the High Middle Ages, innovative China was creating gunpowder and paper money, Vikings were transitioning from raiders to settlers, and it would be nearly 470 years before Christopher Columbus first reached the Americas. That's a long time, and it's still a blip on the screen compared to the everlasting future of the new earth and heavens.

So, how should we live? Should we allow frivolous distractions to deter us from our resolve to build others' lives? Should we treat people with contempt and carry offenses? Should we spend our time fighting for our rights? Should we allow our love to grow cold and selfish? Should we divorce our spouse for simply not getting along? Should we seek only entertainment and pleasure? It seems ridiculous when said out loud. Yet so many believers are setting up their next millennium—and even more importantly, their forever and ever—without considering the outcome.

SOME MENTIONED REWARDS

What are some of the mentioned rewards in Scripture promised to those who overcome the world's attempts to distract or enslave us? To begin, Scripture lists five specifics of the crown(s) God will give to the victors. It could be one of two scenarios: various descriptions of the same crown or multiple crowns. I lean toward various descriptions of the same crown. However, I do believe each crown will vary in glory, depending on the obedience of the believer:

1. The Imperishable Crown (1 Corinthians 9:25)
2. The Crown of Life (Revelation 2:10)
3. The Crown of Eternal Glory and Honor (1 Peter 5:2–4)
4. The Crown of Righteousness (2 Timothy 4:8)
5. The Crown of Rejoicing (1 Thessalonians 2:19–20)

A crown isn't a decoration on top of a person's head; rather, it speaks of authority, rulership, power, and glory. It denotes responsibility of wondrous proportions. These are the promises that Jesus makes to those who endure victoriously to the end, all taken from His words to the seven churches in the book of Revelation:

1. Freely partake of the fruit from the Tree of Life (2:7)
2. Not be harmed by the second death (2:11)

3. The hidden manna in heaven (2:17)
4. A white stone with a new name (2:17)
5. Authority and rulership over the nations (2:26–27)
6. The same authority Jesus received from the Father (2:28)
7. The morning star (2:28)
8. Be clothed in white (3:5)
9. Be pillars in the temple of God (3:12)
10. Never have to leave the temple of God (3:12)
11. The name of God written on them (3:12)
12. Citizenship in the City of God (3:12)
13. Jesus will write His new name on them (3:12)
14. Share a meal with Jesus as friends (3:20)
15. Sit with Jesus on His throne (3:21)

In Luke's gospel, we find the parable of the minas. It reveals a servant who is faithful and multiplies his or her entrustments ten times and consequently receives authority over ten cities, whereas the one who multiplied his five times is entrusted with five cities. This clearly illustrates there is a correlation between how we apply ourselves in this life and the magnitude of our authority and responsibility in the millennium, as well as later on in the new earth and heavens (see Luke 19:11–19, 24–26).

Here is the bottom line: The Lord desires to reward you with abundance, power, authority, and blessing. I know as a dad of four sons, it was my desire to reward them when they were growing up, but I learned from the wisdom of God that rewards are not to be given unless they are earned or deserved. However, I longed to do it and cheered them on in my heart and soul to act, behave, and speak in a way that would be rewarded.

This is Jesus' heart for you. He sincerely hopes you respond to the call to occupy for the kingdom's glory until He comes. He's cheering you on to stay alert, sober, and humble before Him. He longs for you to take the call to holiness seriously, keeping yourself set apart for Him until He returns for you. He deeply loves you, desires you, and is full of hope for you. In fact, there is no one who is more hopeful for you in all the world. He's your greatest admirer. How can we not respond to such love, desire, and hope? Don't let the Enemy lie that you're insignificant or that your role is trivial. We all need you to finish well.

He's coming! Soon He'll catch away His beloved bride, and we'll celebrate like never before. In fact, Isaiah gives us a window into the celebration that will occur at the marriage supper of the Lamb—when all is completed:

> In Jerusalem, the LORD of Heaven's Armies will spread a wonderful feast for all the people of the world. It will be a delicious banquet with clear, well-aged wine and choice meat. There he will remove the cloud of gloom, the shadow of death that hangs over the earth. He will swallow up death forever! The Sovereign LORD will wipe away all tears. He will remove forever all insults and mockery against his land and people. The LORD has spoken!
>
> ISAIAH 25:6–8

What joy and happiness await your faithfulness to the end! I look forward to rejoicing when you're eternally rewarded at His judgment seat and we celebrate together at the marriage supper. Our faithful Lord, Savior, and Bridegroom leaves us with these words:

> "Yes, I am coming soon!"

And our response is:

> "Amen! Come, Lord Jesus!"
>
> REVELATION 22:20

PASSAGE: "If the master returns and finds that the servant has done a good job, there will be a reward." (Luke 12:43)

POINT: There are *full* reward, as well as *partial* and *no* reward, scenarios at the judgment seat of Christ for believers. Live in such a way that you will receive the full reward.

PONDER: Am I living for the Lord's glory or my own benefit in my labor? Am I allowing the Word of God to discern the thoughts and intentions of my heart? What private motives need to be changed? How can I do this?

PRAYER: Dear Father, I open my heart and life to Your Word to discern the deepest thoughts and intentions of my heart. May my thoughts and motives be pleasing in Your sight. May I deeply love those You bring to me each and every day with the same love that my Lord Jesus loves me. In Jesus' name I pray, amen.

PROFESSION: Come quickly, Lord Jesus!

AT JUST THE RIGHT TIME CHRIST WILL BE REVEALED FROM HEAVEN BY THE BLESSED AND ONLY ALMIGHTY GOD, THE KING OF ALL KINGS AND LORD OF ALL LORDS.

1 TIMOTHY 6:15

A CLOSING EXHORTATION

Rewind from the believer's judgment seat back to this very moment. Even though time doesn't permit us to live backward, we can surely imagine it. How does this vantage point affect your life now? How does it shape your perspective for the days ahead?

Many believe that studying, pondering, and discussing the prophetic scriptures promotes an escape mentality, which leads to an unproductive life. But this only occurs if the second coming is incorrectly taught or heard about!

The imminent return of Jesus and the ensuing judgment seat should foster a "hustle-up" mentality. Paul discusses running to win in 1 Corinthians 9:24, so in the same light, let's consider a sports team that's behind halfway through a game compared to a team that has only minutes left on the clock.

I'll never forget a pastor inviting me to the final English Premier League football game of the 2011–2012 season. To my delight, he had magnificent seats on the second row. My host was a huge Manchester (Man) City fan, and they hadn't won the league his entire life. After years of disappointment, they were finally poised to be champions. Man City was hosting the Queen Park Rangers, who happened to be the worst team in the league that season. The league championship would be secured by a Man City win; however, a tie or loss would result in the trophy eluding them once again.

Fast-forward: All ninety minutes of the game had expired, and Man

City was behind 2–1. It seemed they were headed for an unexpected and disastrous loss, but there remained a glimmer of hope: Five extra minutes of stoppage time would be added to the end of regulation. Most of the home fans had already given up; they were livid with their team's performance, booing and yelling profanity, and a third of them had already departed the stadium out of disgust.

Against all odds, and to everyone's surprise, just one minute and twenty seconds into extra time, Man City scored. The fans still in attendance were exuberant with joy; their explosive cheers were deafening. However, the team didn't celebrate—the striker who'd scored didn't rip off his shirt, slide to his knees, jump up, and hug his nearby teammates. Time was too short for any celebration. Instead, he ran into the goal (something I've never heard of or seen before in a professional league), grabbed the ball, quickly handed it to the ref, and rushed to midfield for the kickoff and an unlikely, but still possible, second goal with three minutes and forty seconds remaining. He never would have done this had there still been forty minutes left in regulation. With the time so short, urgency and intensity were demanded on the entire team's part. They forgot the goal that was behind them and pressed "toward the goal for the prize" (Philippians 3:14 NKJV).

Two minutes and five seconds later, Man City surprisingly scored again with only one minute and twenty seconds left in added time and won the game 3–2. Against all odds, this focused and determined team won the Premier League for the first time in forty-four years. That final match was later referred to by sportscasters as "the game of the century."

Now consider a much greater scenario, one that carries weight not just for one football season, or even for one century, but for the rest of eternity. In this event, we are in the final seconds of "stoppage time." With Jesus stating on three different occasions, "I am coming quickly," a greater intensity and urgency should be ignited in us than Man City displayed in the final minutes of that memorable game. Let's live as if we have only a very short time left—as if He is coming today! But at the same time, let's strategize and plan for the next one hundred years.

The prophecies of His second coming are not meant to scare us; they are to be taken seriously. It's the most written-about time period in the Holy Bible for a reason. God wants you to understand it, hope for it, and be prepared.

Since this has been important to God from the beginning, make it important to you today and every day ahead as we draw closer. Let us, like the sons of Issachar, Simeon, and Anna, understand the times.

Dear reader and friend, the King is coming very soon. It's time to prepare for His return!

With you in Christ,

John Bevere

APPENDIX: A TIMELINE AND OUTLINE OF WHAT'S COMING

AN OUTLINE OF WHAT'S COMING

Scripture gives us a general timeline of events that will take place in the near future. If Scripture reveals these events, we should have a good understanding of them and what they will look like. I've organized these for your personal study. (Note: This is not exhaustive.)

1. **The "Catching Away" of the Bride** (John 14:1–3; 1 Corinthians 1:7–8; 15:51–58; 16:22; Philippians 3:20–21; Colossians 3:4; 1 Thessalonians 1:10; 2:19; 4:13–18; 5:9, 23; 2 Thessalonians 2:1; 1 Timothy 6:14; Titus 2:13; Hebrews 9:28; James 5:7–9; 1 John 2:28–3:2; Revelation 2:25; 4:1)
2. **The 7-Year Tribulation** (on earth)
   a. The Seven Seal Judgments (Revelation 6:1–8:5)
   b. The Seven Trumpet Judgments (Revelation 8:7–11:19)

   c. The Seven Bowl Judgments (Revelation 15:1–16:21)
   d. Other important details (Revelation 6–18)
3. **The 7-Year Tribulation** (in heaven)
   a. The Judgment Seat of Christ for believers (1 Corinthians 3:11–15; 2 Corinthians 5:10; Romans 14:10–12)
   b. Option 1: The Marriage Supper of the Lamb (Revelation 19:7–9; Isaiah 25:6–10)
4. **The Glorious Second Coming**
   a. Occurs immediately after the tribulation (Matthew 13:41; 24:15–31; 26:64; Mark 13:14–27; 14:62; Luke 21:25–28; Acts 1:9–11; 3:19–21; 2 Thessalonians 1:6–10; 2 Peter 3:1–14; Jude vv. 14–15; Revelation 1:7)
   b. Jesus will be seen by all (Matthew 24:30; Revelation 1:7)
   c. Jesus and His saints will appear on white horses (Revelation 19:11–14; Jude v. 14 NKJV; Zechariah 14:5 NKJV; 1 Thessalonians 3:13 NKJV)
   d. The swift defeat of the rebels at Armageddon (Revelation 16:12–16; 19:19–21; Zechariah 14:12)
   e. Jesus will stand upon the Mount of Olives (Zechariah 14:3–5)
   f. Jesus will cast the Antichrist, the false prophet, Satan, and his fallen angels and demons into the bottomless pit for 1,000 years (Revelation 19:20; 20:1–3)
   g. Jesus will establish His kingdom with the capital being Jerusalem, and His saints will rule with Him for 1,000 years (Daniel 2:44–45; 7:13–14; Revelation 20:4–6)
5. **The Establishment of the 1,000-Year Kingdom Age** (Revelation 20:1–9; Isaiah 2:2–4; 11:6–9; 65:18–25; Jeremiah 31:10–14; 31–40; Ezekiel 34:25–31; 40–48; Daniel 2:35; 7:13–14; Joel 2:21–27; Amos 9:13–15; Micah 4:1–7; Zechariah 8:1–3; Zephaniah 3:9–20).
   a. Option 2: The Kingdom Age's Inaugural Event: The Marriage Supper of the Lamb (Revelation 19:7–9; Isaiah 25:6–10)
6. **Satan will be loosed at the end of the 1,000 years** (Revelation 20:7–10; 2 Peter 3:11–12)

   a. He will tempt the nations of the earth (this will be people with natural bodies, much like Adam and Eve had; they will have survived the great tribulation). Satan will incite some nations to come against the King and His bride in the Holy City of Jerusalem.
   b. Fire will come down from heaven, devour the rebels, and purge the earth and heaven.
   c. Satan and his forces will forever be cast into the eternal lake of fire.
7. **The Great White Throne Judgment** (Revelation 20:11–15; Daniel 7:9–14)
8. **The Eternal Earth and Heaven Will Come Forth** (Isaiah 65:17–25; 66:22–24; Revelation 21–22; 1 Corinthians 15:24–28; 2 Peter 3:13)
   a. The heavenly Jerusalem will come to earth and God the Father will make His home among us.
   b. Option 3: The New Heaven's Inaugural Event: The Marriage Supper of the Lamb (Revelation 19:7–9; Isaiah 25:6–10)

ACKNOWLEDGMENTS

I love the team that has been assembled to make this book possible and to get its critical message out.

First, to dear Holy Spirit. How could anyone write anything of eternal value without Your assistance. Of all people, I am most aware of Your help. As one whose worst subject in high school was creative writing and language, I stood in awe of You throughout each chapter, watching Your wisdom come forth.

Next, my dear wife, Lisa, for sacrificing a lot of time together to give me uninterrupted focus time to pray and write. You are the love of my life. I constantly am amazed that I am privileged to be husband to such a remarkable woman.

My sister, Laura, who is a language expert and a student of ecotheology. You read every chapter the moment it was finished and provided outstanding feedback and encouragement. Thanks, little sister.

My editor, Kyle Olund, you are a man of God, not just an outstanding editor and leader. I'm so honored you had the first input on the content. You made remarkable suggestions that improved the message.

To Don Jacobson, my dear friend, thank you for your belief in Lisa and me as well as your outstanding leadership in all HarperCollins Faith branches.

To Damon Reiss, thank you for your outstanding leadership of the W team, but more importantly, your close walk with Jesus and friendship with our family. You've encouraged me in so many ways.

To Caren Wolfe, thank you for not just being an amazing marketing expert, but for being a woman who has a heart after our Lord Jesus. So proud of you and honored to labor beside you!

To Allison Carter, my sister who is on fire. Thank you for exploring the most effective ways to get this message out. Your joy and zeal are contagious.

To Brooke Hill, you, with efficiency, coordinated all the complex details of publishing this book in such a magnificent way. Thank you also for helping with the editing; your suggestions were outstanding.

To Jill Jones, thank you for the outstanding line editing you provided. I was amazed by the fine details you spotted that needed attention. I admire your gift.

To Lauren Ash and Madison Baird, thank you for all the behind-the-scenes details that you both address. You make everything look easy, when in reality, your expert labor makes something very complex come together.

To Mark Weising, thanks to you and your team for the excellence in creating the complementary study to this book. It was a fun two days we had in the studio, and I believe many will benefit from your expertise in developing the study.

To Meg Schmidt, thank you for overseeing the stunning cover that your team came up with for the book.

To our faithful son Addison Bevere and my dear friend Tom Gehring. Addison, thank you for being a great leader of our team and working on the details of the publishing agreement of this book, along with Tom. Tom, you have been such a support to Lisa, me, and our entire family. I love you, brother.

To Bryson Liu, Casey Thorton, and Abby Drown of the Messenger International Team. A massive thank-you for the excellence and hard work you put into getting our messages out to the people of God. Each of you amaze me with your expertise and diligence. I'm so grateful for you.

To Chris Pace, thank you for helping me with research and preparing the study for this book. Your encouragement and competence are gold.

To our entire Messenger team, serving our Lord Jesus with you all is a treasure. May your eternal reward for the selfless labor of love you've consistently walked in be much greater than you could have imagined. Lisa and I love you all.

ACKNOWLEDGMENTS

To our dear heavenly Father, Lord Jesus, and Holy Spirit, thank You for the honor of being a part of Your family forever. I give You all the praise, glory, honor, and thanksgiving for the lives that will be impacted for eternity through this message.

And finally, to you, dear reader, please, if this message impacts you, pull together a group of friends and go through the study together. Stay strong to the end and keep making disciples.

NOTES

Chapter 1

1. Dean C. Halverson, "88 Reasons: What Went Wrong?" Christian Research Institute, updated May 30, 2025, https://www.equip.org/articles/88-reasons-what-went-wrong/.
2. Tim LaHaye and Thomas Ice, *Charting the End Times: A Visual Guide to Understanding Bible Prophecy* (Harvest House, 2021), 24–26.

Chapter 2

1. Dr. Delena Norris-Tull, "History: Are We Doomed to Repeat It?", Management of Invasive Plants in the Western USA, July 2020, https://www.invasiveplantswesternusa.org/history-are-we-doomed-to-repeat-it.html.
2. Spiros Zodhiates, *The Complete Word Study Dictionary: New Testament* (AMG Publishers, 2000), under "*díkaios*."
3. Zodhiates, *The Complete Word Study Dictionary*, under "*eulabes*."
4. Johannes P. Louw and Eugene Albert Nida, eds., *Greek-English Lexicon of the New Testament: Based on Semantic Domains* (United Bible Societies, 1996), 532.

Chapter 3

1. Tyler Perry, "The Siege of Jerusalem in 70 CE," *World History Encyclopedia*, May 2, 2022, https://www.worldhistory.org/article/1993/the-siege-of-jerusalem-in-70-ce/.
2. Walter A. Elwell and Barry J. Beitzel, *Baker Encyclopedia of the Bible* (Baker Book House, 1988), under "Nebuchadnezzar, Nebuchadrezzar."
3. Loring W. Batten, *A Critical and Exegetical Commentary on the Books of Ezra and Nehemiah*, International Critical Commentary (T. & T. Clark, 1913), 190.
4. Ken Johnson, *The Ancient Dead Sea Scroll Calendar: And the Prophecies It*

Reveals (independent, 2020), 87. Other sources can be found at Historum, https://historum.com/t/fall-of-jerusalem-70-ad.39734/.

Chapter 4

1. "Signs of Decline & Hope Amid Key Metrics of Faith," Barna Group, March 4, 2020, https://www.barna.com/research/changing-state-of-the-church/.

Chapter 5

1. A few others include 2 Timothy 1:9; Hebrews 4:3; and Titus 1:2.

Chapter 6

1. WebMD editorial contributors, "What Is Hematidrosis?," WebMD, April 7, 2024, https://www.webmd.com/a-to-z-guides/hematidrosis-hematohidrosis.
2. Leon Morris, *The Gospel According to John*, The New International Commentary on the New Testament (William B. Eerdmans, 1995), 699.
3. Rick Renner, *Easter: The Rest of the Story* (Harrison House, 2025), 135.

Chapter 7

1. Association for Psychological Science, "Shared Pain Brings People Together, Study Concludes," ScienceDaily, September 9, 2014, https://www.sciencedaily.com/releases/2014/09/140909113340.htm.
2. Johannes P. Louw and Eugene Albert Nida, eds., *Greek-English Lexicon of the New Testament: Based on Semantic Domains* (United Bible Societies, 1996), 654.
3. Association for Psychological Science, "Shared Pain Brings People Together, Study Concludes."

Chapter 8

1. Spiros Zodhiates, *The Complete Word Study Dictionary: New Testament* (AMG Publishers, 2000), under "*μονή*." Some translations don't use the word *mansions*, but the Greek word is μονή (*monḗ*), and one of its definitions is "mansions."
2. Johannes P. Louw and Eugene Albert Nida, eds., *Greek-English Lexicon of the New Testament: Based on Semantic* Domains (United Bible Societies, 1996), 375.
3. Warren Baker and Eugene E. Carpenter, *The Complete Word Study Dictionary: Old Testament* (AMG Publishers, 2003), under "*māṣā*."

Chapter 9

1. Information about ancient Jewish weddings comes from: Jamie Lash, *The Ancient Jewish Wedding* (Jewish Jewels, 2012); Mo Tizzard, *The Jewish Wedding and the Bride of Christ* (Storehouse Books, 2013); Chuck Missler, *The Rapture: Christianity's Most Preposterous Belief* (Koinonia House, 2014); and Katie Beehn, *Unveiled: Ancient Jewish Wedding Traditions and the Bride of Christ* (pub. by author, 2023).
2. Spiros Zodhiates, *The Complete Word Study Dictionary: New Testament* (AMG, 2000) under "*paralambánō*."
3. Henry Morris, *The Revelation Record* (Tyndale House, 1983), 451.
4. Louw and Nida, *Greek-English Lexicon of the New Testament: Based on Semantic Domains* (United Bible Societies, 1996), 706.

Chapter 11

1. Johannes P. Louw and Eugene Albert Nida, *Greek-English Lexicon of the New Testament: Based on Semantic Domains* (United Bible Societies, 1996), 654.
2. Spiros Zodhiates, *The Complete Word Study Dictionary: New Testament* (AMG Publishers, 2000), under "*anakúptō*."
3. Zodhiates, *The Complete Word Study Dictionary*, under "*epaírō*."
4. Ronald F. Youngblood et al. eds., *Nelson's New Illustrated Bible Dictionary* (Thomas Nelson, 1995).

Chapter 12

1. Note for Hosea 5:15: The NLT version uses the word "Then" at the beginning of verse 15, making it appear that the events are in sequential order. However, this word is not found in the original language; this is reflected by the way the NKJV and ESV translate the verse.

Chapter 13

1. Johannes P. Louw and Eugene Albert Nida, *Greek-English Lexicon of the New Testament: Based on Semantic* Domains (United Bible Societies, 1996), 352.

Chapter 14

1. Spiros Zodhiates, *The Complete Word Study Dictionary: New Testament* (AMG Publishers, 2000), under "*átomos*."
2. Science and Technology Facilities Council (STFC), "Walking the Planck: The Weird World of the Littlest Measure," Medium, January 12, 2024, https://

medium.com/big-science-at-stfc/walking-the-planck-the-weird-world-of-the-littlest-measure-607583a5bede#.

3. Louw and Nida, *Greek-English Lexicon of the New Testament*, 220.
4. Zodhiates, *The Complete Word Study Dictionary.*
5. Zodhiates, *The Complete Word Study Dictionary.*

Chapter 15

1. Spiros Zodhiates, *The Complete Word Study Dictionary: New Testament* (AMG Publishers, 2000), under "*thumós.*"
2. Zodhiates, *The Complete Word Study Dictionary.*
3. Johannes P. Louw and Eugene Albert Nida, *Greek-English Lexicon of the New Testament: Based on Semantic* Domains (United Bible Societies, 1996), 489.
4. "Billy Graham 'My Answer,'" Billy Graham Evangelistic Association, https://billygraham.org/answers/is-it-true-that-more-christians-have-died-for-their-faith-in-the-last-century-than-in-all-history-before-it.

Chapter 16

1. Zodhiates, ἡμάς hēmás; personal pron., acc. pl. of emé (1691), Our, us, we. To be distinguished from humás (5209), your, you. *The Complete Word Study Dictionary: New Testament*(Chattanooga, TN: AMG Publishers, 2000).
2. "Indigenous Peoples: Respect NOT Dehumanization," United Nations, accessed October 22, 2025, https://www.un.org/en/fight-racism/vulnerable-groups/indigenous-peoples.

Chapter 17

1. Johannes P. Louw and Eugene Albert Nida, *Greek-English Lexicon of the New Testament: Based on Semantic Domains* (United Bible Societies, 1996), 757.
2. Rick Renner, *The Rapture, the Antichrist, and the Tribulation: An End-Times Countdown and What Happens Next* (Harrison House, 2025), 127.
3. William Arndt et al., *A Greek-English Lexicon of the New Testament and Other Early Christian Literature* (University of Chicago Press, 2000), 276.

Chapter 18

1. Spiros Zodhiates, *The Complete Word Study Dictionary: New Testament* (AMG Publishers, 2000).
2. "Over Half of Practicing Christians Admit They Use Pornography," Barna, October 17, 2024, https://www.barna.com/trends/over-half-of-practicing

-christians-admit-they-use-pornography/; Ken Ham, "54% of Christians Admit to Viewing Pornography—Over Half Are Okay with It," Answers in Genesis, October 31, 2024, https://answersingenesis.org/christianity/christians-admit-to-viewing-pornography-over-half-are-okay-with-it/.

3. Ted E. Bunch et al., "Retracted Article: A Tunguska Sized Airburst Destroyed Tall el-Hammam, a Middle Bronze Age City in the Jordan Valley Near the Dead Sea," *Scientific Reports* 11 (2021), September 20, 2021, https://www.nature.com/articles/s41598-021-97778-3.
4. Lee W. Brainard, *Recent Pre-Trib Findings in the Early Church Fathers* (Soothkeep Press, 2023), 10.

Chapter 19

1. Spiros Zodhiates, *The Complete Word Study Dictionary: New Testament* (AMG Publishers, 2000), under "*ménō*."
2. Johannes P. Louw and Eugene Albert Nida, *Greek-English Lexicon of the New Testament: Based on Semantic Domains* (United Bible Societies, 1996).
3. Louw and Nida, *Greek-English Lexicon of the New Testament*, 155.

Chapter 20

1. Johannes P. Louw and Eugene Albert Nida, *Greek-English Lexicon of the New Testament: Based on Semantic Domains* (United Bible Societies, 1996), 743.
2. Arndt et al., *A Greek-English Lexicon of the New Testament and Other Early Christian Literature*, (University of Chicago Press, 2000), 249.
3. Oswald Chambers, *The Philosophy of Sin*, in *Biblical Ethics; The Moral Foundations of Life; The Philosophy of Sin* (Discovery House, 1998), 314.
4. Lewis to Mary Willis Shelburne, August 1, 1953, in *The Collected Letters of C. S. Lewis*, vol. 3, *Narnia, Cambridge, and Joy, 1950–1963*, ed. by Walter Hooper (HarperCollins, 2007), 351.
5. Joseph H. Thayer, *Thayer's Greek-English Lexicon of the New Testament* (Hendrickson Academic, 1995).

Chapter 21

1. Johannes P. Louw and Eugene Albert Nida, *Greek-English Lexicon of the New Testament: Based on Semantic Domains* (United Bible Societies, 1996), 662.

Chapter 22

1. Information on the life of John in this chapter is from Rick Renner, *A Light in the Darkness: Seven Messages to the Seven Churches* (Harrison House, 2018), 15–26, 65.

2. Information on the Isle of Patmos in this chapter is from Renner, *A Light in the Darkness*, 5–14.
3. Information on the seven churches in this chapter is from: Renner, *A Light in the Darkness*, 15–26, 65; *Book of Revelation Made Easy* (Rose Publishing, 2015); *The Seven Churches of Revelation* (Rose Publishing, 2015); Tim LaHaye, *Revelation Unveiled* (Zondervan, 1999), 17; Clinton Wahlen, "Letters to the Seven Churches: Historical or Prophetic?" *Ministry: International Journal for Pastors*, November 2007, https://www.ministrymagazine.org/archive/2007/11/letters-to-the-seven-churches.html; and Alexander Kurian, "Do the Seven Churches in Revelation Represent Seven Stages of Church History?," AlexKurian.org, https://www.alexkurian.org/articles-1/do-the-seven-churches-in-revelation-represent-seven-stages-of-church-history%3F.
4. Spiros Zodhiates, *The Complete Word Study Dictionary: New Testament* (AMG Publishers, 2000), under "*ággelos.*"

Chapter 23

1. *Merriam-Webster Dictionary*, "legalism," accessed October 23, 2025, https://www.merriam-webster.com/dictionary/legalism.
2. Warren W. Wiersbe, *The Bible Exposition Commentary: New Testament*, vol. 2 (Victor Books, 2003), 574–75; Grant R. Osborne, *Revelation: Verse by Verse*, Osborne New Testament Commentaries (Lexham Press, 2016), 60.

Chapter 24

1. Mark Allan Powell, ed., *The HarperCollins Bible Dictionary* rev. ed. (HarperCollins, 2011), under "Sardis."
2. Chuck D. Pierce, *God's Unfolding Battle Plan: A Field Manual for Advancing the Kingdom of God* (Regal Books, 2007), 130.
3. Johannes P. Louw and Eugene Albert Nida, *Greek-English Lexicon of the New Testament: Based on Semantic Domains* (United Bible Societies, 1996), 159.

Chapter 25

1. Chad Brand et al., eds., *Holman Illustrated Bible Dictionary*, (Holman Reference, 2003), under "Laodicea."
2. Johannes P. Louw and Eugene Albert Nida, *Greek-English Lexicon of the New Testament: Based on Semantic Domains* (United Bible Societies, 1996), 254.
3. Leon Morris, *Revelation: An Introduction and Commentary*, vol. 20, Tyndale New Testament Commentaries (InterVarsity Press, 1987), 80.

Chapter 27

1. Johannes P. Louw and Eugene Albert Nida, *Greek-English Lexicon of the New Testament: Based on Semantic Domains* (United Bible Societies, 1996), 677.
2. Eric W. Weisstein, "Midnight," Wolfram Research, accessed October 24, 2025, https://scienceworld.wolfram.com/astronomy/Midnight.html.
3. Obianuju Mbah, "Growing Interest in the Bible and Jesus Raises Hopes of Transatlantic Revival Among Young Adults," *Christian Today*, April 15, 2025, https://www.christiantoday.com/news/growing-interest-in-the-bible-and-jesus-raises-hopes-of-transatlantic-revival-among-young-adults.
4. Benjamin L. Gladd, *From Adam and Israel to the Church: A Biblical Theology of the People of God*, Essential Studies in Biblical Theology (IVP Academic, 2019), 157.

Chapter 28

1. Johannes P. Louw and Eugene Albert Nida, *Greek-English Lexicon of the New Testament: Based on Semantic Domains* (United Bible Societies, 1996), 90.
2. Spiros Zodhiates, *The Complete Word Study Dictionary: New Testament* (AMG Publishers, 2000), under "*kakós.*"

ABOUT THE AUTHOR

John Bevere is an international minister, bestselling author, and cofounder of Messenger International—a ministry dedicated to developing uncompromising followers of Christ who transform their world. For more than forty years, John has carried a burning passion to see believers walk in holy awe, living out their faith with purpose and conviction.

Known for his bold, uncompromising approach to God's Word, John has written twenty-five books that have sold millions of copies and been translated into more than 150 languages. Through Messenger International, John and his wife, Lisa, have equipped the global church by distributing over seventy million resources across 240 nations. Their revolutionary MessengerX app provides free digital discipleship resources in over 120 languages, currently reaching users in more than 30,000 cities worldwide.

John hosts "The John Bevere Podcast," where he shares timeless truths for changing times, helping believers live empowered and prepared. His ability to communicate challenging biblical concepts with clarity and conviction has made him a sought-after speaker at conferences and churches globally.

When John is home in Franklin, Tennessee, and not crafting his next message, you'll find him on the pickleball court holding his own against his four sons, loving on his grandchildren, or trying to convince Lisa to take up golf.

ALSO AVAILABLE FROM

JOHN BEVERE

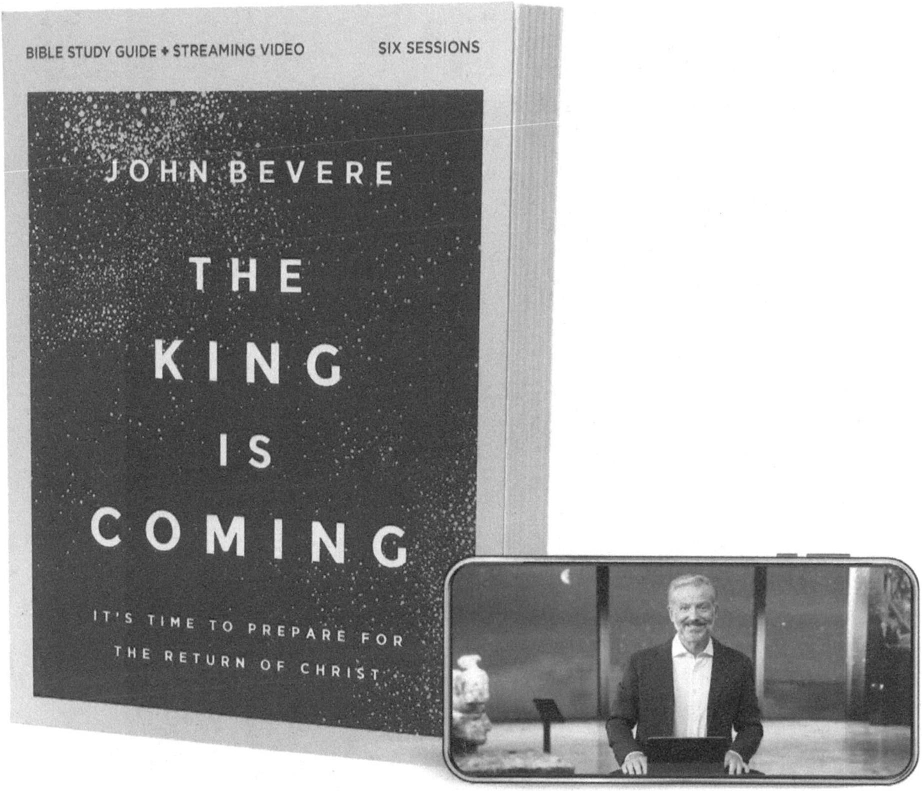

BIBLE STUDY GUIDE + STREAMING VIDEO SIX SESSIONS

JOHN BEVERE

THE KING IS COMING

IT'S TIME TO PREPARE FOR THE RETURN OF CHRIST

Available now at your favorite bookstore,
or streaming video on StudyGateway.com.

OTHER BOOKS BY JOHN BEVERE

A Heart Ablaze
The Awe of God*
The Bait of Satan*
Breaking Intimidation*
Called*
Drawing Near*
Driven by Eternity*
Enemy Access Denied
Everyday Courage*
Extraordinary*
The Fear of the Lord*
God, Where Are You?!*
Good or God?*
The Holy Spirit: An Introduction*
Honor's Reward*
How to Respond When You Feel Mistreated
Killing Kryptonite*
Relentless*
Rescued
The Story of Marriage*
Thus Saith the Lord?
Under Cover*
The Voice of One Crying
X: Multiply Your God-Given Potential*

POPULAR BOOKS BY LISA BEVERE

Adamant*
Girls with Swords*
Lioness Arising*
The Fight for Female*
Without Rival*

---

*Also available as a course

If this message impacted you, consider leading a group study to bring others along your journey!

Find the group video study, bulk ordering discounts, and more at:

johnbevere.com/thekingiscoming

www.ingramcontent.com/pod-product-compliance
Lightning Source LLC
LaVergne TN
LVHW030917080826
845145LV00013B/2930

* 9 7 8 1 4 0 0 3 5 5 6 7 9 *